ZsaZsc + Dave

Stepping off

REWILDING AND BELONGING IN THE SOUTH-WEST

THOMAS M. WILSON

FREMANTLE PRESS

Thomas M. Wilson has spent his life writing about the human relationship with our home: the natural world. He has a PhD in Literature and the Environment, and is an Honorary Research Fellow at the University of Western Australia. As well as being the author of *The Recurrent Green Universe of John Fowles* (Rodopi, 2006), Thomas has made numerous contributions to environmental journalism.

Visit the author at **www.tmwilson.org**

Stepping off

REWILDING AND BELONGING IN THE SOUTH-WEST

THOMAS M. WILSON

FREMANTLE PRESS

Because we have not made our lives to fit
Our places, the forests are ruined, the fields eroded,
The streams polluted, the mountains overturned. Hope
Then to belong to your place by your own knowledge
Of what it is that no other place is, and by
Your caring for it as you care for no other place, this
Place that you belong to though it is not yours,
For it was from the beginning and will be to the end.

– Wendell Berry, '2007, VI'

INTRODUCTION
THE BOOK MY PARENTS
DID NOT GIVE ME

Perhaps it's no surprise that I'm attracted to the natural world. My father always enjoyed exploring untamed land and, before I was born, had spent much of his spare time in the Kimberley or along the southern coast of Western Australia. My mother's guiding star was always nature. She was born in England to parents who owned a small dairy farm near Land's End in Cornwall, and then later in the 70s an orchard on the Spanish island of Menorca. Her father, my grandfather, took Wordsworth's poem 'Tintern Abbey' as the closest to gospel our atheist lineage would ever countenance. When I look back at photos from my childhood most of them were taken outdoors. Some of these photos were from a farm on Mt Shadforth, a wild piece of land behind the small town of Denmark on the south coast of Western Australia, where we lived briefly before my brother was born. I'm pictured climbing an apricot tree, at a time when I would not yet have been able to walk. By the age of eight I was avidly reading Gerald Durrell's book *My Family and Other Animals*, and telling interested passers-by that I wanted to be a zoologist when I grew up.

And yet, in my teenage years, skateboarding, girls and hip-hop became more interesting to me than fields and trees. I never lost affection for animals and the natural world, but such matters slunk into the background, and things stayed this way till my mid-twenties.

When I was studying for a BA at the Australian National University in the late 90s, I remember enjoying writing an essay on the way in which the English tradition of landscape gardening reflected relations between humans and nature over the centuries. However it was only during my PhD studies at the University of Western Australia that I really discovered and confirmed the importance of the biosphere for my view of the world. For my PhD I was researching the writings of naturalist and nature writer John Fowles. At this time, during an extended visit to the French colony of Réunion Island, a volcanic island in the middle of the Indian Ocean, someone mailed me a paperback edition of *The Diversity of Life*, by the premier prose stylist of modern ecology, Edward O. Wilson. This moment turned out to be my Road to Damascus. Although, considering the circumstances, it would be more accurate to call it my Voyage of the *Beagle*.

Wilson's elegant prose traced the way in which every living species has taken a long journey to become exquisitely adapted to the ecological niche it inhabits. As I trod the precipitous volcanic slopes of a geologically young tropical island, I for the first time really began to see and understand the long evolutionary history of the palms and trees, crabs and spiders, coral and fish around me. What had previously been little more than hieroglyphics jumped into meaningful relief. Further I realised that I too was a biological organism making up one strand in this ancient yet recurrent web of species diversity. Those few weeks were pivotal. Standing on the dark basalt shore of Réunion Island, backed by tall palm-covered crags, with Edward O. Wilson's evolutionary primer in my pocket, I felt a deep sense of reverence and of belonging, in my body and on the planet.

Later, I left Réunion Island, and travelled north across the equator, to the temperate forests and fields of south-west England. I found myself in the basement of Exeter University library, poring over the unpublished journals of John Fowles for my PhD. One afternoon I asked a librarian there if I could photocopy a page of the journals. The librarian called Fowles' agent. The agent turned out to be Sarah Fowles, John's wife. Then I found myself on the end of the phone chatting with Sarah and, moments later, being invited to lunch at their house. I couldn't believe my good fortune.

On Sunday I found myself at a small regional train station in Dorset where a red-haired elderly woman smiled at me from across the platform. Sarah and I exchanged greetings, and then, as we passed the train station entrance to buy tickets for the return journey, Sarah remarked: 'Oh, that's the famous writer.' For a moment two worlds collided. The godlike figure whose name was embossed on the spines of countless hardbacks on shelves throughout the English-speaking world was also a very frail old man waiting in a parked Mazda.

That day, my friendship with John and Sarah Fowles began. In 2003, I stayed with them in the seaside village of Lyme Regis for a few weeks. While staying at Belmont House and studying Fowles' journals, I took the opportunity to walk daily in the Underwood, an area of topographically topsy-turvy coastal wilderness and beech wood to the west of Lyme. This period, like my time on Réunion Island, reinforced my sense of belonging in the global biosphere.

I returned home. Like most people in Perth, I was living in suburbia, but I made regular visits to Kings Park, Bold Park, and other areas where I could feel connected to natural ecosystems, and I started to try to identify a few species of plant and tree, and of bird and flower.

However it began to be apparent to me that I didn't really understand the natural environment of the place where I was born. I found myself wishing that my parents had given me a book as I was growing up that revealed to me my homeland beyond the suburbs and the city. I went looking for a comprehensive guide that did just this, but found nothing beyond a few field guides to the plants and animals, a few scholarly bricks on Western Australia's geological history, a journal article or two on its evolutionary history. There was no single volume primer to introduce the traveller or curious local to the identity of this place, to quickly acquaint them with the contours of both its environmental and human history.

Traditionally, we use the empirical method developed during the Enlightenment to understand the physical world around us. I have found many opportunities to develop a connection with the landscape of my home through the lens of biological science. However, seeing this landscape through only the physical sciences is incomplete. For this reason this book links the insights of biology to those of literature and culture. It connects understanding from geology and evolutionary science with the letters and journals, poems and paintings of the people who have lived here. It seeks to return memory to its current inhabitants, and to take its cues from ecological realities just as much as from social ones. It seeks to provide a broader view, so that we can construct a meaningful relationship with our home.

*

Environmental history is the study of the human interactions with the natural world at different times. Environmental historians discuss subjects as diverse as the causes of the dustbowl of 1930s America and the development of agriculture in ancient Egypt. This book contains environmental history, but it is also a guide to the stones and rivers, plants and animals of this place – it blends geology, anthropology, and cultural history, in ways that traditional, anthropocentric, human histories of Australia do not. In reading this book, you may be acquiring knowledge but, more than that, it may give you the opportunity to deepen your relationship with your home. The American essayist Scott Russell Sanders writes, 'I cannot have a spiritual center without having a geographical one; I cannot live a grounded life without being grounded in a place'.[1] Part of what this book seeks to create is a sense of self that is grounded in a place, and is meaningful.

There are elements of my history in this book, but every personal history is part of a much bigger one. Although, like most people, I live in the city, this book looks beyond the urban bubble. And although I am a product of my time, this book's purview reaches far beyond that time, in both directions.

If you live somewhere else, then this story won't be your story. However, you may still recognise the feeling of not truly knowing where you live. I encourage you too to make a journey of discovery in similar ways.

*

Western Australia is a place of new arrivals. More than fifty per cent of us are likely to have been born, or have parents that were born, overseas. Most of us who arrive in Perth, recently or a generation ago, have our own traditions, and cultural and geographical baggage.

In 1830, my family got off their ship at present day South Beach south of Fremantle with their sheep, pigs and other trappings of traditional British agriculture. The baggage my forebears arrived with has done great damage to Australia. My forebears, and many like them, tried to remake this country in the image they knew and understood. But this was not their homeland of rich, dark soils and heavy annual rainfalls. Things work differently here.

'Perth' itself is a relatively recent invention. It only assumed the size and status of a city in the twentieth century. By 1962 the isolated city was clearly visible to John Glenn, an American astronaut whose spaceship crossed the Australian continent at night. Perth became 'the city of light'.

In a state of 2.5 million square kilometres, most of us live in a space that is 6,500 square kilometres, in suburbs that sprawl north, east and south. We live on the grid, and that means not only having the essentials of life piped into our houses, such as power and water, but, for many, being connected to an American culture machine through the medium of our TV sets and electronic devices. For those who live in contemporary Perth, circumstances do not facilitate a deep connection with the land.

Even for those born here and attentive to its ecological and human history, the knowledge we receive about our home may be only two or three generations old. Because although human beings have been living here for more than 47,000 years, there is a strange collective amnesia about what has come before. When my grandmother was in her twenties she might have gone camping in the hills and, while lying on a camp stretcher at night, have heard a range of strange thuddings and scufflings outside in the dark. These were the sounds of quendas, boodies, bilbies, chuditch and other original inhabitants of the forest, hopping and waddling along their nocturnal paths. In the space of two generations, these animals have nearly all gone, along with their habitat around Perth: woodland, swampland and heath. Sprawling suburbs and shopping centres, paved roads and grassy ovals have replaced what came before. Most of these animals are today not even a memory in the minds of those of us who live here. Collectively, we have forgotten what this land looked like, even quite recently, and how it was lived in for thousands of years before that.

*

In 2003, I stood looking out over John and Sarah Fowles' vast and botanically diverse garden that rambled down the hill in front of his eighteenth century home. On that very first day I arrived, I noticed a kangaroo paw sitting in a small pot in the sun at the back of Belmont House. The plant had been positioned in pride of place above the lawn.

The red-and-green kangaroo paw (*Anigozanthos manglesii*) is named after Robert Mangles, who raised a specimen from seed in his English garden in the late 1830s.[2] The stems of these flowers are a vivid red, while the ends of the flowers are a deep green, and the plant covered with a fine, wool-like hair. This is Western Australia's floral emblem. Back in the 1830s, at the same time as my ancestors arrived in Australia, Robert Mangles had succeeded in growing this plant in murky English weather. More than a century and a half later, John Fowles was following a historically old English yearning towards the exotic and the antipodean by growing this bright flowering herb in his garden.

On that day in south-west England, I looked at that plant with interest. I was also oddly comforted by its hint at another vivid, botanical universe, far across the seas to the south. However, if Fowles had talked to me over lunch that day of cowslip orchids, I would have struggled to tell him the name of a Western Australian plant in return.

Thankfully things are different now.

CHAPTER 1
GETTING THE LAY OF THE LAND

We will never have a proper relationship with the land if we do not understand its subtle contours. I am about to condense more than four billion years of geological history and the establishment of an entire ecosystem into a single chapter. Be prepared to move quickly! We have a lot of territory to cover, and the journey begins at a gallop.

The oldest fragments of the earth's crust at the surface of the planet are found in Western Australia, 800 kilometres north of Perth. They are tiny crystals of zircon 4.374 billion years old, formed quite soon after the planet came into being as an ocean of magma. The rocks of the Pilbara in the state's north-west are around 3.4 billion years old and those of the Darling plateau near the city of Perth are between 2.5 and 2.9 billion years old. Living in Perth, you can look east to the Darling Scarp and look backwards in time, in deep time, to areas of continental plate that emerged from ancient seas in the very depths of geological history. In Eastern Australia, the oldest rocks are only 600 million years old or younger.[1]

Western Australia also boasts the oldest fossils visible to the naked eye yet to be found on earth. These are the fossilised stromatolites that are 3.5 billion years old at North Pole in the Pilbara (considering the temperature of the location, the place was clearly named with a sense of irony). Stromatolites are domes of sediment trapped in shallow water and built up by layers of microbes growing towards the sunlight. The surface of the dome is the photosynthesising microbial mat, a veneer one centimetre thick with a viscous texture. The early earth had coastlines dotted with stromatolites, but today they are rare and only survive in lagoons where the water is too salty for the fish and snails that would otherwise devour them. Thrombolites are similar domes but without the layering of accretions. Lake Clifton south of Perth is full of such reminders of what the early earth looked like.

About 2,000 million years ago, the seas turned red as great masses of iron oxide drifted to the bottom of the ocean, a red that is today seen in the Hamersley Ranges in the Pilbara. Around 500 million years ago came an explosion in the diversity of multicellular forms of life, known as the Cambrian explosion. In sandstone in the Murchison River Gorge near Kalbarri you can see 420 million year old tracks of scorpion-like predators about the size of a cat moving about the intertidal zone. Here you are seeing the first movement of animals onto the land.

Around 430 million years ago, the long Darling Fault, which runs from Shark Bay all the way to the south coast, formed one edge of a basin that filled with as much as fifteen kilometres of sedimentary rock – on which Perth now sits.[2]

Mountains may look immutable but they can walk, and they can melt. Great mountains once rose from the land, but they were worn down long ago by the elements, and their sediments carried by large rivers out to the sea. From 330 to 250 million years ago, huge glaciers moved over much of Western Australia, flattening the country. There hasn't been much mountain building since then and so the place has stayed flat. Fifteen million years after the ice melted, plant matter accumulated in wetlands and eventually formed coal, as for example near the town of Collie in the south-west.[3]

The continents drift slowly about the face of earth, like surface scum sliding over the molten soup at the core of the planet. Australia's biography includes a continent that has slipped around the surface of the planet many times. Some 200 million years ago, Pangea, the supercontinent that contained all the present continents, split apart and separated into Laurasia in the north and Gondwana in the south. At this time, a little fish still found in the peaty waters of Western Australia's southern forests, a salamander fish of the family Lepidogalaxiidae, was already burrowing into dry creeks beds to escape desiccation.

*

Early in the history of animal life, amphibians and frogs left the oceans where life began, but they still had to stay close to bodies of water to lay their eggs and avoid drying out from the heat of the sun. When lizards evolved around 330 million years ago, they came with watertight skin and amniotic eggs, which let them trek far inland, across the sun-baked plains. They would have an advantage in a future Australia, low in bioproductivity, as they were cold-blooded and didn't need to eat as much as mammals. Lizards, dinosaurs and warm-blooded mammals were already on the scene as Pangea broke up. One hundred and fifty million years ago, birds, the direct descendants of dinosaurs, first appeared in the sky. Then 120 million years ago, angiosperms, the flowering plants, first appeared. These plants had highly efficient leaves for photosynthesis, and sophisticated means of reproduction, and today they dominate the flora of the south-west.[4] Australia split from the Indian Plate 118 million years ago, and the rocks of modern Tibet pulled apart from the Darling Scarp and the Leeuwin-Naturaliste Ridge.[5] Not many current Perth dwellers would know that the scarp they see to their east used to be attached to the Dalai Lama's traditional homeland now far to the north. When the Indian Plate pulled free from the Australian Continental Plate and drifted west and north, the rocks to the west of the Darling Fault dropped down, and it is thanks to this movement that the 1,000 kilometre long Darling Fault can be seen from space. Sixty-five million years ago a giant meteor hit earth and ended the great age of the dinosaurs.

By this time, marsupials, placental mammals and even primates had arrived, and those best adapted to the changed conditions managed to make it through the extinction bottleneck that followed the far-reaching impact of this meteor. Gondwana had begun to break up into India and Africa and South America. Some biological relics from this far distant time still abide in what was once Gondwana. For example, the trapdoor spider, family Migidae, is found on all the southern continents and New Zealand.[6] These spiders can't make ocean crossings but with a little understanding of continental drift, one can figure out the rest of the story. Perhaps as late as thirty-five million years ago, Australia pulled apart from Antarctica and started to drift north, ultimately to where it sits today.[7] The apes were not even a figment of evolution's imagination at this time. But Australia had begun. When the continents split apart, so did the river channels. Rivers of the south coast have been traced from this state to their old courses still preserved under ice in Antarctica.[8] And the story isn't over. Our southern continent continues to drift north at the rate of about eight to ten centimetres a year, roughly the rate at which fingernails grow.

*

If you had gone exploring in Australia twenty million years ago, you would have found yourself in a dim, warm and wet world, walking in the shade of the canopy of the ubiquitous *Nothofagus* trees that made up a rainforest that covered the land. There would have been cycads, ferns, lichens and mosses all around. Today, if you enter the remaining pockets of rainforest dotted along Australia's eastern edge, you can still have a taste of this ancient, long-gone land.

Since Australia broke away from Antarctica, there have been cycles of greenhouse to icehouse climates, with changing temperatures and rainfalls. As Australia rafted northwards into warmer latitudes there was a general global cooling. The Antarctic ice sheets formed, reflecting more sunlight and heat back out to space. With this general cooling, Australia became more arid. At various times in the last ten million years the advent of drier conditions allowed grasses, casuarinas, acacias and eucalypts to take the upper hand and dominate the landscape. Heath plants took over the sandy soils, daisies (Asteraceae) periodically set blazes of colour to the sandy areas of the land, and saltbushes learned how to take salt out of the ancient ground.[9]

There was never a clear break between a Western Australia covered in rainforests and today's flora. For example, today's sclerophyllous plants have been here a long, long time, even if they haven't always dominated the scene. A fossil banksia cone that was found near

Carnarvon is forty million years old, and looks just like the banksia cones you might see on trees around Perth today. Rather than one flora suddenly emerging and replacing the other, the warming of the region over many millions of years eventually favoured the growth, dispersion and dominance of flora more adapted to aridity than rainforest species.

Remnants of lusher times can be found in tiny pockets of palm-lined monsoon forest in shady gorges in the Kimberley region in north-western Australia. Or elsewhere, in spiders and other many-legged invertebrates scuttling in damp gullies up on the slopes of the Stirling Ranges, whose closest genetic relatives live not at the base of the Ranges but as far away as another fragment of Gondwana: South America. But these are biological relicts hanging on in their own little refuge. One relict from our rainforest days is the beautiful little sunset frog found in tiny peat swamps in the south-west. Another is the majestic tingle tree, rising like a pillar holding up the sky in the southern forests, or the spider that lives in the bark at its base. Another is the underground orchid, *Rhizanthella gardneri*, a plant that escaped the warming climate of Australia by going down and flowering and fruiting underground.[10] The underground orchid never shows its white and mauve beauty to the world, and remains a lover of darkness and seclusion. Some spiders abiding in the moist shade of logs in the southern karri and tingle forests are genetically very similar to ones in Africa. The green and red Albany pitcher plant *Cephalotus*, with its bizarre mouth gaping open for insects, looks like it was pulled out of a tropical rainforest. Some of these relict hangers-on will be the first to be edged off the map as present day global-climate heating inches forward and

Western Australia warms up ever more rapidly.

In the last 2.3 million years there have been more than twenty glacial and interglacial cycles in our climate, with temperature drops of five to ten degrees Celsius. Aridity of the kind we are familiar with in much of Australia developed in eastern parts of the south-west around 500,000 years ago.[11] As the climate became more arid, those plants that could cope with aridity – ones that did not lose moisture easily and that could handle wildfires – spread out over the land. They had the adaptations that were useful and left more offspring as a result. Many eucalypts evolved leaves that hung vertically, letting lots of sunlight through their canopy, as well as leaves that were covered in wax, minimising the loss of moist air around the stomata. Root systems went far down, past the thick, dry crust above, to the deep water table that could be counted on even on the hottest of summer days. The seeds of native peas and wattles required heat for germination, often from a wildfire that killed the parent plant. Fruits of some plants became hard and woody, capable of waiting around until the right combination of rain and sun let them germinate.[12]

As the climate became warmer and more arid, acacias, eucalypts, banksias, casuarinas and tea-trees, to note some prominent examples, covered the land. Warmer and more arid conditions meant more fires. Eucalypts, in particular, are perfectly adapted when it comes to living with wildfires. As historian Eric Rolls points out, the smell of their burning leaves is thirty-five million years old.[13] Their fibrous leaves are full of volatile oils, their bark can hang in inflammable strips, and their fallen leaves, being so low in minerals and falling thickly, can create perfect material to get fires roaring. When the oils in their leaves are burned at extremely high temperatures, the top of the tree can literally explode. If the fire is not too great in intensity, there are always buds, protected by heat resistant bark, ready to sprout in their thousands and get the tree connected to the air again within a few weeks. If the fire is intense and burns the whole tree down, then there is still hope. Even a fire of 1,000 degrees Centigrade will burn no more than about the top three centimetres of the earth. And under this there will be lignotubers – prospective new little trunks primed with just the right proportion of minerals and chemicals in the soil, ready to burst out of the base of the trunk, fresh with vigour. Within three weeks a tree can have a hundred prospective trunks sixty centimetres high, from which it will select one or two.[14] Some other plants resist fire, such as saltbushes and samphires. Some bloom impressively after fires, such as grass trees. When the seeds of ninety-four Western Australian plants proved unwilling to germinate, botanists exposed them to smoke from burning native vegetation, and forty-five germinated readily.[15] It has become clear that some plants need smoke to germinate.

*

Eighteen thousand years ago in parts of Europe, titanic glaciers were ripping away the surface soils and ultimately rejuvenating the soil, while most of south-west Australia hasn't gone through such turbulent glaciation since 320 to 290 million years ago.[16] On the east coast of Australia there has been comparatively more recent mountain building: think, to take an obvious example, of the Great Dividing Range. But here in the south-west, with very little going on geologically for many millions of years, the soils have been leached of nutrients. Does this mean we are digging in poor soils? This is an often-held misconception about this place. But for today's native plants, these soils are not 'deficient' in nutrients, they are just right. Put many native plants in a well-fertilised suburban garden and they may die from the presence of too much phosphorus. Only species that have not been evolving through long, dry summers for hundreds of thousands of years would find this place a 'harsh' environment. In fact, from a global perspective, the genera of plants found in heaths in the south-west of Australia are successfully dealing with the *ultimate* in low fertility soils. Only in parts of South Australia and South Africa will you encounter anything like these examples of ancient and superb adaptation to Mediterranean climate and extremely low-fertility soils.

Evolutionary biologist and botanist Stephen Hopper makes a distinction between old, stable, climatically buffered landscapes (OCBILs), and young, often disturbed, fertile landscapes (YODFELs).[17] OCBILs have endured weathering for many millions of years without much in the way of glaciation, inundation by the ocean, or rapid climate changes. Their soils have been leached of phosphorus, nitrogen and other nutrients necessary for most plant and animal life. Such old landscapes are found in south-west Australia, the Greater Cape of South Africa and parts of South America. Humans come from and have mostly inhabited young, often disturbed, fertile landscapes. South-west Australia has many old landscapes, but some coastal areas, and areas around rivers and creeks are young, fertile landscapes. According to Hopper, only poor or marginalised peoples are pushed into occupying old, climatically buffered, infertile landscapes.[18] The original inhabitants of Australia's south-west, the Noongar people, are comprised of thirteen

'Bridal Rainbow': macro photograph of Drosera macrantha *eating lacewings.* LILLY CAMPE PRIVATE COLLECTION

groups with their own dialects within the same language. The Noongar preferentially occupied the most fertile YODFELs that were locally present in the south-west, such as around estuaries and along the Darling Scarp. Many parts of the Swan Coastal Plain that are not along wetlands or rivers or at the base of the Darling Scarp – not to mention many parts of the eastern Wheatbelt that are in an zone of transitional rainfall – are old, infertile landscapes.

It is important to understand that while in Europe the soils are no older than 45,000 years, plants in Australia manage to grow out of deeply weathered and exhausted sandy soils that are between three million and four million years old.[19] The fact that these sands lack key plant nutrients such as phosphorus, potassium and nitrogen has intriguing repercussions. The beautiful, diminutive sundew plants that you might notice on the ground in Kings Park tell an instructive story.

Sundews are plants that eat insects. The stems and

leaves of these little plants glisten with drops of what smells like nectar but is actually a sticky solution of enzymes full of bacteria.[20] When insects land on the sundew to drink, they get caught in the fluid, and the enzymes and bacteria digest them and feed them to the plant. This system of collecting nutrients means that sundews can outcompete many other plants in places where nutrients are not readily come by in the soil. While there are more than 400 species of sundews found throughout the world, and fifty known species in Australia, forty-two of these are found in Western Australia. On our nutrient-poor sands, sundews have a clear advantage over many other plants. I can't see them without thinking of how symbolic they are of the very nature of this land. They are red stars in the undergrowth, flecked with promise, confidence tricksters of ancient lineage.

Other plants, like acacias, have bacteria living on their roots that capture nitrogen from the air. The handy little bacteria feed the nitrogen straight into the conducting vessels of the plant's roots. The *Macrozamia* species similarly has bunches of cyanobacteria that do the job of supplying nitrogen to them. These underground relationships are a wonder to behold, or at least a wonder to comprehend, as you generally won't see such secretive processes happening with the naked eye. Such processes are part of the reason that undisturbed land in Perth is more than beach sand. Soils analysed in undisturbed stands of one acacia species on Garden Island, soils which would have been similar to many coastal parts of contemporary Perth, showed themselves to be reasonably fertile.[21] With nitrogen-fixing legumes all around, as well as a layer of litter and organic content slowly decomposing, undisturbed native vegetation turns the Swan Coastal Plain into something much more than a developer's barren sandpit.

As in ecosystems everywhere, there are interesting stories of symbiotic relationships to be told. Australian flowers have more nectar than those found in other continents, and more species of bird-pollinated flowers grow in the south-west than in any other place on earth.[22] It is partly for this reason that the flowers are so bright and attractive. Birds have good eyesight and, in the competition to attract pollinators, the plants with the most visually impressive flowers win the evolutionary game. The furry red stem of the kangaroo paw rises from the ground, a bright red made even more vivid by its grey-green background of undergrowth. Furred green fingers sprout from the top of the red stem, curling back one after the other in elegant line and file. Wattlebirds and honeyeaters come to the plant seeking their nectar. Because of the arching shape of the flowers, the stamen brushes the bird as it sticks its long beak deep inside. The bird then unwittingly carries the pollen far away and ensures genetic diversity in the seeds.[23] The flower's beauty, in this way, is bound up in the physiology of local birds and their long beaks, and the life cycle of both plant and animal. Western Australia's floral emblem is an example of the way in which, to paraphrase John Muir, when you try to take one thing out of nature, you find that it is hitched to everything else in the universe.

Another aspect of this country concerns how damn prickly the native flora is. In the course of photographing the wildflowers of south-west Australia, photographer Stanley Breeden wrote:

> Hardness, leatheriness, brittleness, spikiness, protective wax – all these speak of an ability to endure hardship.

In spring the scleromorph's harshness is masked by soft, even delicate flowers, but we could feel it; the prickles, spikes and rough-edged leaves ripped our skin and shredded our clothes.[24]

To understand some of this harshness, it helps to know that Western Australia's flora evolved in the presence of a large number of herbivores. Think of all the great browsing mega fauna, such as the 2.5 metre tall species of kangaroo (*Procoptodon goliah*) that padded this land before the first humans arrived here. But even today there are plenty of herbivores with the urge to take a chew. So the plants need to protect themselves from being eaten, and we are wise to wear long pants when taking a stroll through the undergrowth.

Leaving the grid of electricity and the internet, even for a short while, has become a challenge for many. But for those who do, rewards await. Despite the losses to the environment over the years, there remains much to be discovered by putting down the smartphone, leaving the room, and stepping out into sandy territory.

CHAPTER 2
FORGETTING ABOUT
'WESTERN AUSTRALIA'

My crumbling first edition of W.H. Knight's history of
the state, published in 1870, informs me that, 'Western
Australia, as defined by Her Majesty's commission,
includes all that portion of New Holland situated to the
westward of the 129th degree of longitude, and extends
between the parallels of 13 deg. 44 min. and 35 deg.
South'.[1] The state of 'Western Australia' is a political
and social construct: it is, as Knight tells us, an entity
originally, 'defined by Her Majesty's commission'. But
we can see it with fresh eyes if we also regard the south-
west as an ecologically meaningful entity. It is an island
of fascinating life forms, enisled by desert to the north
and east, and ocean to the south and west. When I write
of 'the south-west' I am referring to an area that may be
delimited by drawing a line from a little south of the town
of Geraldton in the north, to around Esperance in the
south-east. Roughly to the north and east of this inwardly
curving, diagonal line the rainfall drops down below 350
millimetres per year. To the south and west of this line lies
the country in question.

A tour of this region might begin in Kings Park at
Perth's city centre, and move to the northern sand plain
heaths. 'Heath' is normally considered a tract of open,

Image of south-west Australia, highlighting cleared area. NASA

uncultivated land covered by low, usually small-leaved, shrubs; however this is a European term developed for a different landscape. A more local word to use in reference to this sandy, arid, lowly vegetated landscape is the Noongar name, kwongan. If you wander along the Swan Coastal Plain with its white and grey and yellow sands, outcrops of fossilised sand dunes (limestone), and occasional lakes and wetlands, you will notice plenty of orange or yellow or purple banksia flowers up in the branches of trees, their bright spikes held aloft against the blue.

Now turn south. After a long journey, the tall and wet forests of the south coast appear. Here groves of karri constitute some of the tallest forests on earth. Birdsong filters down from an impossibly high canopy above and, looking upwards at the towering trunks, it is easy to lose all sense of height or common proportion. After leaving the forest, you might tread around the kwongan of the south coast for a while, and stand by the ocean with its boundary of granite and spray.

Next to the north-east is mallee country – mallee being lignotuberous, multi-stemmed eucalypts that only rise a few metres tall. Then comes a journey inland to the woodlands and ancient granites of the Wheatbelt. The vegetation here is less dense, as the rainfall declines with distance from the coast. Granite tors seem marooned on hilltops, and banks of long-weathered rust-coloured gravel give way under the feet. Here the antiquity of the land is apparent, the sense of the land having moved steadily through vast tracts of time in a way few other landscapes have.

Further east are the natural salt lakes. Although we call them 'lakes', they are more often dry than full of water. These places are left over from ancient river systems that dried up a long time ago and turned into an uncoordinated maze of brilliant white and red salt lakes with nowhere to drain.

Now the journey turns back towards Perth, passing through pockets of open wandoo woodland. Feeling disoriented? Flowers on the inflorescence of a banksia open first on the warm sunny, northern side of the spike, and most slowly on the cooler southern side.

Granite boulder in Darling Range. THOMAS M. WILSON

Find a banksia flower, and look for the highest point on this sloping line of opening flowers on the banksia spike. You have found true north. Now turn and travel north along the Darling Ranges, a low plateau around 300 metres above sea level, composed of orange-coloured gravel, laterised by the ages, and covered with jarrah trees (*Eucalyptus marginata*). Finally turn west and continue until you reach a broad expanse of flat and slowly flowing water. This is the Swan River, or the Derbarl Yerrigan – those two Noongar words translating as 'estuary' and 'river' respectively. Continue west until you reach a brilliant white sand beach, made of fragments of shells and corals, by azure waters at Fremantle, where the Derbarl Yerrigan joins the Indian Ocean.

*

This south-west bioregion I have taken you through is large, about the size of a medium-sized country in Western Europe. In fact it is made up of a mosaic of many different, overlapping bioregions. Under much of this area sits the Yilgarn block, also known as the Yilgarn Craton or Western Shield, which is a vast and inert piece of the earth's crust. It is an area of granite and gneiss that is between 2,400 to 3,100 million years old. Along with the Pilbara block, this was one of the first bits of the earth's crust to emerge from the seas billions of years ago, and is the foundation upon which the rest of the Australian continent formed.

Here and there projections from this big bit of granite stick up through the soil in the Wheatbelt, creating little refuges with particular microclimates for plants and animals where the rocky terrain has not lent itself to twentieth-century agriculture. The area is tectonically inert. Deep weathering has not only taken away many plant nutrients but left quartz crystals, which have become sand grains, and oxides of iron and aluminium, as well as kaolin which gives the soils of much of the area a pale, white colour.[2] To the west of the Darling Ranges – which could more accurately be called the Darling Plateau – the Yilgarn block drops down and we have the deep sands of the Perth Basin.

And so the walk continues, into the sand and into the coastal margin. It is not for nothing that Western Australians have been colloquially referred to as 'sandgropers'. We live on sand that has been blown by the wind or washed by the ocean over hundreds of thousands of years. The real sandgroper is a large insect, *Cylindracheta*, that worms its way through the sands on the Swan Coastal Plain, much like a smaller version of the mythical beasts in Frank Herbert's science fiction novel *Dune*. However the term sandgroper might just as easily refer to a Western Australian skink such as the blunt-tailed west coast slider (*Lerista praepedita*) whose forelegs have been lost and hind legs reduced to stumps in the course of evolving to allow it to slip through the sand.

Visiting Australia, Thomas Harvey wrote in 1854 that there are 'a few Whistlers, many screamers, Screechers, & yelpers, but no songsters among the birds here'.[3] Wattlebirds and honeyeaters do indeed bring a harsh note to the Australian environment, and their calls are not usually compared favourably to the more mellow qualities of woodland or meadow soundscapes in many other countries. You may have had your morning's sleep interrupted by a paroxysm of screaming, only to find that the noise was coming from cockatoos outside the house. Australian biologist and writer Tim Low explains that many of Australia's birds have loud and aggressive calls because they are nectar eaters. Unlike fruit or insects, a single flower can supply nectar for days at a time, and such rich sources of sugar repay aggressive defence by the birds that live off them.[4] More nectar is available to bird species in Australia than on any other continent, and this country has many large, bird-pollinated flowers. The kangaroo paw is one example, but the enormous banksia flower heads are another with their stiff supporting stems evolved to sustain the weight of large feeding birds. If we look deeper, we find that Australia's depleted soils and large amounts of sunshine predispose plants to generate more sugars than they can use to produce seeds and tissues alone (which require additional minerals). And yet the surfeit of sugars generated by the plants is not wasted. Honeyeaters can get other essential nutrients from eating insects, and so they are happy to inadvertently pollinate the abundantly flowering plants in return for lots of nectar.[5] Thus emerges a link between Australia's geophysical foundations and a raucous gang of avian thugs and screechers. When you next hear a western wattlebird's stapler-like cry pierce the morning's stillness, or you walk down a suburban street and see a wattlebird harry a neighbouring crow, you'll know that such nectar-motivated aggression has its roots deep in the land under your feet.

Australia is the cradle of the songbird in evolutionary history. The term 'songbird' refers not only to birds with a sweet-sounding call, but also to birds with sophisticated songs that are in part learned.[6] The world's birds fall into forty orders, and more than half of the species of bird belong to one of these orders: Passeriformes, or passerines. These 'perching birds' are further divided into suborders, and eighty per cent of them fall into the suborder of oscines or songbirds. Genetic research over the last few decades has revealed that Australia is the base from which songbirds evolved and spread around the globe. According to some estimates, the majority of the world's birds, in terms of sheer numbers of animals, have genetic ancestors in this country.[7] Parrots, too, began in Australia and radiated out across the world. At the level of species, forty-seven per cent of the world's birds have their genetic ancestors in Australia.[8] The song of the nightingale may have conjured up a 'beaker full of the warm south' to Keats in his 'Ode to a Nightingale', but with a knowledge of modern biogeography you could read that famous line from nineteenth-century English literature as referring to the Antipodes, not Italy. Make what you like of it, but Australia was the first continent with song. The planet's bioacoustics would be impoverished if it were not for the ancestors of this country's winged-denizens.

This corner of Australia is enisled in a bioregional and evolutionary sense by the hot and inhospitable desert-like conditions further east and further north. Out beyond the line where the rainfall drops below 350 millimetres per year, there is little other than mulga and saltbush dotted around. The land falls silent. The calcareous Nullarbor Plain has isolated the flora of soils of the south-west from the flora of the soils of the south-east of Australia. The two areas have few higher plant species in common.[9]

*

Here in the south-west, the climate is Mediterranean, with a short, wet winter and a long, hot, dry summer. In summer, high-pressure anti-cyclones are formed in the Great Australian Bight, and bring hot, dry north-easterly winds from the arid interior to the coast-dwellers. Locals long for the natural air-conditioning, also known as the Fremantle Doctor, that blows from the south-west and brings cooling relief. Perth is one of the windiest capitals in the world, and Fremantle is windier. As residents try to find relief from a baking hot day, this desiccating easterly wind knocks at doors at night, wheedling its way in through cracks, and drying eyes and mouths.

Plants, as well as humans, lose their vivacity in this kind of weather. During summer, most of the plants on the Swan Coastal Plain close their stomata to restrict transpiration. These plants are called xerophytes because they have adapted to regular summer drought.[10]

As Timothy Entwisle reminds us, 'since 1788, all Australians have carried the yoke of four European seasons that make no sense in most parts of the country'.[11] European systems divide the year into four three-month-long seasons. However in most of southern Australia, summer is longer than three months. Following Entwisle, we can say that autumn is only April and May (when mushrooms and toadstools fruit across the country), and winter is only June and July (with shorter, wetter days). August and September is 'spring', our flowering season. October and November are a kind of unique, pre-summer season, where the gentle warmth of spring turns to windy, unsettled weather with flushes of heat (Entwisle calls it 'sprummer'). December marks the start of summer; with the beginning of the skink-breeding season one finds tiny skinklets climbing rocks and walls. Summer finishes at the end of March. That makes five seasons to the year.[12]

The first locals, the Noongar people, divided the year into six seasons. Birak (December–January) is hot and dry. Boonaroo (February–March) with its hot easterlies blowing from the desert is the hottest time of the year. Djiran (April–May) is when things finally cool down and some rain arrives. Mookaroo (June–July) is the coldest and wettest time of year, when occasional gales and storms pass over. Djilba (August–September) brings a mixture of wet days and cold, clear days, but overall brings a decrease in rainfall. Kambarang (October–November) is warm, and longer dry spells begin.

This is basically the same as the five seasons previously proposed for southern Australia, except that the local system split 'summer', as proposed by Entwisle, into Birak (December–January) and the very hottest and driest part of the year, Bunuru (February–March).[13] Whichever of the two systems mentioned you may choose, four seasons will not suffice. It is absurd to sit in the heat of a Perth March and speak of 'autumn', just because of a naming convention developed on the other side of the world. It is wrong-headed to witness a profusion of acacia blossom spreading over the land in August whilst maintaining that 'spring' still lies several weeks away. When I use the terms 'summer' or 'winter' in the rest of this book, it is in the spirit of Timothy Entwisle's proposed understanding of these terms.

While spring is the only season bringing new green life in much of the Northern Hemisphere, on this part of the planet there are two periods of increased plant growth and sudden flowerings. The first is when the rains start to fall in autumn (particularly in May), and the second is in spring, which runs through August and September, and even into October and November. During the long, hot summer, it is too dry for plant growth, and for the short, wet and cool winter, plant growth slows down compared to the autumn and spring periods. So in south-west Australia, the start of autumn is purged of northern-European connotations of decline and decay. Rather it can almost be conceived of as a cheerful little pre-winter spring (with cool nights) for us southerners. The old European language we speak doesn't always serve as well here, and this is one example of the disjunction between our language and our landscape. But more on this later.

For roughly half the year in Perth, there is virtually no rain. This said, one should also add that the rainfall in the south-west can range from 1500 millimetres in the extreme south-west corner to 150 millimetres at some spots further inland. For example, there is considerably more rain falling where the westerly weather systems get pushed up in altitude by the Darling Ranges, than there is where I live, close to the coast where air is pushed up by the scarp, causing rain to fall more often. In winter every few days a cold front brings sometimes heavy rains from the south-west. The nights are cold, but the days can be bright and warm. September, October and November are idyllic, with warm airs and often blue skies. 'The luxuriant vegetation, and the flower-enamelled plains of a nearly tropical spring, combine to dispel melancholy,' wrote one early settler.[14] The correspondent was right about the emotional effects of this flower-enamelled season (he was borrowing the term from Wordsworth's poem 'The River Duddon'). At this time of year, south-western Australians experience what is arguably the ideal climate on earth for human habitation.

The original inhabitants of the area that runs from Esperance to Jurien were known as the Bibbulmun, a local word that may translate as 'many breasts'. The Irish proto-anthropologist and writer, Daisy Bates, supposed that this word may be derived from the fecundity of the region.[15] It was indeed teeming with fish such as black bream and spectacular kingfish in the estuaries, and with other edible plant and animal life on land. Stephen Hopper notes that biodiversity is usually considered by evolutionary biologists to be greatest in the tropics, with high solar radiation and abundant water. For such researchers:

> the species-rich temperate regions in the Southwest Australian Floristic Region and Greater Cape [of South Africa] continue to challenge global modellers focussed on latitudinal gradients in the world's biota.[16]

The high number of plant species and the great amount of endemism (species found here and nowhere else) in the south-west shows that the biological rule of thumb, used by most who study global patterns of biodiversity, doesn't always apply.

Hopper emphasises that to understand the diversity of the south-west's plants, we need to understand history. As I have already mentioned, for the last 250 million years the south-west corner of Australia hasn't been doing much, geologically speaking, and has been worn down and leached of minerals. This has allowed the plant species to quietly diversify in their geologically stable and varied ecological niches.

In much of the south-west, away from the coast, plants are generally not in the business of distributing themselves over a wide area. It makes sense to fall close to your mother if you're a plant, as just over the hill there will be a plant species that has had millions of years to become exquisitely adapted to growing in the different soil type there. If you get blown there by the wind, your survival is unlikely, as you'll be in competition with those other better adapted plants. For this reason many plants don't specialise in getting blown far by the wind; they stay close to home.

For proof, look at the shape of the seeds of the south-west. Except for a few plants such as orchids, daisies, some native grasses, and she-oaks (*Casuarina* and *Allocasuarina,* Casuarinaceae), very few species have seeds with large wings and light weights that would adapt them to riding the winds. As Hopper writes:

> The seeds of most eucalypts, kangaroo paws (*Anigo-zanthos, Haemodoraceae*), or most shrubs and perennial herbs that dominate Southwest Australian Floristic Region plant communities are unlikely to disperse from the maternal plant more than a few metres, unless picked up by cyclonic winds, firestorms, sheet-flooding or animals.[17]

Similarly, in the south-west you will not find a lot of fleshy fruits hanging from the trees (apart from quandongs and sandalwoods: *Santalum, Santalaceae*). Such fruits act in nature as a way of enticing birds and animals to eat them, and then follows a wide dispersal of the seeds in the droppings of the animals.

With reduced dispersability of flora come high levels of local genetic divergence and endemism. The south-west is carpeted by a mosaic of ancient populations with great amounts of genetic diversity, each population well adapted to its particular soil region and environmental niche.

Knowing this, it can be argued that bioregional consciousness is even more important in south-western Australia than in other places in the world. In a northern pine forest, for example, you could know your ecosystem and its ways and then head off a thousand kilometres to another part of the forest where the knowledge that you have already acquired would be sufficient to understand much of the natural history. In south-west Australia, on the other hand, there is a fine-grained mosaic of soil types and vegetation types, so that very local knowledge of the biota is crucial. Here you really do need to think locally, down to even a few hectares, to do justice to nature.

*

Today the land of the Bibbulmun is still a remarkable centre of biodiversity with around 8,000 species of plants. The number of known and classified plant species on earth is 310,000, and is expected to reach 350,000.[18] As you can see, the south-west contains a significant proportion of the plant species in existence. South-west Australia covers only around five per cent of Australia's total surface area, but it contains almost a third of the country's 25,000 plant species. In the year 2000, the south-west bioregion was labelled a 'biodiversity hotspot', one of twenty-three concentrations of unique and threatened species of life on the planet. What is more, there remain organisms to be discovered; an exciting prospect for the future. As Edward O. Wilson writes, 'biologists and naturalists, both professional and amateur, who set out to find species and map the biosphere, [remain] … among Earth's true explorers'.[19] Just in one year, from 2012 to 2013, the names of 283 vascular plant were added to the Western Australian census of plant names by the WA Herbarium.[20] Here there are dark spots on the map. True exploration continues.

Yes, this area is botanically very diverse, but at the next level up from species, the same basic genera predominate as in south-eastern Australia: casuarina, acacias, banksias and eucalypts. The result of this is that many of the plants of this place can look similar to the untutored or casually inattentive eye. Having given this proviso, *within* the genera, the south-west does, in many cases, have a majority share of species diversity in the Australian context. Nearly all species of banksia trees are endemic to Australia – sixty-one of the seventy-eight species in existence are found in the south-west of this country. One hundred and ten of the 250 species of *Grevillea* are restricted to the south-west corner of Australia. Ninety of the 140 species of *Hakea*, sixty of the seventy species of *Persoonia*, 100 of the 150 species of *Melaleuca* … the picture that emerges is of a very high rate of endemism at the species level.[21]

*

Most of the banksias in Australia are concentrated in the south-west, so if anywhere should be called banksia country, then it is here. *Banksia menziesii* and candlestick banksia (*B. attenuata)* stand ten metres tall and raise glowing orbs of pink or yellow to the sky. Their bright colours are vivid against an often peerlessly blue sky. *B. menziesii* have been known as firewood banksia. The pink and purple flowers of *B. menziesii* blossom in autumn and winter, while the yellow candlestick banksia flowers in summer. In this way the two species don't have to compete for pollinators.

Western Australia has more species of ground orchids than any other state. In the south-west there are more species of *Melaleuca*, trigger plants and insectivorous sundews than in the rest of the country. New species of flowering plants are discovered each year in the south-west. It is true that there aren't a huge number of tree species (only twenty-three on the Swan Coastal Plain, while there are hundreds of species in the rainforest of Australia's north-east), but the shrubby ground vegetation is as diverse as any roaming Charles Darwin or Alfred Wallace could wish for. Squat down amongst the shrubs and the bushes. Open your eyes. All this tangled, growing green life has tales to tell. In areas of kwongan there is a richness of plant species that rivals tropical rainforests, the major storehouses of the planet's biodiversity.

While you will find 3,700 species of plants in the rainforests of north-east Queensland, the south-west has well over twice this number.[22] Lesueur National Park is a good example. A few hours drive north of Perth, the park contains kwongan that boasts an incredible density of species across each hectare of ground. But although it is an acknowledged centre of biological diversity, the uninformed tourist might pick a path through the prickles and miss the interest of the area, if they knew nothing of botany, or if they failed to stop and look closely. To quote Thomas Huxley, 'To a person uninstructed in natural history, his country or seaside stroll is a walk through a gallery filled with wonderful works of art, nine-tenths of which have their faces turned to the wall'.[23]

What of the flying, hopping, and crawling inhabitants of this place? Compared to land in most developed nations, it isn't all that well-known an area when it comes to the animals. For example, the tiny orange-bellied sunset frog was only discovered in 1994, in a swamp on the south coast near Walpole. I've seen one of these squirming little creatures, about the size of a fifty cent coin, held delicately in the gloved hand of a breeder at the Perth Zoo. The frog is dark on top but glows a brilliant orange on its belly, a colouration that has given it its English language name. These secretive animals live in relict peat bogs in burrows under the water, digging up to the surface when they need to. They have been doing so since long, long ago when the south-west was covered in a thick blanket of rainforest.

In the south-west there are twelve species of mammals, ten species of birds, twenty-seven species of reptiles and twenty-two species of frogs that are endemic to the region. I can't tell you how many species of insects live here. Invertebrates and non-vascular plants (mosses, lichens, and the like) are poorly known. The state has hundreds of species of reptile, those contemporaries of the dinosaurs that abide with us still, and these are coping better with European colonisation than other animals, and few are endangered. Perth itself has seventy species within its boundaries, making it the top city globally in terms of number of reptile species.[24]

A screeching sound comes from above. A mob of black cockatoos wheels and swings across the blue sky, red tail feathers flashing in the light. Most people associate parrots with the tropics. However Australia has a greater diversity of parrots than any other landmass. Parrots are the seed-eaters of the south-west. The mob lands in the crown of a marri tree (*Corymbia calophylla*), and the birds begin, excitedly, to balance on thin branches and take large marri nuts in their specially elongated beaks and tease out the seeds within. The seeds from the marri nuts are especially nutritious. This is because these trees cast a deeper shade than most other eucalypts and, to aid their seedlings' growth, marri seeds contain extra starch.[25] This land has plenty of hard nuts to crack, and the long story of evolution has granted this ecosystem the big, powerful beaks of these birds to crack them open. Interestingly, these nuts may have been partly the cause of the high level of intelligence found in birds such as the black cockatoo. While the kernels of the nuts became bigger to defend against marauding mobs of cockatoos, the birds evolved yet larger jaws to attack them. Such large jaws require large skulls. Parrots, uniquely among birds, have two muscles, Musculus ethmomandibularis and Musculus pseudomasseter, that control their large mandibles. They have associated areas of their brain devoted to the control of these muscles.[26] As the evolutionary race between the nuts and the parrots continued across the millennia, the parrots developed larger skulls with more complex brains.

In general, the bird and mammal species in the south-west aren't that different from the ones found in the eastern states. However this place *is* notable in that it is often the only place where some of the country's mammals have hung on, in many cases living meekly on the sunny side of extinction. The small, carnivorous and cat-like chuditch, for example, used to scurry over eighty per cent of Australia's surface. The chuditch now occupies less than two per cent of its former range.[27] These days you may only find one, if you're very lucky, in a few pockets of forest or woodland in south-west Australia.

The Swan Coastal Plain is the large area of parallel sand dunes, originally fragments of shell and coral and other skeletal remains, built up by prevailing westerly winds over thousands of years, with low relief and patches of wetland dotted here and there. This long patch of sand borders the Indian Ocean. Where it isn't flat, this area takes the shape of gently undulating north-south dunes, which stops rivers such as Ellen Brook and the Serpentine River from running directly west and causes them to meander south for many kilometres before meeting the Indian Ocean.

Where there is rock, it is usually limestone. This rock was formed only a few thousands of years ago when rainwater seeped down through the dunes and quartz sands, and shell fragments cemented into sandy stone. Lime sands became lime stones. Tuart trees (*Eucalyptus gomphocephala*) love this lime-rich environment, and some have survived the wholesale land clearing of the coastal plain.

Compared to many places in the world, the land is pretty flat. Because of this low relief, the rains that fall in the cool months don't always flow straight off into the river or the ocean but have the chance to pool in a scattered mosaic of wetlands across the plain, and trickle down into underground aquifers that are drawn from for much of Perth's water supply. In the hot months the top few metres of the land dry out, too, but for many metres below this, the sand is saturated from past winters' rainfall. The transition from the dry sand to the wet sand is referred to as the 'water table'. Where the land's surface dips below this level, wetlands form. Many of these wetlands appear as long north-south grooves, such as the Beeliar Chain south of the Swan River. Walk through these wetlands, or wade through them, and you'll see the soft, ancient trunks of paperbarks (*Melaleuca rhaphiophylla*) bending and twisting over themselves, their ragged flaps of soft bark hanging limp on a still day or flapping in a south-westerly. Long-necked tortoises (if feral foxes haven't eaten them) might peer up at you from the dark, flat surface of the water as you stand perched on a prostrate log. The sound of the breeze soughs through the fine leaves above. It is a peaceful place. A flag of light might catch your eye on the silky trunk of a nearby paperbark, and you can hear a babble of honkings, tweetings, and the repeated splash of wings on water further out on the lake. These dark, shaded places are naturally air-conditioned oases, wetlands to be treasured amidst the hot, arid and sandy plain by which they are encircled.

When water falls from the sky in the Darling Ranges and forms a river, it is usually stopped by a concrete dam on its way to the sea. In the dry months, much of the Swan, one of the only rivers that has not been dammed from the Darling Ranges, becomes stagnant in shallow pools. The Noongar man, Weeip, said of local rivers around Perth in 1835, 'they are now dead, but when the rain comes they shall be alive, & walk into the sea.'[28] The Swan 'walks' for sixty kilometres across the Swan Coastal Plain and eventually enters into the Indian Ocean, at Fremantle. Here beach spinifex clings to the white sand above the clear blue waters, and behind the dunes, moonah and native cypress huddle under relentless salty sea breezes. Further back again, tuart trees rise tall and thickly trunked. This coastal vegetation comes from a more youthful landscape than the ancient hills that the inhabitants of Perth can see to the east. Over the past two million years, periods of higher and lower sea level have been experienced, and the coastal flora and fauna are well adapted to dispersing widely. This, as Stephen Hopper notes, is great for Coastcare volunteers trying to restore the land with newly established plantings.[29]

The south-west is a place of contrasts and diversity. The images that would come to the mind of a wandering naturalist are many. Acacia kwongan: bird-haunted and amorphous. Peppermint grove: cool and shady. Banksia woodland: bright torches of colour held aloft over a riot of other flowering species beneath. Karri forest: giant, white-pillared temple of Australia. A Noongar lizard trap, a slab of rock propped up by two smaller rocks by long-dead hands, poised and still, immemorially waiting for prey on a granite outcrop in the Wheatbelt. Never to fall.

*

It is December, close to Perth in John Forrest National Park, the season of birak for the Noongar. Someone is walking through the jarrah, wandoo and dryandra clothed slopes of the Darling Scarp in late afternoon light. Less rain falls here than in the jarrah forests further south, and thus less grows in the way of a tangled understorey. The walker enjoys the freedom of movement that such openness allows. This is not a gushing, romantic, landscape. The crackle of dry leaves follow steps over the ground. This land is spartan and dry, ancient and philosophical. Unlike soft temperate forests, it has an intense and stark lucidity and openness. It is not a place of gentle excrescences. It is a place of dry open shrubs and light-shunning eucalyptus leaves that point down towards earth, and let the

49

sunshine slip past. Evening light falls on the dry bark and white trunks of old wandoo trees. Granite monadnocks squat like unlettered runestones. Perhaps next time this walker recalls that they live in 'Western Australia', thoughts of stark lucidity and rounded granite will come to mind, the old bones of the planet, sticking up through the surface. This is no pastoral idyll. This is a land that requires recognition of hard and ancient truths.

CHAPTER 3
THE FIRST LOCALS OF
THE SOUTH-WEST

A country without a memory is a country of madmen.

– *George Santayana*

Edward O. Wilson wrote that, 'although exalted in many ways, we remain an animal species of the global fauna.'[1] We humans are a variety of African ape, and our story need not be radically separated from that of other animals. Before we get to the first humans to live in the south-west, a quick note on the history of animal life that had already co-opted this part of the globe.

As far as vertebrates go, Australia has a representative of the ratites (flightless birds such as the emu), and mammals of the class Monotremata. The latter include the echidna, an animal which is really a mammal, but which gives birth by laying eggs, and anatomically in many ways gives the impression of being halfway between reptiles and mammals; these animals have a truly ancient evolutionary lineage. Then comes our real Australian speciality: marsupials. These animals give birth to their young without using a placenta, and their tiny babies do much of their development in the pouch (in Latin, the marsupium) rather than the womb.

When Australia separated from Antarctica many

millions of years ago, there may have been just one founder species of marsupial, perhaps possums of some kind. They were stepping into the vacant shoes that the dinosaurs had left after their mass extinction. Over the next forty million years, marsupials, with Australia all to themselves, diversified impressively. Of the planet's approximately 270 species of marsupial, Meganesia (Australia and its tropical wing, New Guinea) has around 200.[2] They fill the roles, or 'trades', filled by mammals in other corners of the globe. In the Pliocene (five to 1.6 million years ago) the kangaroo genus emerged.[3] Later in the story, some bats and rodents jumped onto the continental island when Australia started to bump into the islands to its north (for the rodents this was first around five million and then one million years ago), and who have since diversified into their own suites of local Australian animals.

Finally we get to the two-legged ones. Around six million years ago in East Africa an upright ape emerged from the other ape species. While big-eared marsupials had been adapting to a drier, more arid Australia, proto-humans had stepped out of the forest and into an increasingly drier, more open woodland environment in their African homeland. By around two million years ago this evolutionary line gave birth to a creature that looked roughly, at least from the neck down, like humans do today. Brain sizes steadily increased over the next two million years until *Homo sapiens,* our species, had very large brains indeed in proportion to body size. At this point there were only around 10,000 to 100,000 of us on the planet. Only in the last 100,000 years or less is there evidence of human art.

If the toucan can be thought of as a South American species, then humans can be thought of as an African species; these are our origins. However some humans eventually left Africa and spread around the Indian Ocean, into Australia.

As archaeological remains in a cave known as Devil's Lair demonstrate, humans have been in south-west Australia for more than 47,000 years.[4] To speak of Australia as a 'young country' is to show a profound ignorance not only of the geological and biological nature of this land, but also of the human history here. For most of our history, humans have lived in a tightly co-evolved situation with other large mammals, which we've hunted and eaten, or in some cases been eaten by. Australia was the first continent where we stepped into a world in which this situation was absent, where gentle megafauna browsed the vegetation, where hunting was at first easy, and where the previous evolutionary constraints, imposed by gradual coevolution alongside our prey, were released. Australia was in this sense the first New World. Sadly the huge marsupial herbivores, such as the two metre tall *Diprotodon optatum* (a wombat-shaped creature that was the size of a large rhinoceros) that roamed Australia, were not to survive into recent millennia of human habitation. Gone also from that time are koala-sized possums (*Pseudokoala*) and seven-metre long goannas (*Megalania prisca*). You can still see spidery claw marks scratched into the wall by marsupial lions (*Thylacoleo carnifex*) in the main chamber of a cave near Margaret River.[5] The use of fire by the first Australians may have crucially changed the vegetation they were used to eating (this remains an active area of investigation and controversy).[6] Today such animals only remain as rare bones in underground caves or fossilised footprints in inland lakes. Humans today can never know Australia as a land of browsing giants.

So forget Willem Janszoon or James Cook, at least for the time being. The bold explorer and mariner who set foot upon a virgin continent was not a feted European, but a long-forgotten Aborigine. This was truly the first time in the history of the human race that humans had discovered a habitable and distinct continent, and gone forth to explore it. We don't know exactly when that great event took place, but we do know that humans have lived in the south-west for more than 470 centuries (maybe even 600 centuries or longer), gathering and gossiping, hunting and orating, teaching and fighting, loving and creating art. Hundreds of millions of humans, over the course of many thousands of years, may have talked with each other and walked this continent before the first European set foot ashore here.[7] That's a lot of people, and adds up to a lot of human history and heritage.

Around 18,000 to 22,000 years ago, global temperatures fell and the earth's polar icecaps expanded significantly. This dropped the sea level 130 metres, and meant it was possible to walk from Perth to Rottnest on dry land. Around 15,000 years ago, the sea level began to rise again. By 9,000 years ago the coast had a similar shape to today.[8] One early European settler described an Aboriginal story that told of how Rottnest, Carnac and Garden islands (Wadjemup, Ngooloormayup and Meeandip) were once part of the mainland, until the land caught fire and splintered off into the sea. Such a high-fidelity oral history telling of a post-glacial shoreline inundation, a story that must have been passed down hundreds of human generations, has recently been corroborated. Researchers have analysed the region's bathymetry, and dated this story back 7,500 to 8,900 years ago.[9]

The other aspect of the south-west that changed

during this glacial period was the vegetation cover. As in the south-east, vegetation cover was reduced overall – although not as drastically as in the south-east.[10] The bands of vegetation shifted around, with arid conditions coming in further west than today, with woodland replacing forest, and with forest replacing tall open forest. Further east, in what is today the Wheatbelt, we can suppose that humans abandoned particularly arid areas, and congregated around the remaining resources. At the end of the Pleistocene, around 12,000 to 10,000 years ago, these changes were reversed and vegetation patterns returned to something like what we see today in the south-west. Australian societies developed new and smaller types of stone tools around 4,000 to 5,000 years ago.[11] The dingo also entered the country from the north around this time.

Today most of the world thinks of the first Australians as desert peoples. In fact most of them lived in the wetter parts of the continent, such as south-western Australia, and not in the extremely arid desert areas.[12] Around 5,000 years ago there seems to have been an increase in the production and complexity of stone technology, as well as a general increase in the human population in Australia.[13] Around this time, more of the arid regions show evidence of human occupation. The increase in the continent's population may have pushed some people out into the desert but these people were still the minority.

There were several cultural groups in the south-west of Australia, but they spoke a mutually intelligible language – Noongar – with only mild regional variations. Unlike the Western Desert groups to the north and east, the people of the south-west did not practise circumcision and teeth-pulling (avulsion) as part of male initiation.[14]

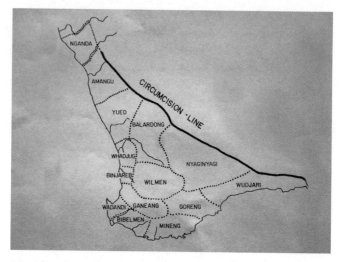

Map of south-west language groups bordered by the 'circumcision line'.
NEVILLE GREEN

Only a few thousands years ago, the Swan Coastal Plain was much larger than it is today. Sea level was lower and the Derbarl Yerrigan wound over a longer plain as it travelled west to the sea. The shoreline was fifty-one kilometres west of the current suburb of Cottesloe.[15] Tennyson's famous words on loss and change could be a coda for the submerged hunting grounds to Perth's west: 'there rolls the deep where grew the tree'.[16] The Derbarl Yerrigan formed what is now known as the Perth Canyon, which incises a deep gorge now underwater about twenty-five kilometres west of Rottnest. If one could drain the Indian Ocean and walk to the edge of the Perth Canyon, a dramatic scene would be revealed. Formed millions of years ago, the canyon is 100 kilometres long, and is around four kilometres deep, which is deeper than the Grand Canyon in America.[17] For longer than we will know, the largest organism that has ever lived on the face of the planet, the blue whale, has hung and drifted in this vast blue canyon and used it as a feeding ground. You can picture the blue whales singing their unique songs together in this lost world, while just a few kilometres away Noongar men waded through the sandy shallows of the Derbarl Yerrigan spearing tailor on a warm summer's evening.

*

Just prior to white settlement there were more people on the Swan Coastal Plain than, for example, in the thick karri forests to the far south. These people didn't live in tribes, but in what is more accurately described as large extended families of up to fifty people (most often these groups were of twenty to thirty people). Each of these nomadic groups used the word 'kaalak' to describe their 'hearth' – literally, their 'place of fire'. A family might make their 'fire' under a rock or a bush or near to water, and it was the fire, rather than any structure that constituted 'home'.[18] One's kaalak was also the country that one set on fire each year to produce a fresh crop of grass for grazing kangaroo. Another use for fire was to burn a break around an area of trees where berries were known to grow.[19] If somebody wanted to set fire to some land to hunt kangaroo, they must first get the permission of the owner, otherwise, according to the law, they should be speared.[20] Some people say that where they hang their hat is where they call home. These people would say that where they set their fire is their home. This unique conception of home is radically different to modern European linguistic and mental constructions of a home place.

By 1836, British settlers in the Middle and Upper Swan could declare that they had 'accomplished the arduous task of transforming a wilderness into a fruitful and civilized district'.[21] This kind of language was almost reminiscent of the *hortus conclusus*, or enclosed garden, of medieval Europe, where the world outside the cultivated natural enclosure was a howling wilderness of chaos and danger, only of value when it had been turned into a human garden of some kind. Through their seasonal burning of large parts of the south-west, the first Australians were already resident ecosystem engineers. Much of the wilderness had been transformed into a fruitful district many thousands of years before white settlers arrived; they simply failed to see it with their European eyes.

Most of the forest trees in this part of the world can easily cope with fire, unless it is a very, very intense fire that destroys the overstorey. Fire actually benefits native grasses, annual and biennial herbs, large macropods, some fungi and some invertebrates.[22] It was the large macropods, or kangaroos, that most interested the early human burners of the bush. Fire can be bad for some late-maturing obligate seeders (plants that put lots of seeds out after the fire has passed through), and mammals, birds and invertebrates that prefer mature vegetation.[23] The current wisdom is that the best outcome for biodiversity in the south-west is not to entirely exclude fire from the landscape, (apart from very rare and intense fires that tear through everything including human property), and rather to have a mosaic of fine-scaled patches of vegetation that have experienced fire at different points in the past. This creates a complex diversity of post-fire habitats. Smaller patches are better than larger ones, and having a broad range of post-fire stages represented is better than having narrower ones.[24] A patchwork of flame-licked vegetation has a long history in this region.

That said, species and ecosystems easily killed off by

frequent or large and intense fires need protection. Such species might include plants that have long juvenile periods and depend on seeds stored on the plant to regenerate.[25] In a jarrah forest, around ninety-seven per cent of understorey species reach flowering age within three years of a fire, and all species reach flowering age within five to six years of a fire.[26] This suggests that if the jarrah forest were to be burnt more frequently than every three years, great damage would be done to the floral biodiversity contained within. Examples of the animals in the south-west that don't do well with too frequent-fires include quokkas (*Setonix brachyurus*), mardos (yellow-footed antechinus, *Antechinus flavipes*), honey possums (*Tarsipes rostratus*), and quenda (bandicoot, *Isoodon obesulus*). These generally prefer the less flammable parts of the landscape, such as areas bordering wetlands. Quokkas are stumpy-limbed little wallabies, commonly known to tourists on Rottnest Island. Although most tourists would not know this, quokkas like to hide in swamps or along rivers during the day. Quokkas also like recently burnt areas being near their hideouts so they can go there at night to feed. Even such damp and sheltered habitats need fire every few decades to regenerate, as they begin to get old and die thirty to forty years after fire, and that they no longer give good cover to quokkas for fifteen to twenty years after fire.[27] Thus a good fire management practice, where quokkas are found, would require controlled burning in moist, spring conditions, so that the upland forests burn mildly and the swamps and creeklines don't burn at all.[28]

*

In the summer of 1826, Major Edmund Lockyer was on the deck of the *Amity*, bound to establish a military garrison at present day Albany. As the ship approached Western Australia, he saw on land, 'a great fire was made as if by persons requiring assistance'.[29] The irony is only apparent to us now. Commander John Lort Stokes recorded a picture of the first Australians managing fire:

> The dexterity with which they manage so proverbially a dangerous agent as fire is indeed astonishing. Those to whom this duty is especially entrusted, and who guide or stop the running flame, are armed with large green boughs, with which, if it moves in a wrong direction, they beat out. [...] The whole scene is a most animated one, and the eager savage, every muscle in action and every faculty called forth, then appears to the utmost advantage, and indeed almost another being. I can conceive of no finer subject for a picture than a party of these swarthy beings engaged in kindling, moderating and directing the destructive element, which under their care seems almost to change its nature, acquiring, as it were, complete docility, instead of the ungovernable fury we are accustomed to ascribe to it. Dashing through the thick underwood amidst volumes of smoke, – their dark active limbs and excited features burnished by the fierce glow of the fire, – they present a spectacle [...] which it is impossible to convey any adequate idea by words.[30]

Jarrah trees are scorched and scarred by very hot fires. Transverse cuts have been made in jarrah trees, which show that very few fire-scars were made before 1850. This is, interestingly, the approximate date that a major measles epidemic swept the Aboriginal population, and the date at which the government banned the setting of fires in summer.[31] As a result, fuel load was allowed to build up on the forest floor, after which a simple lightning strike would be enough to create more infrequent but much more intense fires than in earlier times. Again, the dark wood inside a tree trunk proves to be the best environmental historian we have for this changing Australia. The very frequent burning of the jarrah forest before 1850 would have encouraged grasses and grazing wallabies and kangaroos – exactly what the Noongar hunters wanted – however, there were still areas left unburnt to which fire-sensitive animals could retreat. Another study, this time of the insides of the balga (grass tree), also showed a decrease in fire frequency from the time when the first Australians inhabited the woods, to contemporary times.[32] When my great-great-grandfather William Shakespeare Hall walked around the jarrah and marri forest along the Darling Scarp, he would have strolled over a carpet of fresh grass. Today, where suburban development hasn't erased all history, one faces a densely packed understorey beneath jarrah and marri trees.

The first human locals slept on dried sheets of paperbark (bewel) or mindar (balga leaves) in their miya – a small beehive-shaped dwelling made from the spears of balgas or sticks, and thatched with the leaves of balgas, or with paperbark or other nearby foliage. Three balga flower spears were made to lean together, whereupon twigs were leant on the frame and woven together tightly at the top, and the mindar were mounded up as thatch to keep the rain out.

Early settler George Fletcher Moore wrote:

in the midst of night we were awoken by maturing thunder and flashes of lightning. With the assistance of the natives, a hut was soon erected and thatched with the leaves of the grass tree under which we slept secure from wind and rain. So much comfort was derived from this hut that the same practice was pursued almost every night afterwards; it is easily and readily made, & is a complete preservative from rheumatism or the effects of cold, wind, rain or dew. With a quantity of the tops of the grass tree, or small twigs of bushes spread upon the ground as a bed, a hut over the head, & fire at your feet, there is little to be apprehended from exposure in the bush.[33]

Although Moore didn't know it, the savannah shelter of our African ancestors was made in similar way and, along with the nests made in trees by other great apes, ranks as a candidate for extreme antiquity.[34] Usually there would be two or three of these little shelters together, but sometimes up to seven could be found clustered in a group.[35] At the mouths of these huts, arranged in a semi-circle facing inwards, would sometimes be flat stones on which to grind yams and seeds.

For thousands of years the south-western Australians reclined in their huts for part of the day and looked out past the smouldering fire and the flat stone to the backs of other huts and to trees and clouds and sand and bird movement. The huts faced away from the wind, and no hut overlooked another.[36] If it was summer, they would be camped close to the coast by a wetland, looking out over a tangled thicket of paperbarks and tea trees. As the most common wind is a south-westerly, the shelters would be facing north-east. This perspective, this window frame, an A-frame of a miya's entrance pointing north-east with loose ends of vegetation hanging along its edge, is more than 470 centuries old.

A group of miya clustered beneath a tree. NOT TITLED [ABORIGINAL CAMP], *RICHARD ATHERTON FFARINGTON, STATE ART COLLECTION, ART GALLERY OF WESTERN AUSTRALIA*

Of course sometimes on summer nights these first Western Australians just slept behind a windbreak of bushes. To keep water in the camp they made a depression in the sand and used paperbark to line it. Single men camped away from the married men, women and children. When a woman had her period, she too slept away from the rest of the camp for a few days. Dingos slept with the people, among their feet and legs.[37] When leaving their miya for a day, the people would sweep around the shelter with a bunch of leaves. This allowed them to observe the footprints of any strangers who passed by in their absence.[38] Eyre wrote that the men were:

> well built and muscular, with proportionate upper and lower extremities … fine broad chests, indicating great bodily strength, and are remarkably erect and upright in their carriage, with much natural grace and dignity of demeanour.[39]

They walked naked in summer. The men were bearded. The women made yarn from kangaroo and possum fur which the men then wrapped many times around their waists: their kadjo or stone axes, hung behind them like a tail, hanging down between their buttocks. They might also have hung their kyli, or boomerang, from this belt. Often the men would walk ahead carrying three hunting spears and a mero (throwing board), while the women brought up the rear carrying the stone axes, bags for roots and other burdens.[40]

They hunted wetj; the emu (*Dromaius novaehollandiae*) that with its huge, liquid brown eyes stood tall, looking down. Sometimes a nest with eight large, green, dinosaur-like eggs was found. One can picture a hunter facing the proudly arched neck of the wetj up close, lightly coated in black feathers at the top, with a jagged pyramid of menacing, dark beak, darting down in defence of its progeny. As well as the meat and eggs taken, emu oil from the fat of the great bird was used as a skin moisturiser. The kernels from the sandalwood tree were also pounded and the resulting sandalwood oil was applied to the skin.[41]

The language of these south-westerners was responsive to their green home. Their names for birds and animals often contained onomatopoeic echoes of the sounds those birds or animals made. The Noongar people called the willy-wagtail 'djiti-djiti', which is an imitation of one of its calls. They called the red-tailed black cockatoos 'karak', a word which, when spoken, sounds much more like nature speaking than its English equivalent, 'cockatoo' (in fact the word 'cockatoo' comes from the Malay language, and reflects the fact that many of the parrots that first reached London were taken from the Spice Islands, or present day Maluku[42]). 'Chuditch' is supposedly the sound that the 'native cat' of the same name makes when cornered or in danger.

In winter, Noongar people retreated to the area inland just below the Darling Ranges, away from the strong and chilly winds coming off the ocean. Here the soils were richer than towards the coast, and open woodland of stately marri trees stood tall. And there they found hard stone for their hafted axes and sharp knifes. The kadjo (stone axes) had ground edges and were strong enough to cut into the dense hardwood trunks of the native trees. To keep warm the people wore booka, long cloaks made of three or so female kangaroo furs sewn together and fastened with a bone or wooden pin in front. Yongka (kangaroos) are fattest in June. Noongars hunted yongka, leaving the camp in the morning in groups of two or three,

Detail from Panoramic view of King George's Sound, part of the Colony of Swan River, *1834. ROBERT DALE, ENGRAVED BY ROBERT HAVELL. KERRY STOKES COLLECTION*

and using the noise of the wind and the rain to provide cover. They would stalk the animals from downwind to avoid having their scent detected, and run low and silently behind bushes, spears clasped in one fist, the other hand sometimes touching the ground and sometimes forming hand signals to communicate with their fellow hunters. Although such kills may not have been the main source of calories for the group, when yongka or wetj were speared it would have been a big event in the camp. As Lorna Marshall remarked after spending time in another gathering and hunting society:

> there is no splendid excitement and triumph in returning with vegetables. The return of the hunter from a successful hunt is vastly different. The intense craving for meat, the uncertainty and anxiety that attend the hunt, the deep excitement of the kill, and finally, the eating and the satisfaction engage powerful emotions in the people.[43]

One can imagine that a sense of excitement and pleasure that accompanied the return of the successful hunter. The kangaroo was cut into pieces and grilled on red-hot coals.[44] Most of the time, smaller prey and food items such as frogs, snakes, grubs and roots were eaten.

Unlike for modern residents of suburban Perth, life for these people was profoundly seasonal. As the year progressed and summer approached, the people moved westwards towards the coast and towards what is now Fremantle. The profuse yellow and orange flowerings of the moodjar, the Western Australian Christmas tree (*Nuytsia floribunda*), give forth some of the most spectacular blooms of any tree in the world. Apart from being the world's largest parasitic plant, if you dig up the suckers underground and peel back the pale yellow outer bark, you can eat the moist, brittle centre, which tastes like candy. But the orange blossoms have something to say; they have spoken another of the changes in the year's calendar. As the nomads moved in single file, the women carried bags made from kangaroo skins, some containing roots and resin and some containing babies.[45] One can imagine the perspective of such infants: hanging in a bag, against their mother's warm body, feeling the delicate soft fur against their naked skin, peeking out at the green world slowly revolving by, and hearing the murmur and chattering voices of their tribe, a sense of deep belonging absorbed from the very beginning.

In this early time of summer, thousands of tall candle-stick banksia flowers start to glow yellow in the sun. The people collected the flowers of the mangatj, steeping them in paperbark-lined holes filled with fresh water to create a sweet liquid drink. This time, December to February, was known as the yellow season in banksia country.

Towards the coast the banksias disappear and the tuart forests take over. Here, every spring, men climbed ancient tuart trees by tapping and chipping foot holds in vast, grey trunks with stone axes, and then ascending foot-after-hand, to collect the eggs of parrots from holes in twisting branches far above the ground. The lakes and wetlands such as today's Lake Claremont, Lake Monger, Herdsman's Lake, North Lake, Bibra Lake and Manning Lake provided digging grounds for frogs and tortoises in the mud at their edges. The frogs' eggs were a delicacy. Women killed norn, the highly venomous yellow-bellied tiger snakes (*Notechis scutatus*), for food, not to mention all the other legless lizards in the leaf litter and the sand. The people ate a long white root called warran, and other roots and tubers that the women dug up with their wonars, hard-tipped digging sticks (although there are more warran in the damp clay soils, amongst rocks, to the east close to the Darling Scarp). It was best to dig for them after the first rains, but they were eaten throughout the year. Sometimes the people returned to a few square kilometres of warran fields again and again. Warran were known to grow up to three feet in length and made an excellent meal, raw or cooked.[46]

In March the rhizomes of the bulrush (*Typha domingensis*) were dug up, pounded to get rid of the fibrous bits, then moulded into damper to roast. At this time, the bulbous, bright red, pineapple-like fruits of the zamia palm were also ready to be harvested, but they were soaked in water for two weeks, then dried and roasted, a process that leached out enough toxins to enable the fruit be eaten. Small cakes were made from koonart (acacia) seeds and saved for leaner times.

In the trunks of decaying balga, they found fat, white bardi (beetle larvae) and they also ate the white-coloured pith of the balga.

As summer came on, fishing became their main source of protein. The Derbarl Yerrigan was alive in a way modern inhabitants of Perth could barely guess at. A report from the time states that, 'The river abounds with fish, white salmon, snappers, gard fish, smelts, mullet, and a variety of other sorts'.[47]

According to another early settler:

Exceedingly expert in spearing fish, [the Noongar] some-times pass the tents with a load, one of which is generally entangled in their hair. They are very inoffensive, and appear to have no idea of possessing any thing beyond sufficiency for present want.[48]

The small detail in this passage of a fish entangled in the locks of a Noongar man as he lugs his catch homewards takes us to a time of sheer abundance for the Swan River. George Fletcher Moore wrote in 1832 that, 'at Guildford, the people were on one occasion actually alarmed by the noise of fish leaping and rushing up the river'.[49]

As cold, fresh water stops flowing down from the hills, the river lets more of the ocean's waters into its lower reaches. The creatures that live out in the sea, the prawns, crabs, fish and plankton and the like, come into the warm salty waters of the river (this trend has increased in the twentieth century since the entrance to Fremantle Harbour has had a reef removed from its mouth). In winter a skin of cold, fresh water lies at the surface, supporting flounder, black bream and the odd errant long-necked tortoise in the reeds. But now it is summer and the Derbarl Yerrigan is alive with healthy shoals of big tailor, cobbler (*Tandanus bostocki*), tiger shark, snapper and even the occasional two-metre long kingfish with powerful, muscular blue-and-white body twisting like lightning through the water. Blue manna crabs slink along the sandy bottom of the river with their large spread-eagled, iridescent arms held aloft. Seahorses back and ferry into spinneys of brown weed. The locals fished by herding fish into the sandy shallows and spearing them with their gidgees. A gidgee is a handheld spear rather than a throwing spear. On a still evening on the bilya, men stood motionless above the dead calm water, burning sticks held aloft in one hand, gidgee ready to strike at fish attracted to the light. Canoes and fishing hooks were not to be seen, but here and there weirs made of bark and twigs were used to trap fish.

*

Imagine a bank of the Derbarl Yerrigan one late afternoon in 1827. A quenda ambles along through the understorey, twitching his long, black nose. A shy honey possum creeps through the leafy canopy above, three long brown stripes running down her back, cream-coloured belly just visible. She flicks her long, agile tongue into a yellow candlestick banksia's flower, clinging to the flower spike with tiny, almost human-like hands. From above you can hear the sound of kwel (casuarina) needles soughing and singing in the wind. The day passes quietly, as it has for thousands of years.

At the water's edge, a group of about twenty men, women, children, and half a dozen dingos, are assembled. Roots, quandong and fish have been collected and hunted during the day. Nobody bothers to gather for a meal during the day, but as evening begins everybody looks forward to coming together.[50] A tale is being told around a campfire at the slow-flowing river's sandy shore. Behind the narrator, the western sky is lighting up a tapestry of cumulus. The narrator's long-bearded face is animated, and his hands dart left and right to further articulate his story of adventure on the trail of prey. Dingos lounge, and their tails wag languidly. A honeyeater looks down on the group from a branch above in the dusk. The audience put their hands out to the feel the warmth from the smouldering logs in the fire. Someone wraps a tailor in a shroud of paperbark, covered with hot ashes then left to cook in the coals. At their backs, stands a grove of encircling native cypress (*Callitris preissii*), dark-green sprays rising upwards, at their feet a dull navy green tangle of hakeas and acacias.

Attention returns to the story around the fire. The steaming fish is lifted from the coals and unwrapped. The aroma pervades the clearing and sharpens appetite. A young boy laughs as somebody cracks a joke.

Around the fire the first Australians form a discontinuous ring, squatting, half kneeling or sitting cross-legged. Time passes. The evening lengthens. Red light from the fire reflects and flickers on the underside of native cypress branches.

It is a dark night with a new moon. Out on the dark water, a huge flock of black swans, hundreds and hundreds of them, begins to move. The dingos turn their heads sharply. Snouts point out into the darkness, nostrils flaring, gulping in scent. The people look out, into the darkness. It is a black night, but the rush from the surface of the water is palpable. The swans are taking off.

CHAPTER 4
'OLD WORLD' ENCOUNTERS

Amongst globalised men and women on the streetscapes of Perth, knowledge of the place they inhabit is often limited to the top layer: concrete, metal and glass. Such metropolitan vision is nothing new. For a long time, Western European culture, and its transplanted colonial progeny, has been largely a product of the city. Disinterest about the land in south-western Australia by Europeans has a long history. First of all it had a Dutch accent:

Christmas Day. 1696.
Came to the Southland …

Walked northwards. Lizards,
Reptiles. A rat-like creature
Hunching its back; droppings
Like loathsome birds eggs.
Spiky bracken. Limestone.
No signs of habitation.
Returned to the ship after
Three days. The Southland
Hazy in the morning sun.
Set sail. [1]

These lines from Nicholas Hasluck's poem 'Rottnest Island' envisage the early Dutch encounter with the Western half of Australia, an encounter characterised here by disinterest on behalf of the visitors. In fact when Willem de Vlamingh anchored with three Dutch ships off the north coast of Rottnest in 1696, he recorded enjoying the 'scented groves' of native cypress, and the 'pleasant song' of what were probably singing honeyeaters (*Lichenostomus virescens*).[2] However, in the ship's log written by Mandrop Torst, the island is described as covered in white sand and rock and unsuitable for cultivation.[3] It is unfortunate that this land should have entered into written history in the second millennium of the Common Era with what proved ultimately to be a fizzle. There were no low-bulk and high value substances here that might be traded by the Dutch East India Company. And so the Dutch set sail for the horizon.

The French were also to visit the Swan River, but they did not extol its beauties. Perhaps most significant was the voyage of Nicolas Baudin of 1800 to 1804, that left a legacy of more than 250 French place names on the Western Australian coastline.[4] French interest in the region was one of the spurs to British colonisation. On a small British expedition up the river in 1827, James Stirling was more excited by what he saw, dubbing it rich and romantic country. 'Rich and romantic' isn't a negative initial impression of the Western Australian landscape by English eyes accustomed to fields, woods and hedgerows. However Stirling was here exposed to the profuse vegetation growing in the alluvial flats built up over thousands of years of the river flooding its banks and leaving sediments, creating much more fertile soils than are typical for the Swan Coastal Plain in

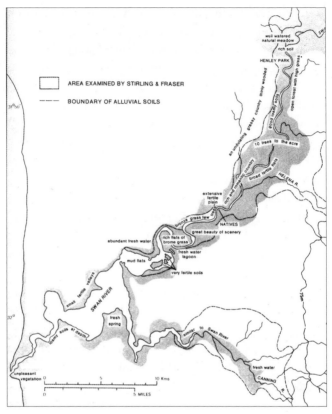

Detail of map of Swan River, as seen by Stirling. J.M.R. CAMERON

general, and thus an atypically exuberant show of flora.
As historian J.M.R. Cameron notes:

> Stirling and his men spent six out of the nine days they
> were on the Swan River in the area north of Heirisson
> Island, largely in the fertile area known today as the Swan
> Valley. Earlier explorers had turned back before spending
> time in the Swan Valley and so it is no wonder that Stirling
> received a more favourable impression of this region than
> the Dutch or the French had done.[5]

Charles Fraser, the botanist who was with Stirling on their little wooden boat, was as excited as Stirling by what he saw:

> The contrast dark blue of the distant mountains and the vivid green of the surrounding forest is such as must in a peculiar manner strike the attention of a person long accustomed to the monotonous brown of vegetation in Port Jackson [Sydney].[6]

This passage seemed strange when I first read it. The colour of the leaves around here appears to be a million different shades of olive-green. Surely most of south-east and south-west Australia is predominantly grey or olive green in colour? However, George Seddon notes that Fraser must have seen plenty of darkly green native cypress trees and peppermints along the banks of the river to have written this, as the leaves of jarrah, marri and tuart appear to be a much duller green.[7] The peppermints are at the northern limit of their natural distribution here, and would have enlivened the landscape that the rowing men observed on their journey east and north into mystery. But there is more to be said about the beauty seen by Fraser in 1827.

Rather than George Seddon, the humble native cypress may well take the prize for being the greatest environmental historian of Western Australia. In 2009, Louise E. Cullen and Pauline F. Grierson took cores from the trunks of thirty very old native cypress by an inland lake north of Esperance in the south-west. They analysed the tree's patterns of growth as reflected in the spacing of the annual growth rings. The autumn–winter period is when the southern region receives much of its rainfall (around seventy per cent) and it was during this time that the significant increase in tree growth occurred each year. From reading the tree rings, they could see a history of rainfall in the south-west. The most interesting thing to me was the discovery that it had been very wet in the period 1815 to 1830. In fact, the 1820s was the wettest period since the 1660s (as far back in time as they could look) when rainfall was around twenty-three millimetres above average.[8] Stirling had arrived in 1827. The trees Cullen and Grierson sampled were east of the Swan River, but there may well have been a connection to the rainfall at that time: after more than ten years of very good winter rains the flora may well have been in very good shape and helped to further mislead Stirling and his band as to the fertility of the country. The natural cycles of rainfall patterns in this part of the world had led Britain's errant captain down the wrong garden path. However, as Cullen and Grierson also found, dry conditions followed from 1830 to 1860, exactly the period when white settlers arrived, began farming and became in many instances disillusioned with the nature of south-western Australia as a place for growing crops. In this case, recent advances in science may well throw light on traditionally understood social and economic history.

Stirling and Fraser's very favourable description of the land around the river was widely reported in the London press. From mid-1829 until some point in 1830, three or four ships per month were arriving. This was the 'Swan River Mania' of the early 1830s. After this time the letters of the settlers reached Britain revealed that it was not an agricultural paradise by any means, and immigration largely dried up.[9] As one settler wrote, 'What could our friend Frazier have been thinking of, when he stated the soil to be good, and the place to be well watered? 'Tis all a farce'.[10] But James Stirling was not a misty-eyed Romantic, despite possibly having read William Wordsworth's great poem 'The Prelude', and revelling in the sinuous 'romantic' beauty of the Swan (wooded Darling Scarp rising as its backdrop) on his 1827 visit. In 1829, the year the British arrived in Western Australia, he wrote that 'it is a fearfully dangerous experiment to come so far to a country wholly unknown, and with habits formed in other modes of life as wide from this as Earth and Heaven'.[11]

Coming here was 'a fearfully dangerous experiment': with these words the captain was sober and prescient. Take for example Thomas Peel and his ship full of men and women who arrived at the Swan River settlement in December of 1829. In July 1830, Dr Alexander Collie, surgeon of the H.M.S. *Sulphur*, visited them at their camp by today's Woodman's Point south of Fremantle, and reported that twenty-eight of Peel's 400 settlers had died (five from scurvy and fourteen from dysentery), and that a very large number were suffering from scurvy.[12] A few metres from where Peel's emigrants were languishing on the sand or in small wooden huts grew the vitamin C-rich, bright red fruit of quandong trees (*Santalum acuminatum*), acacia cyclops seeds, underground tubers and the flowers and fruits of the succulent samphire or pigface; all largely untouched by emaciated and severely vitamin-deficient emigrants. For reasons other than personal survival in early white history, we can see that Stirling was inadvertently prescient when he wrote of what a dangerous experiment it was to bring European habits to Terra Australis; today our biodiversity is in crisis largely due to habitat destruction wrought by European-style agriculture.

During the Napoleonic Wars at the end of the eighteenth

and the start of the nineteenth centuries, Britain worried that the French exploration taking place sporadically along the south-west coast of Australia might lead to the French colonising the area.[13] This, combined with Britain's rapidly expanding population, and the long-term prospect of further markets and commodities for the British Empire, led to the 1827 British colonisation of the land of the Minang Noongar, renamed King George's Sound (and today known as Albany). This was followed by the colonisation of the area around the Swan River in 1829. This was to be the first agricultural colonisation of a new land by the British since the eighteenth century. Lines written by one early settler take us straight back into the newly experienced southern hemisphere with startling immediacy:

> I sit at this present moment on the side of my stretcher,
> I write on the top of a trunk – above my head a bell tent,
> and rushes below my feet. The heat at this season in the
> middle of the day is very great, so that till the evening I
> seldom put on any clothes but a shirt and trousers.[14]

Most very early white settlers to the Swan River area of Western Australia spent their first few weeks in tents on Garden Island, and then on the beach at Fremantle. Above the white sands would have been a ridge of dunes covered in long-leaved spinifex (*Spinifex longifolius*). They might have seen the spiny ball of one of the brown flower heads of the spinifex being blown by a south-westerly, bumping haphazardly over the sand, dropping its seeds as it goes. Elsewhere the newcomers would have seen satin-leaved spinifex (*S. hirsutus*) give off a pale, satiny sheen. If they had looked closely they would have seen that these plants are covered in tiny, white hairs which protect the leaves from moving sand, salt and the drying effects of much wind and sun. Having had hundreds of thousands of years to adapt to Western Australian conditions was not a luxury afforded to these English men and women.

Having camped on a nearby beach, I know that the earliest weeks, when they were in tents on the beach, would have been awful. You can't keep sand out of your tent; the tide is always hinting with an insistent slap of its waves on the sand that it might come up further than you had anticipated when you first pitched your tent. Mosquitoes buzz and the heat turns your tent into an inferno if you're inside it during the day. At least I didn't have to eat salt beef and ship's biscuit.

But after five months or so on a rocking wooden ship, these men and women would have been eager to see what the land held in store for them. Picture this: walking over the first ridge of sand, they see a mixture of spinifex and sword-sedge (*Lepidosperma gladiatum*). Sword-sedge has long, dark-green leaves, and brown, fruiting panicles. The edges of its leaves are sharp, and perhaps cut the exposed skin of the new arrivals. They walk further through the dunes, stepping over a large patch of native pigface (*Carpobrotus virescens*), a creeping plant that spreads its three-sided, fleshy leaves in low, upright clumps, and bursts out into bright purple flowers here and there. Clumps of bright yellow flowers (grey cottonhead, or *Conostylis candicans*), with pale grey-blue stems, pass unnoticed underfoot. They step with trepidation over sea spinach (*Tetragonia decumbens*), another succulent and a hardy coloniser of sand.

Looking up into the canopy of a tea tree grove. THOMAS M. WILSON

After the last ridge of sand they come upon a stand of native cypress (*Callitris preissii*), huddled and bent away from the sea and the wind. Their dead lower twigs are grey and ghostly, bleached by years of salt exposure, but they provide a windbreak for the soft, dark-green foliage above.[15] Walking underneath this stand of cypresses, the newcomers step through the shade over a litter of brown pine needles.

They feel momentarily reassured, standing amongst trees that remind them, more or less, of pine woods back in Europe. The trees open out onto a clearing. They weave through stands of acacias (*Acacia rostellifera*) and under the twisting limbs of tea trees (*Melaleuca lanceolata*). Suddenly there is movement.

It is the first glimpse of a kangaroo bounding away to safety. Sixty years previously, botanist Joseph Banks had seen a kangaroo for the first time and written, 'what to liken him to I could not tell, nothing certainly that I have seen resembles him'.[16] In seeing their first kangaroo, the early colonists may have experienced a thrill of extreme Otherness.

The newcomers walk on. Looking into the branches of the chenille honey-myrtle (*Melaleuca huegelii*), they see native bees sitting on cream-coloured brushes of flower high on its branches: brushes of flower, not garlands, coming forth in shapes not seen before. Further on they walk into the shade of a tuart (*Eucalyptus gomphocephala*) woodland. Some of these trees are up to 500 years old and appear so with their wide girths. But this is no time to be admiring botany. There is work to be done.

According to W.B. Kimberly, writing in 1897, 'Western Australia had for its pioneers more highly educated men of good society than perhaps any other British dependency'.[17] Although there were labourers and tradesmen, many of the early settlers to Western Australia were middle-class British professionals. Kimberly might have overstated his case but it is true that this was not predominantly a tale of a sandstone harbour full of cockney criminals, the kind of tale most people are accustomed to when they learn about white Australian history. Since the feudal era, when military responsibility was devolved by the king of the realm onto various land-owning noblemen with military capacities, land had meant power in England. Ownership of a country estate was equated with social prestige. Only the eldest son inherited the family estate, so there were plenty of younger brothers from well-to-do families who were forced to take on a profession, such as lawyer or doctor. When Captain James Stirling spread the word that there was a beautiful, fertile, open new part of the British Empire waiting to be owned and farmed, many of these middle-class professionals decided to take some money and servants (the more money and people you brought out, the more land you were 'entitled' to) and become landed gentry like their ancestors.

In the early years, the settlers had long ribbon-like strips of land granted to them, spreading out at right angles to the Swan River. This was so that everybody had a piece of that lovely, fertile alluvial soil which spread out a mile or two along the banks of the Swan, before the land turned into a bona fide sandpit again (it also meant that the Swan could be used as a transport route for produce). The early farming gentry could go and have afternoon tea at each other's houses more easily than when they were in Britain on large family estates. The picture is of charmingly shabby gentility: fine glasses and plates, but the pianoforte was standing on a clay floor and there were curtains for doors. Of course, what these fine fellows had done in annexing 'private property' in this part of the planet was to dispossess semi-nomadic Australian families of their rightful territory. It was little poetic justice that there was wind blowing through the window and sand in the china.

Some emigrants sought adventure and wealth. Some, from the ranks of the British poor, were trying to escape an unhappy situation. Due to a variety of factors, including advances in medicine and hygiene, the population of England doubled from around eight million in 1800, to around sixteen million in 1850. The enclosure movement saw Britain's ancient open-field system replaced by an agricultural revolution and a loss of the commons, both factors that marginalised the cottagers and small farmers. Between 1702 and 1797, the British Parliament passed some 17,776 enclosure acts which moved around three million acres from a model that went back to the feudal era into the era of capitalism.[18] Deprived of their share of the commons, small farmers often moved to the city to join urban slums later described by Dickens and decried by Engels and Marx. With the Industrial Revolution continuing apace in England, the world of the yeoman farmer and the independent craftsman was rapidly being replaced by the stench of the town and the monotony of long days in noisy cotton mills. Many a craftsman had been disinherited of his ancient skill by the new machines, and would have been attracted to a land where such skills would still be needed.[19]

Thus there were varying motives for emigration, but ultimately many who made the journey to the new colony sought land to cultivate as their own. And for those who thought they were journeying to an agricultural 'paradise', disappointment followed their experience of this geologically ancient land. A newspaper correspondent from the time wrote that:

> Some few have set to in earnest in cultivating their allotments, but the majority sit staring at one another. The country for miles around exhibits no feature of capability for cultivation; it is one arid sandy formation.[20]

The following verse from a Swan river settler in 1832 sums up the mood:

> Beside the Swan, beneath a time-worn gum,
> A squatter sat dejected, pale and glum,
> Speared were his pigs, and poisoned were his flock,
> Far in the bush had strayed his other stock,
> His wheat, his pride, was blighted by the smut,
> A native fire had burnt his mud-built hut;
> He thought on times by Thames' silvery stream,
> And drew from Memory's page a pleasing dream.

'Twas evening: and the pelican began to leave
The sedge, and screamed the black swan ...
The squatter mused on what he might have been.
Ambition's fire, wrecked on barren sand. [21]

A squatter is someone who illegally occupies crown land, and squatting was common in early white Australian history. The pastoral idyll of the Swan River settlement was quickly disrobed and shown to be built on false presumptions. For example, the beautiful *Oxylobium* and *Gastrolobium* species of pea-flowered shrubs, highly toxic in even a few grams, poisoned many flocks of squatters' sheep in 1830s Perth. The original pastoral image of the British Romantics, the 'Thames' silvery stream', had been projected onto the marine and aeolian sands of the Swan Coastal Plain and found wanting. At this time settlers languished in Fremantle, drinking grog, and suffering scurvy, dysentery and a shortage of drinking water. Government stores of food were all that stopped many dying of starvation.[22] Centuries of agrarian culture developed on the deep top-soils of the British Isles were ill-suited to south-west Australia.

Poetry tells the story:

... cast by Fortune on a frowning coast,
Which can no groves nor happy valleys boast
... these are scenes where Nature's niggard hand
Gave a spare portion to the famished land ...

In fact these words come from not from colonial Australia, but from George Crabbe's famous anti-pastoral poem 'The Village'.[23] Crabbe was an eighteenth-century poet who, here, gives the world an unsentimental portrait of life in a rural English village. Although these lines were written about English soil, they are easily co-opted to describe the anti-pastoral experience of life on the land for many new arrivals to Western Australia.

There is a key difference. And it makes all the difference. I have already mentioned Stephen Hopper's distinction between old, stable, climatically buffered landscapes (OCBILs), and young, often disturbed, fertile landscapes (YODFELs).[24] Such old landscapes, leached of nutrients, are found in south-west Australia, the Greater Cape of South Africa and certain parts of South America. We know that humans come from and have mostly inhabited young, often disturbed, fertile landscapes. Many parts of the Swan Coastal Plain that are not along wetlands or rivers or at the base of the Darling Scarp – not to mention many areas in the eastern Wheatbelt that are in an area of transitional rainfall – are old, infertile landscapes. The British emigrants who found themselves 'wrecked on barren sands' were organisms who hailed from YODFELs, and who were unable to either flourish in, or properly appreciate, OCBILs. One of the canonical poets of these emigrants was John Milton, who in Book 4 of the verse epic *Paradise Lost* paints paradise as a parkland full of rich trees, 'whose fruit burnished with golden rind hung'. Fleshy fruits are uncommon in the old landscapes of the south-west, and could not have inspired this European ideal of Eden. Milton, and the entire cultural traditional the new emigrants hailed from, developed in a YODFEL. Andrew Marvell's classic vision of a garden is worth quoting:

> What wond'rous Life is this I lead!
> Ripe Apples drop about my head;
> The Luscious Clusters of the Vine;

Upon my Mouth do crush their Wine;
The Nectarine, and curious Peach,
Into my hands themselves do reach.[25]

No such pastoral romance was ever penned by a European poet about one of the world's OCBILs. As I have already hinted, south-west Australia gave birth to anti-pastoral literature, writings which measure human life in this old landscape against a European tradition of rural ease in Arcadia and find the Antipodes lacking. Ecology informs a reading of culture. Much of the distrust of Australian landscape – distrust still often evident today – springs from human emigrants hailing from very different evolutionary and biogeographical backgrounds to the ones frequently present in south-west Australia. Only in the past few decades have we, thanks to the help of evolutionary biology, begun to properly comprehend the unique, species-rich nature of the ancient land Western Australians inhabit. As we do so, some of the disharmonies between a European cultural heritage and the profoundly alien nature of the Australian landscape are thrown into relief.

*

George Fletcher Moore was less enamoured by the flora of the south-west than had been Captain Stirling and his intrepid party a few years earlier. On 8 December 1830, soon after arriving, Moore wrote, 'The country is most singular, but does not possess those features of extreme interest I expected; there is (as far as I have seen) great sameness in the scenery'.[26] The low topography of the ancient Western Australian lands, as well as the hundreds of species of often structurally similar looking trees such as *Eucalyptus* or *Acacia* species, might well give the appearance of homogeneity or 'sameness' to an early visitor. On the other hand, to an experienced, local naturalist the biodiversity of the natural world here is obvious, as it would have been to the Noongar people. Even the hard-to-impress Moore changed his verdict in his diaries after further explorations, later pronouncing it an 'interesting landscape, rather than of sublime or grand scenery'.[27] Moore did not complain as much as some of the settlers, perhaps because his land at Millendon in the Upper Swan district had alluvial soils and enabled him to produce food without as much difficulty as those who had ended up with land grants on areas of sandy banksia woodland.

In her letters, the early settler Eliza Brown admires the native flowers, but found the trees 'not handsome': 'It is seldom we meet with a perfect tree, they nearly all show a great number of naked branches and the trunks in most instance are blackened in consequence of the native fires.'[28]

The priest John Wollaston's first impression of the trees was that they 'want freshness; their foliage is of the most sombre uniform hue imaginable'.[29] Looking at the Darling Ranges, Wollaston went as far as to write of the flora that it was of one uniform colour, 'a dark dirty green, over which on a hot day the hazy, African-looking atmosphere hangs like a pestilence'.[30] Wollaston also noticed the absence of obvious animal life during the day in summer: 'sometimes not a bird or beast are to be seen for several miles and above all such an awful silence prevails'.[31] Other early explorers noticed the frequent absence of animal life when walking through the wild lands of the Darling Ranges. Like Wollaston, these men had no notion of local ecological relations and the way that it made little sense for large animals to be active in the desiccating heat of midday on the driest inhabited continent on earth. Georgiana Molloy was another early settler who was initially unimpressed by her surroundings. Molloy settled at Augusta, further south than Moore. However for Molloy, as is widely known thanks to Alexandra Hasluck's and then William J. Lines' biographies, an interest in seed collecting for a London-based botanist led to her becoming intimate with the flora of the region and to developing a strong affection for the plants of her new home.

Working on the land does not necessarily lead to an appreciation of rural beauty. The middle- and upper-class emigrants experienced a shortage of servants in the early years of white colonisation in south-western Australia, so, unlike in their English home, such people had to perform tasks like ploughing, digging the vegetable garden, and moving sheep. As Jane Davis notes, this means that characters like Moore and the Tanners in the Upper Swan area were more involved with the land than they would have been back in their native England.[32] And yet these people, as is evidenced in their surviving writings, still appreciated the beauty of the land, at least now and again. They found certain valleys or outlooks beautiful, and sometimes mention this in their writings; the discourse of 'improving' the land in the name of 'progress' and 'civilisation' coexists with this appreciation. As Davis writes:

> While they appreciated the scenery, particularly the spring display of wildflowers, they were also intent on transforming the land to make it productive in familiar ways.

These quite opposite responses though, were not bound together, and indicate the complexity of understanding their relationships with the land.[33]

Such a view suggests that the white nineteenth-century attitude towards the land in south-west Australia is not easily reduced to simple disinterest and dislike, or acceptance and celebration, and that this new environment elicited different responses from different people. If many of these men and women did get their hands dirty, year after year, in forging a basic European-style agriculture on Western Australian sands, while at the same time appreciating some of the land's beauty, then we can at least say that, apart from the Captain Stirling of 1827, these people did not go in for sentimental pastoral notions. Theirs was a sober, realistic pastoral vision, even if it was built on the theft of the land from semi-nomadic hunters and gatherers.

George Grey was a white explorer with a mission to survey and explore north-western Australia in the 1830s. He also walked north of Perth with a white friend and two Aboriginal men during this early period of white settlement. One warm December night by a lake Grey recorded the beauty of the scene:

Our bivouack, this night, had a beauty about it, which would have made any one possessed with the least enthusiasm, fall in love with a bush life. We were sitting on a gently-rising ground, which sloped away gradually to a picturesque lake, surrounded by wooded hills, – whilst the moon shone so brightly on the lake, that the distance was perfectly clear, and we could distinctly see the large flocks of wild-fowl, as they passed over our heads, and then splashed into the water, darkening and agitating its silvery surface; in front of us blazed a cheerful fire, round which were the dark forms of the natives, busily engaged in roasting ducks for us; the foreground was covered with graceful grass trees, and at the moment we commenced supper, I made the natives set fire to the dried tops of these, and by the splendid light of these chandeliers, which threw a red glare over the whole forest in our vicinity, we eat our evening meal; then, closing round the fire, rolled ourselves up in our blankets, and laid down to sleep.[34]

This takes us straight back in time to a world of gloriously wild banksia woodlands and healthy coastal plain ecosystems. Imagine if we were there as his companions, feeling the warmth of the fire and hearing the alien syllables of Noongar being muttered or spoken loudly across the flames. Out beyond this mysterious circle of ancient Australian culture, the wilds of the country agitate the silvery surface of the historical lens. Grey comes from long ago and reminds us that the land around Perth was once a robustly healthy and intact ecosystem. Yes, it is undeniable that Grey's portrayal of 'the natives' uses the now lamentable vocabulary of the master–servant relationship, but in purely environmental terms this is a unique view into our past. Such visions from history might provide inspiration for future efforts to rewild the Swan Coastal Plain. But more of that in a later chapter.

David James, a resident of Forrestdale south-east of Perth, spoke much more recently, in the 1950s and 1960s, of having spent time living by another lake on the Swan Coastal Plain: Forrestdale Lake. Here his comments are transcribed from an oral history:

Being a child down at the Lake I still think of the sound of
the frogs calling. It was wonderful with the sound of the
stilts yapping, and the noise of the waterfowl. When you
get 5 to 20,000 birds in the peak of summer, that's a lot of
racket with, say, 1,000 mountain ducks, 2,000 stilts, night
herons, the sound of swarms of midges at dusk, a lovely
humming sound. All lakes are special.[35]

Another impression of the land in the south-west comes
from an early explorer's correspondence. Dr T.B. Wilson
travelled from King George's Sound towards the Swan
River in 1829. On his journey he records passing through
good, open forest land:

About sunset we reached a valley, almost entirely des-
titute of trees. So much has been said of the scenery in
New South Wales resembling noble English domains,
that the comparison is rather trite. Imagine a rich valley
of considerable width, extending E. and W. as far as the
eye can survey, bounded on the south and north by a
succession of undulating and moderately elevated hills,
thinly but sufficiently ornamented with trees of gigantic
form, and you may have some conception of the spot,
where, near a pool of water, we bivouacked on Saturday
evening.[36]

Such places are no longer to be found in the south-
west of Australia. The gigantic trees have mostly been
logged. T.B. Wilson may find the comparison with the
open woodland environment of an English park trite
through repetition, but we today in Australia are now so
far removed from the time when the settled coastal parts
of this country were fire-stick farmed by Australians,
that the comparison is not trite but deeply instructive.

It was an open, parkland–like environment perfect for hunting kangaroo, and, sadly for the first Australians, also perfect for the grazing habits of the domestic animals of the colonising peoples. Another example comes from Thomas Bannister, a man who made the journey from the Swan River to King George's Sound in 1830. On New Year's Day he wrote:

> We ascended a hill from which we passed over a fine rich undulating country occasionally rising into hills of moderate height, in many places of a park like appearance and covered with an abundance of the finest grass fit for sheep and cattle… Fancy yourself in a highly cultivated wooded district in England in Harvest, and you see this country. The grass which was in large patches was yellow at this season [full summer], and at a distance did not look unlike ripe corn.[37]

Part of the parkland-like environment, seen by early white explorers, was native grasslands. Reference to 'grasslands' in this context is not to a carpet of the low, deep green grass that you might see on an English field, but rather to dull green or brown clumps of stems between which you might see old and leached soil. When stands of such Australian grassland are in seed, their heads sway rhythmically in the wind. On seeing such grasslands early explorers described them elsewhere as resembling a thick 'crop of oats'.[38] This is very far from what most urban Australians see when they think of 'grass'. As much as grassland was suitable for grazing imported sheep and cattle, it is not often seen today as you travel around south-western Australia.

Despite George Grey's almost lyrical description of his

night around a fire in the company of an ancient human culture and a wild Western Australia, most of the early explorers' reports and journals describe the environment through the eyes of those bent on resource exploitation. Jarrah trees of many hundred years growth, beautiful and now largely vanished patriarchs of the forest, are described, again and again, as 'fine timber'. A chief characteristic of places that are travelled through by these explorers is the quality of the soil in light of its use for agriculture. In reading these Australian journals and reports there is a monotonous regularity and lack of descriptive prowess inherent in the use of phrases like 'met with natives', 'found sandy soil', or 'observed fine timber'. The many wetland environments of the Swan Coastal Plain, oases of biodiversity, are mainly of interest to emigrants, even into the twentieth century, as providing surrounding areas of pasture for cows. Here, for example, surveyor general of Western Australia J.S. Roe, and colonial ad-ministrator James Stirling, and others, passed near by what we now call Manning Lake in today's suburb of Hamilton Hill, just south of Fremantle, 'the land here is good … with an abundance of feed on the edge of several lagoons'.[39] Of course the Noongar also saw the wetland environments through the filter of resource exploitation, for example digging for yargan (tortoises), in the summer mud with digging sticks. But the lack of insight into the wetland ecosystems, which is betrayed in throwaway remarks from passing white immigrants about an 'abundance of feed', is telling. These men had come out of the mainstream of the Western European tradition that, since the 1500s, had replaced a vision of the world as a communion of subjects with a theocentrism and anthropocentrism which saw nature as ultimately a collection of external objects to be directed and adjusted for human betterment. Of course one must keep in mind that these were mainly military men whose purpose in making such journeys of exploration was reporting back on potential resource availability to their superiors. That said, reading these journals and letters, a modern reader notices that the anthropocentric nature of the authors' discourse is uniformly unabashed. If such authors had any knowledge of British Romanticism and the writers associated with that intellectual movement in their home country, it is rarely, if ever, apparent. It would be many years before Thoreau would write of finding conviviality in wild swamps, and even more years before such ecocentric philosophy would penetrate the minds and hearts of a significant number of white Western Australians. Arguably it has still not yet done so today, which is why I have written this book.

In reading the early exploration reports of Wilson, Stirling, Roe and others, it is easy to forget the situation these men found themselves in. Google Earth did not exist in 1830. When these men set out in their little parties, with their horses and pack saddles full of flour, rice, pork, dried biscuits, and water, and their dogs and guns, they were heading into the unknown. On the other side of the Darling Scarp, they might find mighty caverns, waterfalls, bleak dunes baking in the sun, or a further range of even grander mountains. They didn't know. No white person knew. That was why they were riding out into it. They were setting out to find out what lay out there, on the dark spot on the map. They rode and they rode. As their visual vantage point was a couple of metres off the ground, they missed seeing many of the hundreds of species of beautifully patterned flowering plants below them. The pack saddles' leather creaked and the shadows flickered among the marris and jarrahs. Sometimes they walked alongside their horses. Sometimes their shoes wore out and spirits flagged as they trudged through endless grey green woodland or kwongan, not seeing that vividly coloured swamp pea their trouser leg had just brushed past. Then one of the men stops and pulls out a bottle of whisky. He drinks. He is 'refreshed'. Invariably the journals record the beneficial effect on morale that alcohol had. Alcohol in this way had an important function for these admittedly courageous men in daunting circumstances. It is hard to guess at what it would have been like with only a few horses, dogs, guns and fellow 'gentleman' to rely on, while meandering through the dry and impossibly remote south-west of Australia in the 1830s. They were alone out there. Although – not entirely. They did receive help from the first Australians at various times in their journeys. Indeed, historian Glen McLaren considers that there was a significantly greater urge to embrace Aboriginal bush skills in Western Australia than on the east coast in the early decades of the nineteenth century.[40] On the other hand, this kind of assistance can be overstated. Frequently the uncontacted peoples would flee the area before the explorers arrived.

The explorers slept on blankets they carried with them, although the Aboriginal guides frequently brought along to help on these trips soon demonstrated many bush skills to them, such as how to make a bed out of balga leaves. After entering the Darling Ranges, they found that the south-west in, its hotter months, does not abound in fresh water. One of the major issues for these explorers was finding water and again the guides would help, although once they were out of the hundred or so square

square kilometres of ground they knew intimately they were of much less help. Finding water in the wandoo woodland was sometimes possible by tapping into the discoloured trunks of old wandoo trees where water accumulated in the hollows that eucalyptus trees are prone to developing as they age. Sometimes water would jet out of the tapped hole, and this hole would be stoppered with bark once the men had slaked their thirst. If they didn't find water, they would die. In this context – the context of surviving while journeying through an arid and completely unknown world – it is perhaps understandable that aesthetic judgements and biocentric considerations are not frequently a part of the discourse of early exploration journals.

Professional botanists have been more appreciative of south-west Australia. George Vancouver's British expedition of 1791 spent a few days during spring around the present day town of Albany. Here the botanist Archibald Menzies climbed a small mountain and regarded

a long extent of country covered with verdant wood as far as the eye could reach. To a contemplative mind this prospect was by no means uninteresting for if we may judge of the fertility of the country in general from the luxuriancy of vegetation in many places, we may pronounce the tract with our view capable with a little labour of sustaining thousands of inhabitants.[41]

Menzies was wrong about the fertility of the soil – as Charles Fraser was to be so fatefully wrong three decades later – and yet he was appreciative of the beauty of the landscape. In 1792, Bruny D'Entrecasteaux's expedition allowed the naturalist Jacques Julien de Labillardiere to go onshore in the area of present day Esperance. He subsequently produced the first published account of the south-west's flora.[42] Among the plants he brought to the attention of Europeans was the kangaroo paw (*Anigozanthos*). Matthew Flinders circumnavigated Australia in 1801 to 1805. His ship visited King George's Sound with three naturalists on board: Robert Brown, Peter Good and Ferdinand Bauer. They collected 633 taxa from the south-west, and made a major and lasting contribution to the taxonomy of the south-west's flora.[43] One exciting discovery was the Albany pitcher plant (*Cephalotus follicularis*). There were other early botanists of note, including those on Thomas Nicolas Baudin's French expedition. Baron Karl von Hügel of Vienna visited the south-west 1833 to 1834. He wrote:

> One of the unique characteristics of the plants of New Holland is that the beautiful shapes and colours of the flowers reveal themselves to the observer only when he views them carefully at close quarters. So, too, the richness and variety of the flora in all its splendour do not strike the eye till you are close up. The cheerless grey-green changed to the most vivid hues, mingled with brilliant flowers of every kind, in untold numbers ...[44]

Von Hügel was right in emphasising that many of the beauties of the south-west become apparent when the viewer looks at the flora and the flowers at close quarters. As I have previously mentioned, many of the early explorers missed this beautiful and variegated botanical landscape as they passed metres away from it, high on horseback.

A taxonomy of 3,600 native species of plant compiled in 1860 was only increased to 3,650 native species by the mid-1960s.[45] In the view of Stephen Hopper, it took until the end of the twentieth century to make significant progress, when a well-funded Western Australian Botanic Garden and a range of Western Australian universities made major advances in developing knowledge of the south-west flora.[46] We now recognise around 8,000 native species in the south-west, thanks to the work of herbaria and university research programs over the last four decades. This huge development so late in the day in understanding the plants of the south-west means that, as Hopper contends, this region should be called the 'Cinderella of the world's temperate floristic regions'.[47] For some, this region of the planet has only been recognised for its biological riches very late in the day.

CHAPTER 5
FAMILY

In the rapidly expanding capital of Western Australia, there are hundreds of thousands of people who may not know the history of their home. This is a serious and particularly contemporary form of amnesia. Personal history is the long, tapering strand that helps constitute a sense of self. In part it may be invented, but it is the story that can in very large part make up personal identity. Group histories can do that for a whole people. One's group history grants one a group narrative.

Like most people, my group narrative has personal DNA woven into its fabric. White colonisation began in earnest on the western third of the continent in 1829. My great-great-great-grandfather Henry Edward Hall was – although he didn't conceptualise it that way – in the vanguard. He brought his family out on a ship to Western Australia in 1830. Henry had a little bit of land at Fremantle, some on Rottnest, and around 16,000 acres given to him south of the Murray River near where the modern city of Mandurah stands. Captain Irwin, the commander of the military stationed in the colony, wrote a book about Western Australia, published in London in 1835. In it he writes of my ancestor Henry:

Mr Hall is a man of singular firmness and intrepidity. He is residing with his wife and children and his servants, on the left bank of the river, the other settlers being located on the opposite side. This gentleman has mingled more with the aborigines in that district, and obtained a greater influence over them than any other settler. He has been known to pass several days together along with them in the bush, and has thus acquired a considerable knowledge of their habits and language ... Mr Hall is of a commanding appearance, and is generally habited in a singular costume, of which a conical hat, usually worn by the Malays, forms not the least conspicuous part.[1]

Was my ancestor a protoanthropologist, or just a rapacious invader trying to 'influence the natives' in order to have power over them? According to my grandmother, Helen Margaret Wilson, the answer was the former. Amongst other things, she adduces the following evidence. One of Henry's children, James Anderton Hall, a five-year-old boy, was lost in 1834 after watching soldiers fishing on the beach at Mandurah. Little James was lost at midday and at four a.m. the next day a party of white men and two Aboriginal trackers, Migo and Mollydobbin, set out:

The natives walked 22 miles with their eyes constantly fixed on the ground for ten consecutive hours of tracking before they saw the little boy lying asleep on the beach, his legs idly washed by the surf. Another hour and he would have perished as the tide was rapidly coming in. The joy and the delight of the Aborigines was said to be beyond description. All through the long search the natives had apparently shown great anxiety for his welfare.[2]

Migo was a prominent member of the Aboriginal community. For the two men to go twenty-two miles in ten hours they must have been practised endurance runners. This fact would not be surprising given that many first Australians used persistence hunting – the most ancient form of hunting – to track and run down prey over long distances. My grandmother thought that the anxiety of the two men was linked to how well they knew the father of the little child. Henry wrote to the newspaper *The Inquirer* for more sympathy to be given to the Aboriginals around Perth, as we have 'driven the kangaroo from their hunting-grounds'.[3] Given his knowledge of bush ways, he would have been an ideal man for the white expedition that killed dozens of Aboriginals on the banks of the Murray River at Pinjarra in October 1834 – the Pinjarra Massacre – but Henry took no part.

One of Henry's sons, Frank Hall, had a cattle station in the karri country near the modern day town of Manjimup (his lease was taken out in 1859). Frank had spent much of his boyhood among Aboriginal people of the Murray district, and knew their language, their customs and their bushlore.[4] He was charged with stealing cattle in September 1860, but immediately escaped on horseback – giving a cheeky goodbye over his shoulder to the policeman – and lived in clandestine peace for a few months with an Aboriginal group in the coastal country that is now D'Entrecasteaux National Park, north-west of the modern town of Walpole.[5] Despite a very generous financial reward for his capture and the efforts of many superbly qualified Aboriginal trackers, Frank Hall could not be found, and was only jailed after he had turned himself in to the police.

Another of Henry's sons was William Shakespeare Hall, my great-great-grandfather. W.S. Hall was a central figure in the white settlement of north-western Australia. His son Aubrey Hall, my great-grandfather, lived with the Ngarluma people around Cossack and Roebourne, working on various sheep stations. I never got to ask my grandmother what life was like on a sheep station in the Pilbara in the early part of the twentieth century and I regret it. In a newspaper article marking the publication of a word-list of the local Aboriginal language by Aubrey in the *Northern Times*, a journalist wrote of how Aboriginal elders in Roebourne remembered Aubrey with great fondness and warmth.[6] My great-grandfather spoke Ngarluma with fluency, and compiled a Ngarluma dictionary which was published posthumously.

William Shakespeare Hall. THOMAS M. WILSON PRIVATE COLLECTION

Today we can see our modern bodies, minds and emotions as having developed in a Pleistocene environment of gathering and hunting in small and extended family groups, moving through a wild biota. The first human inhabitants of Australia's western third were still living this original human lifestyle when my great-grandfather befriended some of them. Although he wouldn't have known this at the time, my great-grandfather was, in some senses, looking into the very functional core of what it means to be a member of the human species.

One physical example of this is that the people he saw would not have needed to wear glasses to recognise something far away in the distance. The Spanish missionary Dom Rosendo Salvado wrote of the Noongar hunter that:

> He scrutinizes every object that comes in sight to see whether it offers him food, bringing into play all his senses, which in his completely natural state are more highly developed than we can easily imagine. In fact, a native will clearly pick out a tiny bird high up on a very tall and thick-leaved tree, or a kangaroo hiding behind scrub and blackboy-trees more than a mile away, or the barely perceptible footmarks of the smallest quadruped. Many a white man who had lost his direction in the bush would never have been heard of again if his tracks had not been picked up by the extraordinarily keen-sighted natives.[7]

Early colonist J.E. Hammond also extolled the perfect sight of the Noongar: 'I have never seen a white man do with the rifle in the bush what I have seen a native do. Seldom did a native miss'.[8]

Sometimes I try to imagine my great-grandfather's life, growing up with Aboriginal companions in the 1880s and 1890s in the north-west of Australia. A lesson learned from cognitive science has been that if you speak a language regularly before you're seven years old, you'll have a perfect accent for the rest of your life. It is intriguing to me that Aubrey was reported to speak Ngarluma as well as native speakers, and knew their culture intimately. I can only just picture this white gentleman leaning against a saddle, feet on the bright red earth, chatting away in the strange (to me) syllables of Ngarluma. He sometimes read Joseph Conrad and Jack London and thought of England as 'home', while never having been there, but he also had many deep and long-running friendships with men who knew the Pilbara with hunter-gatherer intimacy. He was formed by a collection of cultures and places that coalesced at a particular time on the Western edge of the continent. What a different picture of Australia he would have had to people like us in our brick and concrete settlements on the coast of a modern industrialised nation-state.

*

In the south of Western Australia my family practised traditional farming on the eastern side of the Swan Coastal Plain. For much of Australia's history 'a farm' has meant what it meant to my family: a hut to live in, a well for water, a shingle-roofed shed for the fowls, a yard for the horses, land to graze sheep and cows on, and land to grow wheat on. In these early days of white settlement, the plough was usually single furrowed and drawn by one or two big powerful horses or bullocks. Seed was scattered by hand, what little wheat there was in these early days was harvested by sickle, and the grain was threshed with a flail. Most successful settlers produced their own milk, butter and cheese from their own dairy cows; their own pork and bacon from their own pigs; their own beef; their own figs, mulberries, grapes, apples, potatoes, from their own orchards and gardens.[9] It would take a few years to have all of these things established, and in the meantime they might dine on bread and coffee for breakfast, while pining for the butter they were once accustomed to. Their dogs and guns would supply a large proportion of their weekly calories. Much of their relations with nature would consist of shooting things and burning things down. Cockatoo was a classic and favoured Western Australian colonial delicacy, and would often be on the menu.

As the nineteenth century wore on, many white settlers moved further east. If you weren't planting on the Swan Coastal Plain, you might be out there, in the Avon Valley say, shearing sheep, or cutting down sandalwood trees to be shipped off to Singapore for seven pounds a ton. Wherever you were, days were spent in such tasks as making fences, picking fruit, weeding the garden, bringing water from the well or carrying water up the hill from the spring, fretting about your livestock or talking about your livestock, gathering wood for the hearth, making axe handles or ox-yokes, mending things, setting the table for dinner, and maybe writing a long letter to a relation on the other side of the earth. Reading *The Inquirer* and *The Perth Gazette* gave you your news of the colony. If it was very early in the colonial period you might have an occasional visit from a group of the first Australians, and try to placate them by giving them some bread.

Apart from the unsustainable pillaging of sandalwood trees and their persistence in ringbarking and burning most other trees (an immensely girthed and many hundred-year-old jarrah tree was just too hard to cut), Bill Mollison, the father of permaculture, might have been proud of these small-scale and largely autonomous Western Australian farmers.

One of my own ancestors had such a farm, one that he was very happy with. His home was larger than a simple hut, but otherwise it wasn't too dissimilar to what I've described. Henry Edward Hall owned around 400 acres at Wungong Brook. It had originally been run by the Armstrongs, and then the Hall family (remembered at Hall's Head in modern day Mandurah) took it over in the 1840s. They lived in a house with a jarrah frame (they would have called it 'Australian mahogany') and a thatched roof.

They ran cattle on their fertile land. Running cattle would have been the obvious thing to do in this kind of country, which would have been surprisingly open compared to today. One early correspondent gives an idea of the kind of country my ancestors would have encountered around Wungong:

In appearance, the whole country, excepting a belt along the coast, of from one to two miles, is most pleasing – being a fine open forest with but little close underwood, containing a great deal of very fine, and not a little magnificent and venerable looking timber, with a lower shrubbery of many curious trees and bushes … The forest, as before stated, is disposed like the timber of a park or domain, in most places very picturesquely; and wherever a settler sets himself down, he is sure of finding ample space for all agricultural operations for the first two or three years without any clearing. The underwood is very trifling and scattered, and seldom so stout as to require anything more than a bill-hook to clear it.[10]

This was a particularly fertile part of the Swan Coastal Plain that had accumulated sediments from run-off of the Darling Scarp for hundreds of thousands, if not millions of years. Today it is a geological unit known as the Pinjarra Plain, and is made up of clay and lateritic material that has been washed down from the scarp and slopes to the west.[11]

Early on, it was cows and not humans that first experienced the fertility of the land along the base of the Darling Scarp. Cattle confined on the sandy, western edge of the Swan Coastal Plain either wasted away and died, or escaped through makeshift fences and went eastwards. There they found good grazing country, and would be picked up weeks later enjoying the grasses that grew on the loam soils in places such as Wungong Brook, along the base of the scarp.[12] The first incident of this happening was recorded by the lawyer, farmer and diarist George Fletcher Moore in his journal from 1834. He records that Thomas Peel

was one morning himself looking into some agricultural book in which there was an engraving of a cow. A native boy was standing beside him who immediately imitated the lowing of a cow. This struck them as strange, there being no cows among the settlers there now. On enquiry, the boy pointed out to a direction where he said there were plenty of them, &c&c.[13]

And so the cows were discovered on the more fertile land to the east. In one sense at least, cows were proven more quick-witted than white-skinned human beings.

My ancestors did not only run cattle at Wungong. They also cleared the land to grow plants such as fig trees, banana plants and grape vines. On 14 August 1859, Henry Hastings Hall wrote to his brother, my great-great-grandfather William Shakespeare Hall, 'M says we shall have 400 gallons of wine this season, they only made about 50 last year. We are going to clear 15 or 20 acres of land so next year there will be 60 under crop'.[14]

The land my ancestor cleared had huge jarrah and marri trees growing on it. When the Reverend John Wollaston visited the Halls on his way to Perth he wrote:

> The farm is a fine one (as are several others in this direction). Well watered with mountain brooks all year, & a fine run for cattle in the hills. ... Envied Mr Hall (the proprietor) his fine garden, wherein were forty sorts of fruit trees, thriving most luxuriantly. He has quite a herd of pigs & told me in the season he fed them on peaches. I met with much kindness and frank hospitality.[15]

The Halls had indeed found their way to some of the most agriculturally productive land on the entire Swan Coastal Plain. Unlike the sands further to the west, these soils had some ability to retain water. No wonder his fruit trees grew so well.

I would do anything to go back to sit around the dining room table with my great-great-great grandfather Henry Edward Hall at his farm (near present day Armadale) at the end of his life in the 1850s. At this point in time only around 8,000 acres of Western Australia had been cleared for cultivation.[16] The human impact on the environment was still modest. The great jump in the white population of the 1880s and 1890s, precipitated by a gold rush, was still a generation away, and many of the first Australians were still living their traditional lifestyle throughout much of the south-west. Henry would have been in his sixties by this time, and have spent two and a half decades diligently learning the ways of the local land and the ways of the local Noongar people. Perhaps he learned how to hunt quenda, or where to dig for burrowing frogs; we will never know. What seems sure is that Henry's notions of such fundamental concepts as food, land and work would have been utterly different to an urban citizen such as myself, shopping and motoring in the twenty-first century. What my ancestor had seen and learned during his life in the first decades of white settlement in Western Australia would have made this book glow.

At Wungong, Sarah Theodosia (Henry Edward's wife), planted an oak tree which still endures and grows, putting out thousands of green leaves each year in the Western Australian sun. The original acorn came on a wooden ship propelled by the winds from the northern, green island she grew up on. Today I stand near the oak tree and wonder at what a symbol of home, of England, its familiarly shaped leaves must have been to Sarah in a land of hunters and strange flowers.

I let my mind travel back 160 years. I see Henry getting up early one morning, standing by himself for a moment on the large verandah around his house, looking out over shadowy and dew-soaked grass, hearing the first honeyeaters begin their morning song in the nearby trees. He is contemplating repairing a fence later that day and, along with men he has hired for the job, will split wood with an axe. But for the moment he pauses in the early morning light and enjoys a sense of stillness and repose, a sense palpable over the grass and amongst the thick pillars of the marris. He feels the linen shirt on his back, and, then uncomfortably, notices a familiar ache in his knees. He has worked this land, and he feels connected to it; he belongs on this earth. But he knows this land will go on forever, while he will not. He turns, and looks up to the east. There are the looming grey granite domes of Wungong Gorge, still unwarmed by the rising sun.

Today, the house is gone, remaining only as an old watercolour in The City of Armadale's archives. I look up from a citrus orchard on a semi-suburban farming property. The same eastern prospect that my great-great-great-grandfather saw, the same steep and precipitous stone cleft in the Darling Scarp, greets my eyes. Human lives shift and wane. Granite faces clustering together, high up in the sunshine, are indomitable.

Under the midday sun I turn back to the west, and make my way under the boughs of an old oak tree. I stop in the shade and look up amongst the branches. My breath deepens. It is a softer prospect here. Thousands of young green leaves flutter and their edges intermingle. Stone and tree, east and west, history and future. Knowing that every time one of these green leaves unfurls on Sarah's oak tree above me, it is thanks to my great-great-great grandmother's forethought in planting a small acorn in the Western Australian earth, I feel assured that some lines of continuity abide.

CHAPTER 6
SETTLING IN

And the LORD God took the man, and put him into the
garden of Eden to dress it and to keep it.
– *Genesis 2:15, King James Bible*

The newcomers to the Swan River Colony hailed from a
northern island that had been cleared of its wild forests
for more than five centuries. By 1350 only 12.4 per cent of
the land usable for agriculture in England and Wales still
had forest left on it.[1] By 1850 just 1.9 per cent of the land
available for agriculture in England and Wales retained
forest cover.[2] In fact these men and women treading on
Western Australian sands came from a Western Europe
that had been practising widespread agriculture that had
significantly displaced forest cover since 300 BC (with
only small reversals of this trend after the collapse of the
Western Roman Empire and later the Black Death of the
fourteenth century[3]). When they walked the few remaining forests in their home country they would have been
lucky to see large, dead trees lying untouched on the forest
floor. These newcomers hailed from an intensively used
and intensively domesticated part of the planet's surface.

In the early years of white settlement, much of the
land along the banks of the Swan River was cleared for
agriculture. Remember, this was where, over hundreds of

thousands of years, the river had left previously floating sediments, often from periodic flooding. These rich, alluvial soils would have supported tall, open forests of yarri or blackbutt, marri and flooded gum with a shrub understorey. The area today known as the Swan Valley is the area where much early agriculture was assayed. It would have been a special place, rich and verdant, considering the soils on the fertile flats here.

One early correspondent wrote that the

> channels of the three rivers (the third is to be called the Murray) are very serpentine, having meadows of black clayey loam, covered with luxuriant vegetation, in their bends. ... The Swan is the largest river of three. The land on its banks appears the most fertile.[4]

Another settler reported:

> From Guildford to the head of the river, about fifteen miles, the country is rich and beautiful, and in this district the society is considered most select; a large proportion of the banks of the river forms rich alluvial meadows, averaging about six trees to the acre, clear of brush-wood, extending back in some cases about half a mile, and in a state of nature yielding nearly a ton of hay to the acre; behind these meadows you have a park-like, open, forest country, ... The trees are all ever-green and all blossom; some reach one hundred and fifty feet in height, and thirty feet in circumference at the base.[5]

We will never get to walk through this fertile and botanically exuberant Australian ecosystem along the banks of the Swan, as these days the Swan Valley is a solid mosaic of horse paddocks and vineyards. I don't doubt that the more fertile soils along the banks of the Swan were highly valued by the original Australians for hunting and gathering. Perhaps few of those tourists who quaff sweet whites in the shade of the tasting room know that, more so than many other places around Perth, they are standing on what was once a beautiful and fertile hunting ground of a long-dead Australoid family. Further away from the river the land becomes more typical sandy coastal plain, and here today we *can* find remnants of the banksia woodland. Luckily for this lower and more shrubby ecosystem, it grows on land that did not endear itself to white farmer-gentlemen from a northern island. Sadly in more contemporary times it *does* appeal to suburban property developers, catering to an expanding population in Perth, fuelled largely by sizeable annual immigration; the bulldozer side-slips over another living banksia tree.

Earlier on, in 1829, examples of 'first contact' with the first Australians around Perth had been amicable. The Noongar men (the women were not allowed to talk with these new men) had been at first hugely surprised by the white skin colour of the visitors, but gifts of jackets and hats had been exchanged for spears, hammers and the like. Later, when they were displaced from their hunting grounds, they began to realise the impact of the white man. When Aboriginals stole flour or speared cows or horses they were often shot by the white settlers. Aboriginals dug up the potatoes of the white settlers, as these root-like vegetables were not all that different in structure to the edible yams, or warran, they were accustomed to digging for, but were even more packed with calories after centuries of agricultural domestication. Again white vengeance would follow. But these acts encouraged acts of Noongar retribution such as the spearing of white people with Western Australian wood.

The Aboriginal leader Yagan, from the Beeliar tribe south of the Swan River, remonstrated with George Fletcher Moore, with his hand on his shoulder, that such acts of retribution were bound to take place. In a memorable episode from white–black history in Western Australia, Yagan is already known by Moore and by many of the white settlers. He is spotted amongst a group of the Australians. Moore continues the dramatic narrative:

> I had just been taxing Migo with having been present at the murder [a previous killing of a white man], which he warmly denied, when my eyes first fell upon Yagan. I said immediately: 'What name?' They all answered 'Boolgat'. I said, 'No! Yagan.' At first, he was inclined to deny, but seeing that I knew him well, he came forward & avowed himself, and entered into a long argument & defence of his conduct. 'Fremantle, white man shoot Domguin, Yagan brother. Blackman cutyell (two). (Two had been shot.) Yagan gyidyell (to spear) white man cutyell (two).' I said then 'But Domguin quiple (steal) – white man shoot.' 'Yes. Domguin quiple. White man shoot Blackman. Black man 'pear white man.'
>
> I confess he had almost as good of the argument as I had. All grouped round & seemed to consider us as respectively arguing the question. Yagan used emphatic language and graceful gesture with abundant action. I was heated & spoke in the same way. Sometimes he advanced boldly & leaning with his left arm familiarly upon my shoulder he delivered a 'recitative' which I regret I could not understand, but the sound of it was as if we had not acted peaceably & fairly towards them.[6]

When I first read this passage it recalled images to my mind, from another part of Meganesia, of Stone Age Papua New Guinean village life where 'big men' regularly demonstrate their wisdom and leadership through displays of forceful and charismatic public speaking in front of the assembled social group.

Later in July 1833, in an act of horrible and bloody violence, Yagan was shot (and later decapitated) on the banks of the Swan River. His killer was speared and beaten by his Aboriginal kin in turn. A spate of guerrilla skirmishes continued that year, and almost drove the whites out of the south-west.[7] In September 1833, with the assistance of a translator, one of Yagan's brothers, Monday, appealed to the governor in a public forum. According to Moore:

> He stated the number of men belonging to his tribe that were killed several times since we came to the settlement to be 16. Gave a most particular catalogue of the names, places & manner of death, & by whom killed, whether by soldier or otherwise. He complained greatly of our encroachments and interference; that they were straitened for subsistence, treated with rudeness, & prevented from walking with liberty in their own country.[8]

The whites had previously told the Noongar that they were all 'brothers', in order to impress upon them that unlike the Noongar people's deeply tribal mindset, in which violence against another tribe was expected, the white arrivals resented violence against any of their countrymen. Knowing this helps to understand the following extract from Moore's journal:

The conference was very long and interesting. The man made a most affecting appeal. He is the only survivor of 4 brothers of whom Yagan was one. 'You white man brother plenty – you brother, <u>you</u> brother' said he turning to several of the bystanders. 'Carram (time before this time, long ago), me brother <u>plenty</u>. Now, me Garbal <u>one</u>!', holding up his one finger impressively. Poor fellow he killed a pig of mine not long since and I was inclined to be angry with him, but now I forgive, I pity. I respect him for that touching appeal.[9]

The white presence in Western Australia had begun a few years earlier on the south coast at King George Sound. During this time the British presence was a garrison of troops, not an agricultural settlement, and according to John Host and Chris Owen, 'it occupied little land and was not seen by the Aborigines as an intrusion'.[10] From the start of the 1830s, things changed. Early white settlers dismantled fishing traps and weirs of the Aboriginals, often shot or poisoned their dingos, and took their most valuable hunting pastures. Their tracks became the basis of new road networks and their camping grounds became the sites for homesteads and towns.[11] As had already happened in other places such as the Americas, the crowd diseases that had emerged since the invention of agriculture and settled societies spread to the first Australians and caused many deaths. The first Australians had no genetic resistance or developed immunity to diseases which were only able to spread and be maintained in large agglomerations of humans. British germs ultimately left many more corpses lying on the sand than did British guns, but as you can see from the above extract, interracial violence was significant.

In describing the Aboriginal relationship with the environment, Bill Stanner wrote in 1969, 'When we took what we call "land" we took what to them meant hearth, home, the source and locus of life … the aborigines faced a kind of vertigo in living'.[12]

Vertigo is an apt metaphor for the loss of land faced by the first Australians with white colonisation. As the sensory system of the ears regulates the sense of orientation of the body to space, so too the land gave cosmological orientation to the Australian psyche in their perceptions of the world. Dispossession of such land was part of the profound psychic disorientation experienced by many first Australians as they moved from one world to the next.

The whites flew the Union flag on the land, and told themselves that 'the natives' were a lower race of humans than 'civilised' members of the British Empire like themselves ('civilised' fellows were of course civilised enough to die from scurvy while the nearby 'savages' munched contentedly on vitamin C-rich quandongs).

The first Australians wore cloaks in winter, but in summer, or when the cloaks became an obstacle to physical activity, they were thrown back and all walked naked. The British again failed to understand their own cultural identity in a broad evolutionary framework and saw this as another mark of the inferiority of the local people. As Steve Jones has written, the invention and use of clothes, one example of the exceptional behavioural adaptiveness the human brain has facilitated, allowed humans to leave the equatorial regions of high sunlight and warmth and to travel north into the gloom. The invention of clothes has allowed Europeans to 'take the tropics with them'.[13] Again it was a variation from a very functional and long-held human norm. For their cultural norm of – some would say their obsession with – concealing the human body from public view, the white-skinned wayfarers from a far northern island were the 'strange' ones, if such misleadingly essentialist language ever had to be employed.

George Grey's experience with Aborigines in south-western Australia in the late 1830s prompted him to write that in the middle of summer and the middle of winter some hunger was felt by the locals. And yet at all other times of the year, 'they can obtain, in two or three hours, a sufficient supply of food for the day, but their usual custom is to roam indolently from spot to spot, lazily collecting it as they wander along'.[14] Such an experience of long, daily freedom from economically motivated time-urgency is hard for modern citizens to imagine. The early white settlers were likely even more beholden to the ideal of hard work than we are today. As the Roman poet Virgil wrote more than two thousand years ago: *Labor omnia vincit* – 'Work conquers all'.[15] Splitting logs or chopping till the sweat made their shirts stick to their backs in the midday heat; or leaning wearily as they contemplated another furrow to be ploughed in the lengthening evening of a long, long day … this was the reality for many of the newcomers. The locals did work hard for their food – climbing trees, moving heavy stones or carrying zamia palm nuts to salt water for their preparation – however it was not the sun-up to sun-down routine of the European farmer.[16] The Protestant work ethic that motivated these God-fearing emigrants had no great praise for the psychological benefits of relaxation (unless it was the one day a week on which even the Lord rested: the Sabbath). Even the otherwise sage Herman Melville could not understand the freedom from the Protestant work ethic of traditional peoples. When travelling through the

South Pacific in the 1840s he wrote, 'The mechanical and agricultural employment of civilised life requires a kind of exertion altogether too steady and sustained to agree with an indolent people like the Polynesians.'[17]

In fact these people were not indolent, it was just that they had not internalised the work ethic of modern European peoples like those of Melville's European-American tradition. It was not indolence that the Noongars were exhibiting to the questing Grey, but a liberated freedom from a psychologically ingrained work ethic developed in the abstract economy of a cold northern country. In this instance Grey's language indicts his own culture more than the world of the first Australians. Some anthropologists have labelled traditional hunter-gatherer societies who spend a low number of weekly hours on subsistence tasks as 'the original affluent societies'.[18] The first human inhabitants of the south-west enjoyed such affluence, and this was not often comprehended by the first white immigrants.

Grey's account of the use of plants and animals by the first people of south-west Australia is invaluable. In the following excerpt Grey describes an Aboriginal man hunting a kangaroo in the south-west:

> The moment an Australian savage commences his day's hunting, his whole manner and appearance undergo a wondrous change: his eyes, before heavy and listless, brighten up, and are never for a moment fixed on one object; his gait and movements, which were indolent and slow, become quick and restless, yet noiseless; he moves along with a rapid stealthy pace, his glance roving from side to side in a vigilant uneasy manner, arising from his eagerness to detect signs of game, and his fears of hidden

foes. The earth, the water, the trees, the skies, each are in turn subjected to a rigid scrutiny, and from the most insignificant circumstances he deduces omens – his head is held erect, and his progress is uncertain, in a moment his pace is checked, he stands in precisely the position of motion as if suddenly transfixed, nothing about him stirs, but his eyes.[19]

Unlike the newly arrived colonisers, this first Australian was eco-literate. He could not read the Roman alphabet but, as a lifelong hunter-gatherer, he could, with impressive speed and insight, read the sometimes cryptic patterns presented to him by the earth, the water, the trees and the sky.

Historical accounts, such as those of Salvado, demonstrate the huge difference in the abilities of the Noongar people and the newly arrived Europeans. A major difference between the two groups stemmed from the fact that the Noongar had a spatial intelligence developed through lives lived moving through and interacting with a wild biota. Many accounts have verified the ability of traditional first Australian trackers to identify key attributes of the person being tracked such as sex, weight, age, and height.[20] Most importantly they can also estimate the length of time since the track was made. Tracking was a taught and learned ability, and the learning began as early as six years of age. Broken twigs, crushed grass, leaves bent the wrong way, or objects in unexpected places – all signal that a human or animal has passed through the environment.

*

Early British settlers shot and ate many kangaroos. As early as February 1830, kangaroos were not found close to Fremantle, and were depleted in the Upper Swan by 1832.[21] Clearly this deprived the local Noongars of one of their major protein sources. They reacted by killing sheep, pigs and cattle. In 1832 the lawyer George Fletcher Moore wrote in his journal, 'I dare say the natives think they have as good a right to our pigs as we to the kangaroos, and the argument is a strong one', but this didn't stop Moore and his fellow white settlers from answering Noongar livestock predation with aggressive gunfire.[22]

Later in the 1830s sheep were moved out to the Avon Valley (and depopulated the Swan Valley to some extent). In moving out into the Avon Valley, as Tom Griffiths has remarked of the animal in Australia in general, 'sheep were the shock troops of empire'.[23] The empire was on the march and its shock troops were headed to the area around York as their first outpost. As Richard Weller notes, the agricultural settlers were quickly leaving 'the sand plain to the artisans, administrators and entrepreneurs, who would form the kernel of urban settlement that in later years was to grow into the Perth Metropolitan Region'.[24] Fremantle remained a small port with a bad harbour, and a series of two-storey office blocks and shops, as well as smaller cottages, mostly made from limestone that began brilliantly white, and then greyed and hardened as the years passed. Drunkenness, thievery and the jingle of horse harnesses were frequent companions on its hot and sandy streets.

By 1850 the best agricultural and pastoral land in the south-west had been occupied by the whites, and sheep farming was a major enterprise. The arrival of convicts created a building boom in the 1850s (as well as marring the colony's reputation as purely a 'free' settlement), but it was still a small-time boom. Recalling his childhood in Perth in the 1850s one former resident remembered rowing across from Perth to South Perth:

> almost down to the mill was covered with christmas trees and also the large flowering banksia. It was a gorgeous sight to see all the natural beauty of the spot. When the trees were in bloom the natives used to camp here and extract honey from the blossom.[25]

Alexander Taylor's sketch *Perth from St. George's Terrace* made in 1850 shows how much of a rural village Perth was at this time, with the number of whites in the colony numbering only 5,886.[26] Sadly, the Aboriginal population of the south-west was hit by a series of disease epidemics in the 1850s and 1860s, significantly reducing their numbers.

By 1860 the climate ended its period of drier than average years. The economy was doing better than during the first few decades of white colonisation and the figure of the dejected squatter became a memory. Perth was connected to the telegraph system of the world in 1876. In 1881, Perth had just 932 houses.[27] St Georges Terrace finally got gravel.[28] Most manufacturing happened in the eastern states (even today Western Australia is still a primary producing state), while ships at Fremantle were busy loading up with stacks of sandalwood (*Santalum persicarium* and *S. latifolium*) to be sent to India and Singapore and loads of jarrah to be carried to Johannesburg and London. Locals were still importing some wheat and flour from Adelaide. In March 1881 a new railway was opened from Fremantle to Perth, and onwards to Guildford. River traffic declined. Then, with the gold rush of the 1880s and 1890s, came a significant increase in Western Australia's white population. In 1885 the state's white population was about 35,000. Henceforth it began to rapidly increase in size. By 1894, thanks to the discovery of eastern goldfields, the population had jumped to 81,600.[29] That is a five-fold increase in less than a decade. On 20 January 1886, my great-great-great-aunt Dora Hall wrote in a letter to her sister-in-law Sarah Bracher, 'There are so many strangers coming to WA now that houses cannot be found to accommodate them altho' new buildings are being run up everywhere I am afraid of my rent being raised beyond my means …'[30]

Gold production peaked in 1903, and the population continued to boom.[31] This period marked an important shift. Until the 1880s white Western Australia was essentially comprised of agrarian folk loyal to Union flags, surrounded by vibrant human cultures which they, with a few exceptions, failed to understand, and by thousands of kilometres of ocean, woodland and desert. A walk down St Georges Terrace was a walk through a country town, not a city. From the 1890s capitalism, communications and government had all sped up, and the place was starting to look a bit more like a modern Western city.[32]

In 2008, Steve Appleyard from Western Australia's Department of Environment and Conservation discovered human impacts on groundwater and soil acidity from 1890s. He found evidence of sulphur and nitrogen oxide when measuring soil properties in the Gnangara Mound. This large aquifer, just to the north of Perth, was only cleared for pine trees in the 1950s and 1960s, and up until that time was basically pristine land. The only way this increase in soil acidity could have come about is from an early increase of the burning of coal putting sulphur and nitrogen oxide into the air and then either through rain or dust getting into the soil and water of the Gnangara Mound.[33] The Bassendean soils are naturally somewhat acidic, but this was acidity on top of the natural acidity. So we can now see that around the time Western Australia started to speed up its technological and societal tempo – through the late 1880s and into the 1890s – there was a mark left on the land itself. The Western Australian soil remembers the changing times we were entering: the century of earth alteration.

In 1890, Perth was no bustling London or New York. Far from it. It was only that year that it was given its own parliament. Perth was very much a lonely outpost of the British Empire. People were accustomed to the idea that it took a week to reach Melbourne by ship.[34] Electrically powered lighting had only just been introduced in Perth two years before.[35] In the nineteenth century white south-western Australia was just a few little settlements amongst the trees, with a few whale oil or kerosene lanterns swinging in the gloom of the evening. It would not have been visible as a glimmer at night from outer space.

But things were gearing up. Western Australia, as a sizeable Western-style 'civilisation', began life at the start of the twentieth century. Federation of the colonies occurred in 1901. It can be argued that modernity as a whole began at this time for the world more generally. The first radio contact established across the Atlantic in 1901, the first flight made by the Wright brothers in 1903, and Einstein's theory of relativity was published in 1905. Political and cultural changes such as stirrings of universal suffrage (here Australia was at the cutting edge), universal health care in Britain and the beginning of a literary market were being established. These changes mark radical shifts in human experience. As 1901 came to a close, my great-great-great-aunt Dora Hall wrote in a letter:

> I have … lived in Hay St for the last ten years at least. The trams are a great convenience. I think our parents would be very much surprised & pleased if they might be permitted to see all the present improvements in this place, which had for a long time seemed so behind the other parts of Australia.[36]

We may focus in on one single event in Western Australia as heralding our move into the modern age, or modernity. At the turn of the century the engineer C.Y. O'Connor blasted the rock bar at the mouth of the Swan River, ending its million-year old life as largely fresh water system and changing it to an estuary. Until this time tourists and mail had made the 400-kilometre journey up from Albany where there existed a superior deep-water harbour. In the words of Malcolm Tull, 'the first ocean-going vessel to enter the new harbour, the Blue Funnel Line's *Sultan* in May 1897, symbolised Western Australia's economic take-off'.[37] From this point onwards our place in the international web of trade and commerce was firmly established, with serious implications for the forests, plains and deserts of the region. If Tull is accurate in his understanding of this historical detonation of the coastal margin in 1897, then the state's economic growth has a deep historical connection to ecological disruption.

CHAPTER 7
A SNAPSHOT OF PERTH THROUGH MODERN TIMES

The act that founded the city of Perth, Western Australia, in 1829 was the cutting down of a sheoak in the vicinity of the present-day Barrack Street, and the firing of a volley of shots. This was, perhaps, an inauspicious start for the city. Today the Perth metropolitan area has plenty of facilities for automobiles, but not quite so many for ranging biodiversity. And yet, as recently four generations ago, Perth's CBD was an undulation of shallow lakes, sedgelands, and shrubland, where you could see jumping frogs, darting minnows, stalking heron, and lurking marron in the shadows of the tea-coloured water. Closer up you might have watched beetles, dragonflies, spiders, and water mites weaving and scintillating through the waterlogged groves.

This habitat was ideal for water birds such as the black swan (*Cygnus atratus*), a bird first called koltjack. As its habitat and nesting ground has been taken from it (specifically by the very core of Perth's cityscape) the species has suffered a reduction in range and population. The black swan, as it stares out from postage stamps, beer cans, taxis or coats of arms, is now a sad icon for our city. Flocks of up to one hundred swans once sat together on the waters in front of the city. Most contemporary

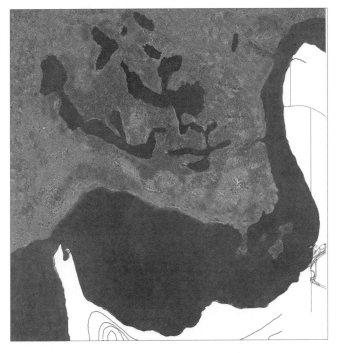

Aerial view of Perth prior to colonisation. Vast spread of wetlands evident. ANDREA TATE

inhabitants are blithely unaware that greater Perth lacks the huge numbers of pelicans and black swans it hosted prior to white colonisation, and quite probably fail to see the unfortunate irony in Perth's choice of symbolic bird.

When the Italian monk Dom Salvado came to Perth in the 1840s he wrote, 'the croaking of the frogs ... within town limits was so loud that we sometimes had to raise our voices, as if talking to the deaf'.[1]

George Fletcher Moore sat in a house further up the river, and one evening in 1832 he finished a letter with the following:

With this I close my answers to the queries in your first letter and finish for the night. I have just looked out on the night – fine weather again but such a croaking, twanging, grating, creaking, blowing, moaning and bellowing of frogs. I never heard such a Dutch concert.[2]

Moore was listening to the soundscape created by the moaning frog (*Heleioporus eyrei*) whose call sounds like a low, rising moan; the beautifully green-hued slender tree frog (*Litoria adelaidensis*) whose call sounds like a screech; the motorbike frog (*Litoria moorei*) whose call sounds like a motorbike changing gears, or as he says 'grating and creaking'; the western banjo frog (*Limnodynastes dorsalis*) whose call sounds like the slow plucking of a banjo's bass string; and other amphibians. 'I have heard frogs … roaring in such a fashion as to make a stranger think that the hills were infested with legions of lions, tigers, bears and rhinoceroses', wrote the English novelist Anthony Trollope on his visit to south-west Australia.[3] Apart from the frogs already mentioned, Salvado, Moore and Trollope might have been listening to the quacking frog (*Crinia georgiana*) whose call sounds like the quack of a duck; the rattling froglet (*Crinia glauerti*) whose call sounds like the rattle of a pea in a can; the squelching froglet (*Crinia insignifera*) whose call sounds like drawing a wet finger over a balloon[4]; the bleating froglet (*Crinia pseudinsignifera*) whose call sounds like the bleating of a goat; or finally the spotted-thigh frog whose call has been described as 'like the distant sound of wood being sawn'.[5] Today eighty per cent of the original wetlands on the Swan Coastal Plain has been cleared, drained or filled. If a lake has been left, it has often had fringing vegetation removed. Today Moore's 'Dutch concert' and Trollope's legion of wild beasts have become symphonies with very few players.

The chain of wetlands that sits beneath modern Perth, running to the north-east of the central business district, was thought to spread miasma and disease, and was filled in very early on in the city's development. The Perth train station was built on low and swampy land, because its undesirability made it available to the government. When the Alexander Library building was constructed in the 1980s, the planned two levels of underground car park were reduced to one because of the high water table.[6] In 2014, diaphragm walls were constructed to provide a watertight construction during the building of the underground Perth train station, located on the site of Lake Kingsford.[7] Constant mechanical pumping is still performed in some city basements. The undulation of shallow lakes that was Perth's past have not entirely passed.

Of course the city has changed over time. The Swan River no longer teems with the same quantity of large fish, prawns and blue manna crabs. Where a forest of nine-to-ten-metre-tall zamia palms once swayed their fronds in the breeze at Burswood, a casino now stands.[8] A suite of marsupials, including the beautiful and shy honey possum, has vacated the area. In our largest remaining patches of woodland, Kings Park and Bold Park, the only native mammal left is the brush-tailed possum. Thankfully, in the small fragments of vegetation that remain, at least many of Perth's fifty-one species of lizard and some of its twenty-four species of snake hang on.

Many great trees are barely a memory. When Salvado walked out of Perth, heading north-east into the unknown in the 1840s, he took shade under a jarrah tree, 'so thick in the trunk that one might well have thought it was there

This photograph, Out of the Mist: A Road Scene at Jolimont, *shows a tuart of the kind that would have been common around Perth in the nineteenth century and later.* FRED FLOOD

before the flood'.[9] In studying landscape art from 1827 to 1950, Andrea Gaynor found a decrease in the prevalence of very large trees around the Swan River.[10] Fred Flood's photograph from the 1920s *Out of the Mist: A Road Scene at Jolimont* shows a tuart of the kind that would have been common around Perth in the nineteenth century and later.

Such trees are almost never encountered around Perth today. Most were dynamited or cut down for timber years ago. All cities displace and replace a particular ecosystem, but it is salutary to remember the ways in which the Perth was once a glorious wildland. A historian pacing through contemporary Perth and its suburbs would be right to echo Joni Mitchell: 'They paved paradise and put up a parking lot.'

*

Anglo-Saxon suburbia has a pedigree reaching back to eighteenth century London. In 1757, Robert Lloyd wrote:

> The wealthy Cit, grown old in trade,
> Now wishes for the rural shade …
> Sir Traffic has a house, you know,
> About a mile from Cheney-Row.[11]

Soon enough Sir Traffic would come to be the proud owner of the Country Box. So, too, Perth's early development of suburbs was encouraged by this wish of the urban citizen for 'the rural shade', and was fostered by the introduction of railways in 1881.

The wooden wagon wheels of white settlers were not well adapted to deep sands. In the nineteenth century the sandy nature of the land around Perth was the cause, for its 'sandgropers', of not infrequent misery. Apart from slowing transport, the sand caused eye diseases in many colonists. The sand would blow into the eyes, often triggering an infection. Even with roads being made of crushed limestone and sand, grit blew into surrounding houses and back gardens much more than it does today.

The building of the railway from Perth to Fremantle provided a new focus for suburban expansion. Claremont station was the first siding, so Claremont saw houses erected amongst the tuarts and the macrozamias. Then Cottesloe siding came into being, and it became a good area to have a house by the sea (it still is for those who can afford it). These early bush blocks fronted a quiet road. From your front verandah you could have looked across the horizon and seen the windmills of your neighbours that pumped up water from Perth's groundwater system via a well in the back garden.

Housing by this time was often a structure made of mass-produced weatherboards and galvanised iron roofing. However, as late as 1911, some cottages in Osborne Park were still built of whitewashed hessian, and roofed with sheets of bark from paperbark trees.[12] Sand fleas were a frequent and unappealing feature of life on the land. The toilet was a privy or outhouse at the end of the back yard. Sand filtered the waste from the septic tanks, but this meant that the water supply was liable to contamination, and cases of dysentery and typhoid were alarmingly high.[13] To solve this, the authorities began to insist that suburban blocks were increased to a bit over a thousand square metres. This legacy of the quarter-acre block left its mark on future generations and is still discernible in the culture of sprawling housing development. Early suburban back yards featured a vegetable patch, a chicken run and coop, a workshop, a woodshed, fruit trees (Perth's isolation meant you could only eat fruit that was in season), with figs and citrus being popular, and a clothes line to hang your washing on after the weekly wash.[14]

One way in which Western Australians have expressed their feelings for the natural world has been through the creation of gardens. Unlike the chaotic complexity and grey-greens of the bush, the suburban gardens of Perth have for the last 100 years, for the most part expressed an attachment to order, colour and uniformity, and the plants of the 'mother country' have been traditionally favoured in Perth's gardens.[15] In the average-sized suburban garden in Perth you may still find around 150 introduced plant species, and only a handful of native plant species.

*

Today Perth has a central business district with a non-residential core, surrounded by car and fossil-fuel dependent suburbs. But the city wasn't always designed this way. Until the 1940s and 1950s the main architecture was composed of two- and three-storey Victorian buildings, much constructed in the gold-rush era, lining long streets like St Georges Terrace and Hay Street. You could stroll along St Georges Terrace and catch flashes of a sun-sparkled river down to the south between the stately facades.

Roses and lawns bravely and incongruously confronted sand and intense midsummer heat. The city looked much as the West End of the port city of Fremantle looks today, except that it was larger and had electric trams rolling up and down the street. From the 1890s till the 1950s, Perth had a tram network with thirty-five different routes, including ones to Subiaco, Nedlands, Leederville, Mt Hawthorn, and Victoria Park, adding up to fifty kilometres in length. Perth of this period had a heart of a kind with boot-makers, grocers, tailors, barbers and the like downtown, and people of average means living close to the centre, in places like West Perth.

My grandmother lived in this city of English values, where 'home' was 13,000 kilometres away. In the late 1920s, when my grandmother was a young woman in Perth, most houses did not have telephones, and when you did make a call you did not dial a number but spoke with women at the switchboard who would connect you to another telephone number. Houses didn't have washing machines, and heating was mostly from wood. Manually worked sewing machines were often part of the household. Women had a large amount of physical toil and domestic isolation to contend with. In many cases, people went to work from Monday to Saturday, mostly walking, riding a bike or using public transport. Rates of immigration were low compared to today, and racism was, lamentably, socially acceptable. It is likely that Perth had a great deal of what American sociologist Robert Putnam has termed 'social capital';[16] people were more likely to have trusted a stranger on the street than today. Levels of civic engagement were higher. The internal combustion engine had been invented, and there were cars around, but the clattering of the hooves of horses and carts was still a reality in the streetscape. There were no traffic lights until 1953. Saturday evening you might go to a dance. Sunday you'd wear your best clothes and head off to the nearest, usually Anglican, church service. Connie Miller reports going to church in Osborne Park where horse-drawn vehicles were tied to shady jarrahs and banksias in front of the church, and where, after Sunday School, children picked hovea, cowslip orchids and stars of Bethlehem beneath tuarts and zamia palms.[17] The man was the head of the house and sat at the head of the table, carving the roast and slicing the bread.[18] That said, women still broke the mould. The adventurous Daisy Bates had been writing as an anthropologist with the first Australians for years, and in 1921 a woman, Edith Cowan, won the election for the seat of West Perth, followed by May Holman in the seat of Forrest in 1925. There was a certain formality about visiting someone, and I still have my great-aunt's silver visiting-card case in a drawer. Bread and milk was home-delivered, as it would be for many decades to come.

Many people knew nature through picnics in Kings Park, swimming in the Swan River, or daytripping to Serpentine Falls. Crabbing, prawning and fishing were popular activities, with large mullet, cobbler, tailor, flounder and flathead there for the catching. John Forrest National Park, the first national park in Western Australia, had been proclaimed at the turn of the last century less than thirty years after Yellowstone, the world's first national park, had been established in America. And yet, national parks were seen more as urban recreation areas than conservation reserves. The Stirling Ranges were declared a national park in 1913 (it was originally more than three times the size it is today, but was reduced in size after pressure from farmers, and was made accessible to visitors in 1928).[19] You could travel by train through much of south-west Australia (much of this railway network was only closed by the government in the 1950s). At the start of the 1920s the person to automobile ratio in the state was around one hundred to one, and at the end of the decade it had grown to around ten to one.[20] Only a train journey across the Nullarbor still hinted to people how silent and huge the land was further east out past the goldfields. The term 'the bush' indicated a lack of sensitivity to the particularities of different bioregions outside of Perth, a linguistic insensitivity that abides into the present day.

I find it fascinating to think that for my grandmother this was her experience of a walk through Perth as a young woman: genteel Victorian stone facades, expansive balconies, trams, bowler hats, bicycles, three-piece suits – through what was a quiet, pretty little town situated on the banks of a river teeming with life (this is not to forget of course that there was also a dark side of institutionalised racism). There were fewer than 200,000 residents of the city, and only sixty-six square kilometres of urban development.

In the 1920s, chuditch and quenda and numbats ambled through the bush around Perth's suburban edges each night. Around this time one woman recalled going from Harborne Street by Lake Monger to Herdsman's Lake and seeing swathes of orchids:

> primrose cowslips, royal blue enamels, pink-threaded or pure white spiders, even the tiny shy green orchids that burrowed into the sand. And the great drifts of the gilded donkey orchids. Lovely mantels of purple hardenbergia and white clematis spilled over shrubs and saplings. There were myrtles, their shining wands thick-starred with pink rosettes. Heaths with perfect flowerets of delicate mauve. Native buttercups of bright saffron, heliotrope fish flowers, creamy waxies, glistening sundews ...[21]

South of the river, what is today known as Canning Highway was 'a limestone track meandering through the bush with the treetops entwined overhead. It was travelled infrequently; in fact to travel the road was regarded as something of an adventure into the unknown. Bush animals were there in plenty'.[22] On a trip down a sandy track such as this north or south of the city, you might see metre-tall bustards, or 'bush turkey' (*Ardeotis australis*), run wildly into the distance, or large goannas swish their long tails as they made a reptilian S-curve into cover. During the 1930s and 1940s, foxes reaped their harvest, and the bush became a more lonely place.

Concrete high-rise buildings appeared in the 1950s, and then really entered the streetscape in the 1960s and 1970s.

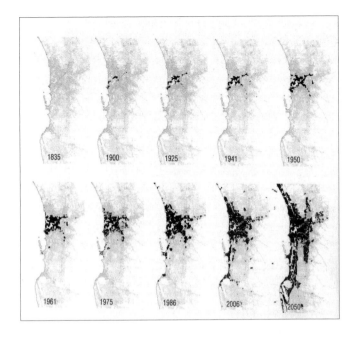

Perth's geographic extent through time. RICHARD WELLER

Busy roads and freeways crisscrossed the Esplanade and you could no longer stroll down to the river's edge with ease. The private automobile reigned supreme; the consumer economy, loaded with cheap petroleum-derived plastic goods, had arrived.

At the start of the 1970s, when my father was a young man, Perth had grown to well over 600,000 inhabitants, and over 350 square kilometres of urban development spread out around the Swan River. But the urban footprint of Perth was far, far smaller than it is today. It was a land of tidy suburban houses with fruit trees out the back and Hills Hoist clothes lines on the back lawn. There were still electricity cables above ground on all the streets and big boxy cars parked out front. Cars had gained the ascendancy over public transport; central Perth had high-rise office buildings, but not the vertiginous skyscrapers of today. Only in the last few years had white Australians discovered that their country had a human history that went back for tens of millennia. People still walked to the local shops for their household needs. Sprinklers watered endless green verges with their click, click, click on hot summer nights. Many people had chickens, and vegetables, in their back garden. Much of the fruit and vegetables people bought were grown in market gardens in Spearwood and South Coogee. A few years before, in 1963, records show that almost one in every four households could hear the sound of clucking coming from out the back.[23] It was many years since these fowl had been harassed by hungry chuditch in the dead of night.

Despite trends towards an increasing culture of consumerism, there emerged a new consciousness at this time, which we might call an ecological enlightenment. This started back in 1962 when the science writer Rachel Carson more or less inaugurated the modern environmental movement with the publication of *Silent Spring*, a book exposing the dangers of pesticides. The Conservation Council for Western Australia was established in 1967. In 1969 a man had looked down on the earth from the moon for the first time in history, and brought back photographs that focused attention on the unified, delicate and irreplaceable nature of the global biosphere. In 1971, a statewide Environmental Protection Authority (EPA) was established as a necessary part of our decision-making process in Western Australia. In the 1960s and 1970s some young people demonstrated against the destruction of the natural environment in the south-west by standing in front of bulldozers.

When my father grew up in Swanbourne in the 1950s and 1960s, there were many more trees to the north of the city. Many more birds than today could be found, and heard, amongst the trees. The eastern-most strip of the Swan Coastal Plain had been cleared for agriculture a long time ago (this was the best soil for agriculture), but only in the last few decades of the twentieth century did the less fertile sand plains further west and north of the older suburbs get subdivided. Those bushlands used to be the home of thousands of birds, plants, reptiles and insects. On a summer's afternoon in those woods you could have stopped and watched what the Noongar called birinbirin, a rainbow bee-eater (*Merops ornatus*) sit, insect in beak, on a branch in the sun. If you looked closely you would have seen a red eye with a black iris sitting in a band of black feathers, but apart from this strip it would all be shimmering colour. Yellow at the crown, turning to light green at the chest, and the light green fading through eggshell blue into a darker aquamarine further down the body, its shape is completed by elegantly elongated black tail feathers. Washes of cinnamon, green, bronze, and blue, so superbly begun with a long black beak and finished with such dark tail feathers, make this one of the most beautiful creatures in all Australia. Noongar people used to celebrate life in that banksia country when, in December each year, they would sit around holes of fresh water full of the nectar of dozens of mangitch, yellow banksia cones. Later Perth's remnant bushlands provided a place to play for young children, like my father, wandering barefoot under the shade of an old tuart in Claremont in the 1950s. In the 1950s, 1960s, and even the early 1970s, *Nuytsia floribunda*, the Western

Australian Christmas tree, set the Perth metropolitan area on fire each Christmas with profuse blooms of golden flowers. Perth was literally wreathed in ribbons of glowing orange.

A black and white aerial photograph of Perth's suburbs south of the Swan River taken in 1965 shows Jandakot Airport surrounded by many square kilometres of undeveloped land. Today Google Earth shows Jandakot Airport firmly hemmed by houses. From the early 1970s onwards the city started to explode, in slow motion, north, south and east away from its cluster of settlements around the Swan River. Today the Perth that was mantled in the annual orange blossom of Christmas trees – known by my father, my grandparents, their parents, and so on backwards in time till European arrival in 1830, and known by the Noongar as moodjar for many thousands of years before that – has gone. Born in 1978, I have never known that city. Children born today will for the most part never know that blaze of colour that lit up the suburbs at Christmas time.

Much of what today's Western Australians think of as 'natural' is in fact a profoundly altered biological world. Without the knowledge of the old biological Perth, we can't lament the loss of this diversity. But perhaps we should. It was our rightful inheritance. The baseline of what Perth's people perceive as environmentally 'normal' or 'natural' has shifted, and shifted downwards, and will continue to shift downwards with each new generation that grows up amongst the ever-sprawling suburbs.

*

After retiring in 1966 after sixteen years as prime minister of Australia, Robert Menzies declared himself to be 'British to my boot-heels'.[24] Perth is now far less ethnically homogenous than it was in the 1950s. There has been considerable immigration. The 2011 Census from the Australian Bureau of Statistics showed that over a quarter of Perth's people were born overseas (the highest of any capital in the country), and approximately half of Western Australia's population had one or both parents born overseas. Fifty-one per cent of Western Australians said that they had non-Australian ancestry in 2006, but amazingly this figure had risen to seventy-five per cent by 2011.[25] This cosmopolitan nature of contemporary Perth is to be welcomed.

Once, the catch-cry among Australian politicians was, 'Populate or Perish'. However, an environmentally informed perspective may today caution that this contemporary immigration is taking place in a corner of Australia where environmental limits are already biting, in the form of water scarcity. This is arguably the most pressing problem facing the current population. From 1911 to 1974, Perth's reservoirs had an average annual inflow of 338 gigalitres. From 1975 to 1996, it was 177 gigalitres. From 1997 to 2004, it was 120 gigalitres.[26] This downward trend continues. In September 2014, I checked the statistics and found that we had had 53.7 gigalitres of stream-flow into our dams since January. In 2015, I checked again in September and found that this figure was down to 7.4 gigalitres. This frightens me. The reality we face is of drastically declining rainfall in an already very dry corner of Australia. If you had sat beside streams in the Darling Ranges every spring in the second half of the twentieth century you would have noticed that from the mid-1970s the waters began to run low. A ten to fifteen per cent drop in south-west rainfall since the 1970s has produced a corresponding fifty per cent reduction in average flows into south-west rivers and streams.[27] Perth's lake systems are becoming swampy flats. Wetlands above climate-sensitive groundwater systems are experiencing more frequent dry states. In light of our drying climate, perhaps the political refrain could now become 'Populate and Perish'.

The Swan flooded the year after white settlement, and one correspondent from the time wrote that 'the overflowing is not that of a rapid torrent, carrying everything before, but merely a gentle rising of the fat muddy river.'[28]

Prior to the 1970s, Perth's annual rainfall would, in some years, be massive. Nowadays the rainfall varies each year, but without the huge variations of the pre-70s; without the occasional year of really heavy annual precipitation. I was born after this time, so I don't have a memory of such years of flooding and large rainfall. My baseline to understand the Swan River has shifted, and into less dramatic territory.

If we found one of the few remaining old flooded gums (*Eucalyptus rudis*) along the Swan and cut deep into its trunk, we would find traces of some years of drought and some years of flooding reflected in the spacing of the rings of the tree. But I don't have the long-running environmental memory that is stored in the trunk of an elder flooded gum. Looking at the graphs and the statistics we can at least know, abstractly, that, linked with global anthropogenic climate warming, our water supply is decreasing in Perth. While considering this fact, we might remind ourselves that Perth citizens are amongst the highest consumers of water per capita in the world. Perth's Water Corporation is faced with a decreasing water supply from dams and

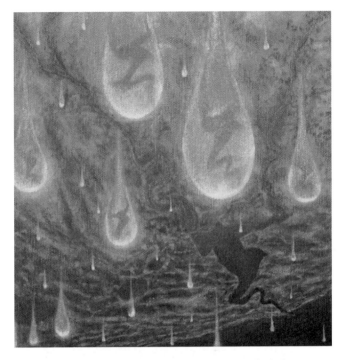

Rain falling over the Swan River, aerial view; Djart Whadjuk Nyoongar Boodja. ALAN MULLER

Mill Point in the 1926 floods, Western Mail, *29 July 1926.*
THE WEST AUSTRALIAN

aquifers as the south-west warms up as a result of climate change. In 2006, Perth became the first Australian city to use a seawater desalination plant, and within a few years another such plant was running. In 2014, almost half of Perth's water supply was coming from water desalinated from the Indian Ocean. These plants produce lots of water but also consume vast amounts of energy. Most of the rest of Perth's drinking water is pumped up through wet sand out of the Gnangara Mound aquifer, a large reserve of underground water, and yet recharge into the aquifer has reduced by twenty-five per cent over the last twenty-five years.

Leaving aside the controversial and politically unpalatable issue of environmental limits to sustainable population growth, we might at least consider that a city made up of a rising population of new Australians may be in danger of lacking a historically and biologically grounded sense of place. It is hard to see the nature of your new home, or develop a sense of belonging amongst it, when such nature is buried beneath Malaysian palms, brick houses and concrete driveways.

*

Today Perth is a city built around motor vehicles and roadways. In 1909 the introduction of the first mass-produced car, the Ford Model T, signalled a massive change in world history. Unlike old world capitals, most of modern Perth has developed in the years since the car became king. Perth is one of the most car-dependent cities in the world, well deserving of John Betjeman's epithet, *Motopolis*; he wrote of the car that 'it poisons the air, endangers the streets, deafens the ears and deadens the senses'.[29] Most trips (eighty per cent) are made by car.

Reliance on private cars has risen to above ninety per cent of all trips in some newer suburbs on the urban fringe of the Perth metropolitan area. If we run out of cheap and abundant energy to run individual people movers, then we could experience a profound crisis dubbed by local sustainability academic Peter Newman as 'Mad Max in the outer suburbs'. Perth is one of the most sprawling cities on earth, with an average density of six homes per hectare. And there are not many people in these houses. In 1961, around thirty per cent of Western Australian households consisted of one or two people. By 1991 this figure had increased to just over fifty per cent, and by 1996 was over fifty-five per cent.[30] We have large houses, with not many people inside them. Household size is still declining.

From south to north, the city is over 120 kilometres long. Perth's air quality is of a high standard compared to other Australian and international cities, but photochemical smog is regularly experienced over the city in summer in the form of a brown haze. In 2006, the Western Australian Department of Planning and Infrastructure released figures for the percentage of work trips made on public transport: Perth 9.7 per cent; Australian average 14.5 per cent; US average nine per cent; European average thirty-nine per cent.[31] Perth people are, considered on a global per capita basis, major contributors to the crisis of global climate warming. What is more, Perth relies on electricity that comes, for the most part, from the burning of coal.

The large freeway that slices through the centre of Perth, dividing east and west, is typical of the modern city. Unlike the bidi, the footpaths of the Noongar, which were born out of generations of humans following contours and landforms on the earth, this perfectly graded, arrow-like route north and south swaps myriad places for hastily traversed and largely anonymous space. As the writer William Least Heat Moon says, 'Life doesn't happen along interstates. It's against the law'.[32] Drive south or north on the freeway, then turn off at a major intersection. Enter what was a few years ago in many cases an unbroken sea of trees and plants, and is now a sea broken repeatedly by angular rooftops. Pass homogenous project home after homogenous project home, each occupying almost a full housing block. The streets are largely treeless, having been subjected to the scrape of the developer's bulldozers a few Christmases past. There is a sense of loneliness along these streets, and within the empty guest bedrooms of many ersatz suburban palaces dust gathers in the gloom. Driving recently through the grid-like streets of one unfortunately named suburb, 'Success', I recalled Gerard Manley Hopkins' poem 'Binsey Poplars' which made me think of venerable old paperbarks:

> My aspens dear, whose airy cages quelled,
> Quelled or quenched in leaves the leaping sun,
> All felled, felled, are all felled;
>
> ...
>
> O if we but knew what we do
> When we delve or hew —
> Hack and rack the growing green!
>
> ...
>
> Where we, even where we mean
> To mend her we end her ...[33]

When George Seddon wrote his book *Sense of Place* in 1972, he was already aware of how much Perth had expanded since the middle of the century (it had roughly doubled its population). Seddon was one person who *could* 'guess the beauty been', in spite of the work of thousands of bulldozers. And in the middle of this current decade, the urban area of Perth has more than doubled since the 1970s. The growth isn't over yet. Today the Perth metropolitan area keeps expanding outwards, knocking down the tiny patches of paperbark wetlands or banksia woodland that are left on the Swan Coastal Plain. Hopkins is more relevant than ever: 'To mend her we end her'.

In 2014 this city reached around two million people. Perth's population is predicted to grow to 2.5 million people by 2020, and around 4.6 million by 2050. Most of this population increase (over seventy per cent at the time of writing) is happening in the outer suburbs of greater Perth, in suburbs where a mosaic of grey, orange and white rooftops creeps out over the landscape. These rooftops are mostly unrelieved by a tree, or even much in the way of space to grow future trees. The people who live beneath them, from Vietnam, China, India, Ireland, England, or whichever nation they have emigrated from, may know little of the nature and history of the land where they now live. As Wendell Berry writes:

> The industrial conquistador, seated in his living room in the evening in front of his TV set, many miles from his work, can easily forget where he is and what he has done. He is everywhere and nowhere.[34]

Real estate billboard. THOMAS M. WILSON

The change in native vegetation cover for the Perth metropolitan area has been estimated for the six years from 1998 to 2004. In this time, around 6,000 hectares were knocked down in the Perth metropolitan region, giving an average of 853 hectares per year.[35] This is over one football oval per day being destroyed in the Perth metropolitan area.

In the last ten years we can see that Perth is exploding outwards, day-by-day, tree-by-bulldozed-tree. Most of this destruction of nature is done for housing developments full of non-native, water-hungry gardens and energy-inefficient, car-dependent houses. Continued loss of nature in the Perth metropolitan area is expected, as many areas have been zoned 'urban' in the planning system but have not yet been cleared and built on. In 2001 there were 266,000 hectares of native vegetation in the Perth Metropolitan Region. Of these, 191,000 hectares were protected and 75,000 hectares were unprotected (many of them on private land).[36]

Shire councils continue to approve the destruction of

Vegetation clearing, aerial view. RICHARD WELLER

areas that may not be pristine natural ecosystems full of endangered species (hopefully Australia's national environmental legislation will prevent this), but which are covered in native trees. A range of studies has demonstrated that proximity to green spaces is good for our mental health and refreshment.[37] Not only is this loss of nature from our city and suburbs bad for our mental health, it also means 'death by a thousand cuts' to the home and feeding grounds of the endangered Carnaby's black cockatoo and many other species besides.

Perth is changing fast, but how much reflection currently attends these changes is debatable. Current residents might not always ponder the changes to their city from the perspective of the nonhumans amongst us. For example, imagine the beautiful and emotionally complex Carnaby's cockatoo, which traditionally visits the Perth area at the end of each summer to feed on the banksia woodlands that are now largely under concrete. In Nandi Chinna's book *Swamp: Walking the Wetlands of the Swan Coastal Plain*, she includes a photo

'All you need is right here'. NANDI CHINNA

of a billboard standing on an area of denuded land that is soon to become a shopping centre. In a perfect piece of unintended poetic irony the billboard spells out in huge letters: 'All you need is right here'.[38] Beneath the sign, the sands of Western Australia lie denuded and disrespected.

The expanding population is great for property developers, builders, the retail and service industries, and politicians who extol the virtues of unlimited economic growth with almost mystical fervour. And yet, while writing this chapter and knowing what has been lost since my father was growing up in the 1950s, I became sad that some historically uninformed members of parliament and local councils could allow insult to be made to already incurred injury in the form of inappropriate housing and retail developments. The stamp of local and state government approval continues the destruction. Whitefellas, or wadjela, as the first Australians called them, are industrious in paving over the wild earth.

For most of its history, Perth has been the administrative centre for the western third of Australia. Even in the early settler years it was halfway between the farmed land in the Upper Swan and the port's trade at Fremantle. Later, wheat and sheep flooded in from different parts of the state. Later still, it was gold and then iron ore and other minerals. For a long time, particularly since the rock bar was blasted at Fremantle at the mouth of the Swan in 1897, and later again when the first purpose-built container ships slipped onto the world's oceans in the 1950s, Perth has been a spider hanging in a web of international trade and global market demand. Go to the top of a skyscraper in the Perth CBD and look down. Below are the concrete canyons of industry and finance. Now look out across the land. The dry landscape is covered in houses glittering under the sun. In the distance you see container ships, vast floating metal warehouses, coming and going into Fremantle Port to the south and west. Imagine for a moment that, in this tranquil and glittering scene, the ships suddenly stopped. What would happen if cheap fossil fuels ran out and these vessels ceased departing, full of wheat and iron ore and nickel and returning with cars and fridges and washing machines? What would happen to this great sparkling city on its dry Australian plain stretching out to the horizon? The very existence of Perth assumes there is limitless cheap oil to burn to haul in the necessities and luxuries and to remove the waste, but it rests upon fragile foundations.

*

Despite all this, I hold to hope. Looking at faded old postcards or consulting current visitor itineraries, Kings Park is clearly a place central to the identity of the city of Perth. In 1894 this area of vegetation at the western edge of the city was reserved, and unlike Centennial Park in Sydney, another famous Australian park, it was not entirely cleared of its native plants. Today Perth boasts one thousand acres of wild organisms, an area larger than the huge Central Park in New York, in the middle of the city. Bold Park is another jewel in the crown of this city. Although you might not always notice it, this settlement still has plenty of native biodiversity. Look at all our lizards, for example. A vast array of species of reptile are, as you read this, minding their own business in the sun, or under a quiet rock.

Even in this city of concrete and bitumen, the living earth has a future. The last three chapters of this book will demonstrate reasons for hope, where I explore the concept of rewilding, both personal and ecological. For now I leave you with the words of Wendell Berry from his poem 'In a Country Once Forested':

> The young woodland remembers
> the old, a dreamer dreaming
>
> of an old holy book,
> an old set of instructions,
>
> and the soil under the grass
> is dreaming of a young forest,
>
> and under the pavement the soil
> is dreaming of grass.[39]

CHAPTER 8
FROM YORK/GUM BELT
TO WHEATBELT

Come Sons of Summer, by whose toile
We are the Lords of Wine and Oile:
By whose tough labours, and rough hands
We rip up first, then reap our lands.
– *Robert Herrick, 1648, 'The Hock-Cart, or Harvest Home'*[1]

It is a sunny afternoon in Perth in 1884. Along a sandy track called Canning Road rolls a dray loaded high with bales of wool. It is pulled by six bullocks. The driver watches their gluteal muscles flex and strain as the heavy-wheeled wooden vehicle tilts forward along the plank-lined track. There is almost no traffic. He can smell the greasy wool behind him, and hear the sounds of honeyeaters singing high, darting across the way in front of him. He swishes a gum tip to fend off persistent flies around his face. He is bound for the jarrah-built docks of Fremantle. He has come from York, miles behind him, to the east. York is land where once millions of York gums (*Eucalyptus loxophleba*) and wattle (*Acacia acuminata*) once grew. This man's father saw these trees as evidence that the soil was first-class (if it was marri and wandoo it was second-class and if it was jarrah, banksia and heath then it was third-class and almost useless). There in the shearing sheds of York, the sharp implements clipped the sweaty merinos, and the wool was scooped and loaded into bales, and ultimately onto his cart. Before that the merinos had grazed amongst the granite tors of the undulating landscape, dotted with gimlet and york gums. In the past, a shepherd would have looked over them, sleeping fitfully, made uneasy by imaginings of meat-hungry Noongar hunters passing in the night. But now paddocks with fences and a diminished traditional human culture were starting to make the wool-laden quadrupeds safer. All that has now passed, and this afternoon in 1884 the wool is bumping down the tree-lined Canning Road parallel and to the south of the Swan River. It is a rural-looking road. Along its margin the yellow tints of spider orchids enliven the grey-green understorey. When it leaves Fremantle, in a few weeks time, the wool will sail over the Indian and Atlantic Oceans and up the Thames and arrive on the docks of London. Who knows on which English man or woman's back it will end up on, in which drawing room, street or factory? For now the driver bumps down the track, moving slowly westwards. He carries a valuable cargo, stacked twenty bags high. This wool was grown where once stood a woodland haunted by numbats and chuditch, emu and bustard ('bush turkey' our cart driver would have called them). That ecosystem was killed by ringbarking and by the roar of flames. A pound is a pound. There is money to be made. The international economy sings out its demands, to every corner of the Empire. For a moment the sea breeze pushes at the driver's towering cargo and the bullocks' shoulders grip harder in their leather harnesses. The moment passes ... they push on.

*

Let us consider the human impact on the land outside of Perth. The early white settlers around the south-west obviously did not have a deeply conservationist mindset. Part of this can be excused through ignorance of the biological and geological nature of the land they were entering and settling. Prior to Darwin, Charles Lyell had published his *Principles of Geology* (1830 to 1833). The Bible ascribes a recent date to Creation (4004 BC). Lyell's book popularised geology with the argument that the earth was – *pace* the Bible – millions of years old. Lyell's work was carried by Darwin on his voyage aboard the *Beagle*, and was indeed instrumental in allowing Charles Darwin to formulate his own theory of evolution by natural selection. And yet Lyell's work was not widely known or his theories widely subscribed to among the general population at the time. This was understandable, as John Fowles reflects: 'Genesis is a great lie; but it is also a great poem; and a six-thousand-year-old womb is much warmer than one that stretches for two thousand million'.[2]

Despite the arrival of Lyell's publications, most early Western Australian white settlers would still have thought that they lived in a snugly accommodated universe. If they had have understood the true age of the earth, and the staggeringly ancient nature of the Western Australian rocks and soil that they were stepping over, as well as the process of biological evolution through which the plants and animals of this place had adapted to this ancient and leached land, then they would have had a greater appreciation for the ecosystems they were encountering. But it would not be until 1859 that Darwin's *The Origin of Species* was published, and even longer before his lessons had permeated widely amongst the minds of god-fearing Australian farmers. Indeed when Europeans arrived at the Swan River in 1829, Darwin had not yet left Plymouth on his voyage of the *Beagle*.

So early agricultural settlers were not much interested in ecology. W.H. Hudson was writing about the Argentinian pampas, but he could have been writing about south-west Australia:

> There is no longer anything to deter the starvelings of the Old World from possessing themselves of this new land of promise, flowing ... with milk and tallow, if not with honey; any emasculated migrant from a[n] [English or Irish] slum is now competent to 'fight the wilderness' out there, with his eight-shilling fowling-piece and the implements of his trade.[3]

Back in Europe where these migrants had come from, a few plant species occupy ranges of many, many thousands of square kilometres. The land is fertile and resilient. Here in the south-west of Australia, on the other hand, there is a fine-grained mosaic of different soil types, just about all with a fragile topsoil. Here in Australia there were and are some plant species that may only exist in a few square kilometres, and have been there for hundreds of thousands of years. Clear the few kilometres of land, and the species is gone. But if you are used to the tenacity of the weedy and widespread flora back in Europe, not to mention entirely uninformed about Lyell's principles of geology or Darwin's principles of evolution, then you won't have the faintest understanding of such subtle ecological dynamics. This was the case for early agricultural migrants. The very use of the phrase 'ecological dynamics' indicates that we hail from a post-Darwinian age cognisant of the complex interactions of biological species. That's a long way from the nineteenth century 'pioneering' perspective graphically characterised by the Bible by the bed, an axe in the hand and bread on the table. These men and women were chiefly concerned with possessing and 'fighting the wilderness'. Of course this historical observation does not excuse all twentieth century exploitation of nature, of which there was plenty, and of which I will come to consider soon enough.

After the Swan Valley, the Avon Valley (just the Swan by another name and further into the Darling Ranges) was next to be cleared. As Jamie Kirkpatrick notes, 'the term "clearance" encapsulates the attitude that sees the bush as an obstacle' as, after all, introduced species were immediately placed in lieu of the native vegetation.[4] Huge sheep runs and small food-growing plots next to the family home was the order of the day for whites for most of the nineteenth century in this part of the world. In 1890, long after Europeans arrived in the south-west, only 500 square kilometres of the area had been cleared.[5] Squatters grazed their cattle far and wide, but what is today known as the Western Australian Wheatbelt hardly existed. It was only in the 1890s, with the introduction of superphosphate, that the red loam soils in the valleys of the Wheatbelt were able to be farmed for crops.[6] The railway soon sprouted lines out into this region and, not coincidentally, this expansion tracked the destruction of the natural vegetation.

Historian Geoffrey Bolton has observed that when Australia became self-governing, there was not much in the way of environmental planning, and that this had much to do with the fact that these governments lacked a skilled civil service, and were primarily under pressure to spend money on developmental works like roads and bridges.[7] And then of course there was the agricultural lobby. Sir John Forrest was the first premier of Western Australia (1890 to 1901). In 1883 he said, 'It is the duty of the State to do everything in its power to encourage cultivation of the soil'.[8] These words tolled a death knell for many of the non-human species of life in this part of the planet.

White Western Australians have a long history of government-championed destruction of native flora. Indeed the Swan River Colony came into being with land regulations that entitled the newcomer who arrived before the end of 1830 to forty acres of land for every three pounds of productive capital (equipment, livestock, plants, etc) they brought with them. Only when the settler had finally brought the whole of their land under some form of cultivation, would they be granted title to the land. Western Australia's state-owned Agricultural Bank came into being in 1894.[9] It was later to become the Rural and Industries Bank, and then Bankwest.[10] To encourage white settlement on the land the bank provided loans to would-be farmers. As historian Geoffrey Blainey says, in those days, 'to own a small farm was a dream as intense as the later dream to own one's house'.[11] Understandably, everybody wanted a bit of land for themselves. Here was the opportunity. From today's perspective, one might say that white Western Australians were being given money by the government to destroy ancient ecosystems. If they failed to destroy the natural habitat by clearing and fencing the land, then they forfeited the land. By 1900 the Inspector of Lands could write triumphantly:

During 1899 there has been much expansion … an enormous area has been cleared … Next to the Agricultural Bank, nothing has pushed on clearing so fast as the system of burning ringbarked timber.[12]

By 1900, seven million acres had been sold for agriculture. By 1920, this had increased to twenty-three million acres.[13]

An early stimulus here came via the availability of land after the gold rush had slumped. To retain thousands of immigrant prospectors, the government offered them 160 acre farms, the uptake of which resulted in an increase in the rate of habitat loss from 1905.[14] A few numbers from Statistical Registers tell an environmental history in a nutshell: the area of land that the *Agricultural Bank Act* had financed to be ringbarked was around: 17,000 acres in 1896; 56,000 acres in 1900; 886,000 acres in 1910; and 2.4 million acres in 1920.[15]

Here we have an important part of the environmental history of south-western Australia: in the first two decades of the twentieth century the vast York gum, gimlet, wandoo and salmon gum woodlands, a few hundreds kilometres east and north-east of Perth, were almost totally obliterated. A large part of Australia, now almost totally forgotten, died. Today people do not speak of the 'York Gum Belt', rather they speak of the 'wheatbelt'. As this phrase slips over the tongue, the identity of this bioregion is profoundly ripped off.

For a long time, wheat growing was mainly to supply flour to the family farm's homestead, but as the railway was being constructed in the 'wheatbelt' in the first couple of decades of the twentieth century, wheat came into widespread commercial production. Between 1904 and 1919, around 3,200 kilometres of track were laid.[16] And as you watch the rapid expansion of the snaking line of the railway moving further east, you can almost simultaneously track the destruction of nature. According to historical ecologist Ian Abbott, published maps demonstrate extensive clearing in the western Wheatbelt in the years 1909 to 1918.[17] If we look at the value of exports of wheat around this time we can see a sharp jump from 130,000 pounds in 1909 to 760,000 pounds worth of wheat leaving Fremantle harbour in 1913.[18] Underneath these figures lies the reality of great ecological losses. At the end of these first two decades of the century the 'wheatbelt' really was belt-shaped, moving out north and south in a very wide band behind the Darling Ranges. Many a dusty railway siding, stacked many metres high with hessian bags full of wheat, witnessed the first and forced productions of a newly denuded land. Many of the grandparents of today's farmers in places like Tammin (a couple of hours drive east of Perth) were unravelling the fabric of the land. They were leaving a gargantuan task of revegetation to their grandchildren in the twenty-first century.

It was also scientific advances in agriculture that allowed this early clearing of the western Wheatbelt. The Department of Agriculture was established in 1898, and by 1911 there were two factories manufacturing superphosphates.[19] These were used as fertilisers on soils that until then hadn't been very good for growing crops or pastures as they were low in phosphate, or on soils that had quickly been exhausted after several seasons of producing crops. A kind of legume, 'sub-clover', was also soon in use to increase the fertility of the soil, and this boosted the wheat and sheep industry in the state's south-west.

By 1912 the problem of salt-affected land had been

noted. That year an engineer for the Goldfields Water Supplies wrote, 'When land is cleared, natural vegetation no longer utilises rainwater, which enters the ground taking salt with it'.[20] For 10,000 years the winds had been blowing salt inland and it had accumulated in the soil.[21] There was also a small amount of salt in the rain that came from the west, and again, over a long enough time, this built up in the soil. Though this hadn't happened in the western Darling Ranges, as the much higher rainfall regularly leaches the soil there of any salt (so no worry about a salinity crisis in the western Darling Ranges, not to mention the southern karri forests). But for most of the Wheatbelt area there had been no regular seepage and stream flow to empty the pallid soils of their ancient salts. The salt had built up. And the engineer O'Brien was right, back in 1912. The native plants did use up the year's rainfall, and when they were removed, the rain washed the salt out of the soil, killing everything that might have been living in the bottomlands where this salty mix ended up.

It is only thanks to the self-regulating effects of biological life that life is possible on the salty geology of much of south-western Australia. Trees put down deep tap roots and keep the salt from entering the topsoil. This lets all the other plants, and thus insects and animals, live. Chop these trees down and replace the deep-rooted perennials with shallow-rooted annuals like wheat, and you've ruined a delicate biological balancing act. The soluble salts in the soil get released by the rising groundwater that is no longer being soaked up by the native vegetation. The flow through the soil flushes the salts to the valley floors, where evaporation concentrates them. This process has given us pockets of moon-like, salty desolation. I have walked

Dead trees in salt-ridden valley. THOMAS M. WILSON

through such valley floors and they are full of the gaunt skeletons of once-living trees.

Despite the fact that the knowledge of the salinity crisis was firmly in the public domain since the 1920s, the clearing continued through most of the twentieth century. The 2007 *State of the Environment Report* estimated that seventy-five per cent of Australia's dryland salinity problem was in Western Australia. The report also noted that about 1.1 million hectares of the south-west was currently salt-affected and that nineteen football-oval-sized areas were being lost to land salinisation every day.[21]

*

Barbara York Main is primarily a scientist. In 1971 she published a collection of literary vignettes of agrarian life in the Wheatbelt area, the area where she grew up as a child. A sadly neglected book of occasional lyrical power, *Twice Trodden Ground* gets its title from the author's return to the area as an adult, over ground that she had trodden as a young girl. During York Main's lifetime, immense clearing of the original vegetation of the area took place – one million acres a year during the 1960s – and the work is infused with a sense of loss as the result. In a chapter entitled 'The Betrayal' we read of a farmer who decides to clear the last patch of bush on his land to extract the maximum economic gain from it. The narrative details his hard work clearing the plants and trees. At the end of the chapter the farmer sees the rise of a silver scum to the surface of the ground after the last season's rains. The account ends with a paradoxical image of whiteness, 'He had betrayed the land for silver – but the silver was ground gone salt'.[22] Very little can live in salt, which is why British surgeons in early white Australian history saw themselves as benevolent when they rubbed salt into the wounds of freshly flogged convicts. This image of the wheat farmer standing amongst a field of silver is the image of a prelude to death on the starkly flayed back of the earth.

By 1930, Western Australia's area of wheat was half of the Australian total.[23] Overseas export markets were ready to take whatever wheat locals could sell them, and it was this that fuelled the continuing destruction of habitat in the Wheatbelt. But in 1930 to 1931, the Depression hit Western Australia hard, as it had built so much of its wealth on the export of primary products such as wheat and timber overseas. By 1931 to 1932, twenty-eight per cent of the workforce didn't have a job, and Edward Shann called the place 'a fine country to starve in'.[24] Labour was sparse for the farmers during the Second World War. However, after the war in 1945 a global increase in wool and wheat prices, as well as more government tax breaks for environmental vandalism, encouraged the clearing of more of the Wheatbelt.[25] After the Second World War the process of land-clearing accelerated, thanks to large machinery coming to the aid of the destroyers. While early on gimlet, wandoo, salmon gum and york gum were ringbarked and burnt in the Western Wheatbelt, now chains were dragged through biodiverse kwongan further east. Finally the role of trace elements such as zinc and copper was understood, and 'light land', that is, Western Australia's enormous sand plains further east, could be farmed with their addition. According to David Coates et. al., 'the fragmentation of south-western Australia's floristically rich heath and shrublands (kwongan) is relatively recent with most clearing occurring between 1949 and 1969.[26] There was official government talk of a victorious clearing of 'a million acres a year' in the 1960s. As Keith Bradby writes, in the 1950s 'survey methods were rough. Often a bulldozer would be set off on a compass bearing, told to maintain it for so many hours, turn onto a different bearing and then again until an area was enclosed'.[27] Such quasi-military imagery of war declared against a recalcitrant natural world could not be any more stark. After chains were pulled through the trees and the shrubs, the land was set on fire. Bradby's 2002 film on the destruction of the Wheatbelt, *A Million Acres A Year*, vividly depicts millions of years of biological evolution going up in enormous clouds of dark smoke into the wide Western Australian sky. As the smoke rose higher, banks, some farmers, machinery manufacturers, fertiliser companies and state exports all enjoyed profits.[28]

In Chapter 4, I mentioned the recent work on recon-structing past rainfall patterns in south-western Australia of Cullen and Grierson. They had read the growth rings of native cypress trees and discovered that, as well as in the 1820s, there was also a wet period in the 1960s to mid-1970s. This is just when agriculture was very rapidly expanding in the transitional zone of rainfall in the Wheatbelt. In the 1960s farmers were still getting tax concessions for clearing the land. With the advent of new agricultural technology, such as the addition of trace elements and fertilisers, land never considered worth farming was all of a sudden being stripped of its delicate life forms. The rains were falling well on a yearly basis. But these farmers and their political backers, did not understand the nature of rainfall in south-western Australia. Just as they did for Stirling, the wet conditions, lasting for around fifteen years, misled the white Australians. As Cullen and Grierson note, dry conditions followed from 1975 to 1985. Again the colonisers had wrongly understood the nature of cyclical rainfall patterns over a span of decades in their home and quite possibly over-estimated the capacities of the land on the eastern edge of the Wheatbelt to grow wheat. Much of the cleared land was later to look like a sandy desert wracked by howling winds.

Into the 1980s the clearing continued. In 1986, farmers were required to notify the Commissioner for Soil and Land Conservation if they wanted to clear their land. If the Commissioner thought it would cause land degradation, he could prevent the clearing taking place. Finally, in the mid-1990s broader environmental assessments including water quality and biodiversity concerns, came into effect. In 1988 to 1989 over 60,000 hectares were legally cleared, but by 1997 to 1998 onwards this had dropped to below 1,500 hectares. From this point onwards, mining and urban expansion in the south-west, particularly as Perth sprawls outwards with new suburban houses, has become the main cause of land clearing.[29] Today the rate

Wheatbelt from above. RICHARD HOBBS PRIVATE COLLECTION

of clearing has slackened, and the twentieth century stands behind us as the true century of chopping trees and killing kwongan in Australia's western third.

Travelling through the rolling Wheatbelt today, one watches dry, weedy road verges giving onto kilometre after kilometre of wheat and sheep fields with the coral-like foliage of york gums stretching up like lone survivors of an earlier Australia here and there. These isolated native tees are sad reminders of what was there before the woodlands were burned and ringbarked, had their seedlings devoured by hungry sheep, or poisoned by rising salt. They appear, as Tim Winton writes, 'like embroidered motifs at the hem of a bleached and threadbare rug'.[30] Sometimes one passes ugly 1960s brick and tile suburban houses with depressing little rose gardens out the front sitting incongruously at the centre of these many-thousand-acre properties. Sometimes lone mesas standing on hills, with laterite capping breaking away into tumbling iron stone down their sides, with delicate grevillea flowers fanning their petals against the lichen-splotched sides of the rocks. Occasionally you may be lucky enough to see a wedge-tailed eagle (*Aquila audax*) spread its vast wing-span and flap up and away from a piece of road-side carrion. Old railway carriages stand useless on the Perth to Albany line at occasional sidings. Large Victorian balconies on the hotels in depopulated towns like Wagin and Katanning. Most of all, hundreds of kilometres of tarmac winding through hundreds of kilometres of fields, denuded of nature.

In contemplating the idea of community, the agrarian essayist Wendell Berry writes:

> we must take care to see how this standard of health enlarges and clarifies the idea of community. If we speak of a *healthy* community, we cannot be speaking of a community that is merely human. We are talking about a neighbourhood of humans in a place, plus the place itself: its soil, its water, its air, and all the families and tribes of the nonhuman creatures that belong to it. If the place is well preserved, if its entire membership, natural and human, is present in it, and if the human economy is in practical harmony with the nature of the place, then the community is healthy.[31]

Using this expanded notion of health, one that includes the surrounding human and nonhuman community of the place, we can say that the Wheatbelt is not a healthy place. With its salt pans in place of gimlet woodlands, its salty rivers and empty high streets, its sometimes lonely farmers, its efficient and expensive machinery, it is the antithesis of the harmonious and healthy communities we might desire to find in rural Australia. Species are locally extinct, and rural counsellers clock up vast distances in their cars talking to deeply unhappy people.[32]

Today around seven per cent of the Wheatbelt is covered in its original vegetation (this is an overall figure;

in the Western Wheatbelt closer to the Darling Ranges it is down to around two to four per cent). But it isn't enough to say that this area has been ninety-three per cent cleared. You need to also add that the approximately seven per cent remaining isn't in a large block of nature sitting comfortably in a well-managed national park, but resides in a scattering of unintentionally conserved remnant patches (like road verges and rocky outcrops), most of which are smaller than twenty hectares and open to invasion by weeds, and most of which are owned by private landholders.[33] If you thought seven per cent was bad, then the broader truth is even worse. The seven per cent that is left is not safe.

According to David Coates and Kingsley Dixon:

> the loss of biodiverse shrub and tree canopies has resulted in estimates that 25 per cent of the landscape and 40 to 50 per cent of valley floors will be salt-affected within the century, and there will be a 4 per cent decrease in rainfall attributable in part to the loss of radiation balance of the native vegetation. Furthermore, 13 per cent of agricultural land is already affected by wind erosion and 11 per cent of soils are degraded.[34]

According to one author, retention of the natural biodiversity, particularly the diverse range of tree species in the Western Australian Wheatbelt, would clearly represent the most cost-effective means for maintaining hydrological processes and sustaining agriculture.[35]

Apart from shareholders in fertiliser companies and some bank balances held by agrarian folk, we can say at least that galahs have enjoyed the changing face of the Wheatbelt. These birds, attracted by all the wheat to eat, have come south from their more arid homelands, but in doing so have taken the tree hollows of other birds. In general, however, the region is haemorrhaging biological diversity. Undoubtedly some species have been lost before scientists even recorded them. Most of the state's many plant extinctions have occurred in the Wheatbelt. Two hundred and fifty square kilometres of this area becomes useless each year for agriculture because of rising salinity. As Bob Beale and Peter Fray remark, in the blink of an eye the region's biodiversity has been, 'replaced by a sea of grain representing just one plant species that is common throughout the world. And within the span of another geological eyeblink, much of this land will be unfit even to provide Australians with their daily bread'.[36]

The South-West Botanical Province accounts for only 0.23 per cent of the earth's land surface. On the other hand it supports 12.6 per cent of the world's rare and threatened flora.[37] According to David Coates:

> Nearly 75 per cent of the 8,000 taxa endemic to this region [Western Australia] are found in the south-west. The majority of these endemic species occur in the kwongan which originally covered around 27 per cent of the south-west. Many of the areas where kwongan predominates occur in the cereal-growing areas where there has been extensive land clearing and habitat degradation.[38]

It is in the kwongan of the sand plains and the Wheatbelt, and not in the high rainfall southern forests, that most of the endangered plant species are found.

Why do we have so many threatened and rare species of plant in a place like the Wheatbelt? To answer this question requires a quick foray into evolutionary biology. Unlike places such as North America and Europe, the south-west flora has existed for hundreds of millions of years without volcanoes, glaciers and mountain-building causing the extinction of many species. The land has been isolated on a little island of high rainfall in the south-west for a long time. After many millions of years of the climate getting wetter and then more arid by turns, moving the edge of the rainfall zone in the south-west sometimes further east, sometimes further west, we've ended up with some plants left over from wetter times in high rainfall refugia, and some more newly evolved species in drier areas. They are all good at living on nutrient-deficient sands and laterites, conditions that, in our Mediterranean climate, have often given rise to a shrubland flora of biodiverse kwongan. But all this evolutionary history has left many species with geographically fragmented distributions. They are here and, many hundreds of kilometres away in some cases, there, often only in small pockets (this pattern is particularly prevalent in the transitional rainfall zone of today's Wheatbelt).

Add massive land clearance in the twentieth century to this story and the result is that today many of the world's threatened, rare and poorly known plant species are living in south-western Australia. As I have discussed in earlier chapters, there isn't a lot of pollen movement or long-distance dispersal of seeds between these often fragmented populations of plants in the south-west. This means that different populations of plants here are often very different on a genetic level. These rare plants often look the same to the ambling naturalist, but they've had a very long time away from the other population a hundred kilometres up the road, so that genetically

Heath plants in the Stirling Ranges. THOMAS M. WILSON

Aerial image: native vegetation versus monoculture. GWEN VELGE

they're actually quite different, and probably better evolved to local conditions than that other population of plants. 'Species' are, we should remember, human-created categories. Sometimes nature is more complex than our retrospectively delineated boundaries and nomenclature. Coates' work suggests that ignoring population-based variation will, 'lead to the loss of evolutionary lineages that may be as unique as many taxonomically recognised entities'.[39] His work shows that we might need to conserve all populations of some plant in one area, as they are genetically quite different, but we should give high priority to conserving only a few populations of the plant in another area, as these populations aren't that different to the norm for that plant species.

Even at the species level, not all threatened plants are safe and sound inside the national park system. According to Coates, '72 per cent of threatened flora populations occur outside the conservation reserve system'.[40] Sadly some of these species of plants are faced with extinction. Some are losing their genetic diversity as fewer and fewer populations are alive. Apart from diminishing the great library of life on the planet we all live on, this is of concern to the timber industry and the cut-flower and horticulture trades and they are losing the genetic diversity with which to work and develop their businesses.[41] Our plants are protected under the *Wildlife Conservation Act* 1950 to 1979. But in order to be protected under this piece of legislation, the plant in question must first be listed under a government notice, and in order for that to happen, knowledge of the conservation status of the plant must be worked out. As Coates makes clear, this, 'excludes the 1708 poorly known taxa until their conservation status is adequately understood'.[42] In other words, if we don't know about it, or know very little about it, then bad luck for that plant species. More surveys need to be done but Coates stresses that 'resources for survey are the critical limiting factor'.[43] Even the plants that are listed and have individual recovery plans in place aren't all safe; many of them are still likely to go extinct without more immediate action. Coates writes that,

> clearly with 350 threatened flora currently listed, and inevitable additions as the list is updated each year as further survey work is undertaken, it is difficult with current resources to prepare and implement individual recovery programs for all taxa.[44]

We might read 'more resources needed' as the state government needing to devote more of its revenue than it usually does to the Department of Environment and Conservation in the yearly budget. But there is little evidence for a priority of this kind. Meanwhile, communities of the few remaining plants of a whole species are growing quietly and unknown at the side of a road under the Western Australian sun.

In 2003 to 2004, fifty-two per cent of Australia's wheat was grown in Western Australia (that was nearly ten per cent of the world's total wheat trade).[45] Eighty per cent of the state's wheat is still not eaten by people in Perth, but rather is sold overseas to make money for Australian farmers. There are very few farmers in this part of the world. In 1951, twenty-seven per cent of the state's workforce worked in agriculture (with around two million hectares under crop). In 2001 only 2.6 per cent of the workforce was working in agriculture (although there was almost eight million hectares under crop).[46] This difference is of course related to the use of huge machines, powered by cheap fossil fuels. So, today, the reality is that only a small percentage of people in Western Australians are involved in agriculture. As Geoffrey Bolton writes, most Australian farming districts are no longer the 'potential home of a bold yeomanry but an increasingly efficient workshop of large-scale rural capitalism'.[47] Towns like Wagin can feel empty, where once their high streets were the scene of gossip, fellowship and community. In some towns it is hard to find anybody under the age of thirty.

As one *State of the Environment: Australia* report put it, 'agriculture is way in front as the continent's worst cause of habitat destruction and species loss'.[48] Our ecosystems have been more damaged by monocultures of wheat and sheep in the twentieth century than by pollution or climate change. After learning about the environmental holocaust that has happened in the Wheatbelt – the largest area of south-west Australia, with seven per cent of native vegetation remaining and the highest proportion of threatened plants and animals in the state – I asked myself a couple of questions: Why does the Western Australian government allow a small number of farmers to make money at the cost of hundreds of threatened, unique and irreplaceable Australian life forms that have taken hundreds of thousands or millions of years to evolve? And secondly: Why don't they buy back at the least fifteen per cent of this area from the farmers and regenerate the vegetation of the area?

Even if it was only in the more marginal and eco-nomically affordable eastern Wheatbelt from Merredin to Ravensthorpe, we would still have a major victory for much-needed rewilding of our homeland. Considering the combination of a biodiversity extinction crisis, a climate change emergency which requires the immediate creation of effective carbon sinks, and the rising scourge of salinisation in the region, which threatens what farming does take place there, such an action appears to be at least worth entertaining. The two major parties in Western Australian politics have never considered such a scheme. Perhaps, one might be led to surmise, these two major parties represent the priorities of an electorate not deeply comprehending of the spiritual or practical value of Australian biological diversity. At the very least one might question why farming and its impact on our country has rarely, if ever, been questioned or challenged by the state's majority of citizens.

In the last three chapters of this book, I offer a list of reasons to be hopeful about the future of this land. But for now the following passage from an English author seems appropriate:

> In numbers they are many – twenty-five millions of sheep in this district, fifty millions in that, a hundred millions in a third – but how few are the species in place of those destroyed? and when the owner of many sheep and much wheat desires variety – for he possesses this instinctive desire, albeit in conflict with and overborne by the perverted instinct of destruction – what is there left to him, beyond his very own, except the weeds that spring up in his fields under all skies, ringing him round with old-world monotonous forms, as tenacious of their undesired union with him as the rats and cockroaches that inhabit his house?[49]

In fact those are the words of W.H. Hudson writing about Argentina – another land vanquished by monoculture. Despite this, such words are fit to purpose. The rural economy as it has developed over the course of the twentieth century in south-western Australia does not represent a healthy and flourishing community, in any broad, ecological or human sense of the term. Unlike city dwellers, the inhabitants of this region are familiar with the world away from the pavement and the electronic screen, but the world that they know lacks ecological conviviality. There is little left of healthy soils, fresh water creeks, familiar animals, and known woodlands. The feast of Creation has few welcome guests at its centre.

CHAPTER 9
DOWN TO THE WOODS TODAY

I see growing over the land and shading it
the great trunks and crowns of the first forest.
– *Wendell Berry, 'The Dream'* [1]

It is a clear and sunny morning in the karri forest near Karridale in 1882. Earlier that year a Mr M.C. Davies had established his first mill in the area.[2] The very biggest karri are being selectively sought for logging. Down in the rich green tangle of karri, sheoak and acacia, sweating men hammer an axe again and again into the cream-coloured base of a 100-metre giant. They have nearly finished their job. And then it happens. The forest elder creaks and tilts from up in its far distant canopy all the way down its long, tapering trunk. Ambient bird song suddenly drops to stillness. Even the sprightly willy-wagtail seems to hold his breath. And now the plunge. Countless tons of wood, accumulated and accreted over centuries in the peace of the forest, slam themselves downwards through tangled space, poleaxing younger karri trees and underlying acacia thickets as they fall. There is a booming crash of flying twigs and branches in the understorey. The forest echoes with the thud of the trunk hitting earth. Then dust in the air, hazing the light. Then stillness. The diminutive primates with their sharp metal tools will soon have ton upon ton of building material to sell on the open market. But there is a hole up above in the forest ceiling on this spring morning in the reign of Queen Victoria. This particular blue rent in the canopy will never be filled by the upper candelabra-like branches of a karri elder of such magnificent proportions again, at least not in my lifetime.

In Western Australia, 25.7 million hectares is classified as forest, representing about ten per cent of the State.[3] Jarrah and marri is the largest forest type. Jarrah originally covered around 3.9 million hectares (today it is down to less than 2 million hectares[4]), running down the back of the Darling Ranges in a rectangular block roughly 400 kilometres north to south and thirty-seven kilometres in width.[5] This forest has around 800 of the plants species in south-west Australia.[6] The forest grows on soils with very low levels of nutrients, and food productivity is low as a consequence, with small fruits, seeds and flowers. Even the animals have low food requirements. Animals are fewer than in other forests, and only the emu and the western grey kangaroo weigh more than ten kilograms.[7] The honey possum lives on nectar and pollen and only weighs twenty grams. A trip to today's jarrah forest in the Perth hills scarcely hints at this once towering and magnificent forest. One hundred and fifty years ago, you would have walked through many groves of straight, grey, forty-metre tall trunks. Today you walk under the canopy of trees that aren't much more than ten metres tall. The difference in walking through the two forests is hard to imagine.

Jarrah is a very useful wood. In her history of forestry in the south-west, Mary Calder wrote:

Newly sawn Jarrah, bright reddish in colour, polishes when dry to a glowing red-brown with handsome grain,

How jarrah forest used to look. POWELL AND EMBERSON

but the major quantity has always been used for practical
outdoor purposes where it weathers under sun and rain to
a gentle grey. Being exceptionally resistant to white ants
(termites) on land and to sea worm under water, it is the
preferred timber for sleepers, dock piles, bridge decking,
telegraph poles, and all uses where there is a direct contact
with water or soil. Great strength and durability combined
with low flammability created a sustained world-demand

for Jarrah, lessening only with the steel-and-concrete age. Even in the late 1970s, Jarrah was used, with Finnish Birch plywood as originally, for re-decking the Hammersmith Bridge over the Thames in London.[8]

White Western Australians soon realised that they had access to one of the finest stands of hardwood in the world.

They also soon discovered the beauties of the karri tree. Karri forest is limited to a smaller area than jarrah. It lives in the very bottom south-western corner of the state. The karri forest is much wetter than the jarrah forest. While the northern jarrah forest might only receive 600 millimetres of rain a year and have an annual drought over summer for four, five, or six months, the towns of Pemberton and Walpole,

Karri from below, with peeling bark strand. THOMAS M. WILSON

deep in karri country, receive 1,400 to 1,450 millimetres of rain and have a nine or ten month rainy season.[9] The karri forest covers around 200,000 hectares.[10] The soils there aren't much richer than in the jarrah forest, but they often retain water better and have a physical structure that enables them to support very large trees.[11] There are more fire scars in karri trunks analysed prior to 1850 than after, suggesting that these forests were burnt more often before than after Europeans arrived on the scene.[12]

Karri trees can shoot up ninety metres before they even start branching, and are one of the tallest flowering plants on earth, following close behind the titanic *Eucalyptus regnans* or mountain ash in the south-east of Australia. The very high, open canopy of the karri forest allows shafts of sunlight to make their long way down to a cool, green understorey. Each year, in late summer and autumn, the karris shed their bark in long strips. Once the bark has peeled back, the silver and pink trunks shine forth again.

Newly sawn karri is bright, pinky-red, and very similar in appearance to jarrah. Unlike jarrah, it is susceptible to termites and dry rot. It is a long-grained timber and hard and tough. It has a greater strength than English oak or Douglas fir (oregon), and a higher breaking strain for structural work than jarrah.[13] A great human structure made from wood could do no better than have karri to provide for its huge supporting beams.

Standing on the forest floor, you see these sturdy trunks shine like the white pillars of a gargantuan temple, and raise your eyes upwards, upwards, upwards, following the line of one tree for a long time until you've reached the tree canopy. It is a humbling experience.

In the later part of the nineteenth century, the Western

Australian government gave large concessions to those with capital to build mills. By the 1870s, logging was under way in earnest, and the export of jarrah and karri was earning substantial amounts of money. The value of exported timber in the last years of the nineteenth century tells an important chapter in the environmental history of the south-west. It went from 88,000 pounds in 1895 to around 500,000 pounds in 1900.[14] The most magnificent old jarrahs of the forest were felled, hewn, and shipped. Often such jarrah made its way to the heart of Empire and became paving blocks under the black tar of London streets. William J. Lines remarks that mostly the 'miller cut the trees to satisfy British imperial ambitions of railway and telegraph line building in India and Africa'.[15] Logging concessions were given away by the government at Canning, Jarrahdale and Lockeville. Logging companies needed to build not only their own mills, but also their own railways and ports in many cases. This ensured that most logging in the early days was close to an already established port, or at least close to the coast. Close to the turn of the century the Perth–Bunbury–Bridgetown railway was constructed, and timber towns like Yarloop and Greenbushes sprang up. By 1909, Nannup was producing wood for the world, and soon afterwards the Manjimup–Pemberton area, deep in the south, started to hear the boom of falling forest elders. In 1913, Western Australian timber production peaked.

But this was uncontrolled chopping down of big trees by enterprising men, rather than sustainable management of natural resources. John Ednie-Brown was appointed Conservator of Forests in 1895, but in all cases his recommendations were rejected. Then the outspoken Charles E. Lane-Poole was appointed Conservator of Forests in 1916, and his approach went against the pro-agriculture mood of the then premier and the unregulated tone of the timber industry.[16] Only in 1918 did the *Forests Act* give forestry officers power to police the over-cutting of timber by private firms.[17] Despairing with the government of the day, Lane-Poole resigned in 1921.

In the 1920s in Western Australia, the British government and the Australian government cooperated to create the Group Settlement Scheme. This scheme saw hundreds of British men and women immigrate to south-west Australia where they were given a bit of land in the tall and wet forests of the south-west. Usually they would start up in a location along with around twenty other families. They were to clear the land, 'improve it', and were given a plot of land to themselves to create a dairy farm. They were paid to clear the land on sixty-four-hectare homestead blocks and the government stocked their farms. When the farm was successful they were to repay the Western Australian government for the assistance they had been given. They would often ringbark the karri and jarrah trees.

Picture the sight of a plot of land, at Northcliffe, say, with a full moon shining down on a field of deathly white trunks and branches. At the end of the square plot of land they had cleared would be the wild, dark forest towering up. It's a ghostly spectacle.

Zamia palms were toxic to cattle. Men would stalk their blocks in narrow strips armed with a small crowbar and an open can of kerosene. When they found a zamia they would drive the bar into the heart of the palm and pour kerosene into the hole to kill the plant.[18] Jarrah trees were dispatched with more fireworks, literally. Men often felled them by boring a hole into the base of the trunk and inserting a stick of dynamite. The men would then light the fuse and retreat for cover nearby to observe the

explosion and the subsequent splintering and fall of the wooden giant.[19]

Of course one should not claim that all clearing of forest is lamentable. In the case of south-west Australia, locals have needed and continue to need European-style agriculture, although they could be using many more native plants as foods than they currently do. However, the group settlement schemes of the 1920s were ultimately a failure. Much of the land was deficient in minerals, waterlogged in winter and sour where heavy timber had been uprooted by explosives[20] Many blocks were eventually deserted.

Sustainable forestry is one of the best uses of the natural world you could imagine: providing valuable building materials to society while at the same time having a lower carbon footprint than concrete. Sustainable use of a forest means adjusting cutting to match forest regrowth so that a smooth flow of wood comes out of the forest, forever. For most of the twentieth century timber was taken out of the jarrah forests of the south-west faster than the rate of regrowth (one must keep in mind that karri takes 100 years to mature, and jarrah 250 years to mature). In other words, for most of the twentieth century, the major forests of Australia's western third have been overcut. This has had impacts on fauna. A third of Australia's terrestrial birds nest in holes, a much higher percentage than anywhere else on earth.[21] After logging, a new forest doesn't have the big, ancient trees here and there with the holes that birds (and also other species) require.

After the Second World War, new technology aided the tree choppers. Diesel trucks replaced the old bullock trains of early decades. Dieback, a soil-born plant pathogen, was spread on the wheels of these trucks far through the jarrah forests. Noisy chainsaws replaced the old axe and saw. Giant karris fell without the human sweat that once poured from the logger's brow. Fossil fuels now provided most of the requisite grunt. In the 1970s Japanese corporations wanted woodchips from Australian forests to feed its expanding pulp, paper and packaging industry. Awe-inspiring karri forests in south-western forests are places that cycle nutrients constantly between the canopy and the forest floor, thus enabling a large biomass to exist on otherwise impoverished soils. The soil here is not deep and fertile, so every fallen twig, leaf, log and animal dropping ultimately gets reprocessed in the forest's economy. But in the 1970s, much of this karri forest was clear-cut, wood-chipped, and headed off for a future as paper and cardboard in Japan. Far fewer nutrients were left to cycle again through the system. Desolation replaced the cathedral of green. One of the sorriest episodes in this history of over-cutting came with woodchipping.

Increasingly, from the 1960s, extensive tree plantations were introduced in the south-west. Blue-gum were grown on a twenty-five-year rotation, which was much shorter than the 100 years or more required to grow jarrah or karri.[22]

By 1990, half all the original forest in the south-west had gone. Only in 1994 did the State Government adopt Ecologically Sustainable Forest Management in native State forests in the south-west as policy.[23] The ALP defeated the Liberal government in February 2001; some consider this win was based largely on their promise to protect old-growth forest.[24] The year 2001 saw an official end to the logging of old growth forest. In 2004 there was another step forward when a new forest management plan formally recognised that logging couldn't take place in conservation reserves, and expanded the amount of forests in conservation reserve with the creation of the Walpole Wilderness Area. Despite all this, logging of the native forests still doesn't leave enough old trees for habitat for wildlife, and it still remains the case that in clear-felling, nutrients are taken out with each cut of the forest and not replaced.

Finally, in the light of the supreme urgency to fix the runaway heating of the earth's atmosphere, in 2009 a new perspective on logging native forests emerged. According to Brendan Mackey:

> the remaining intact natural forests constitute a significant standing stock of carbon that should be protected from carbon emitting land-use activities. There is substantial potential for carbon sequestration in forest areas that have been logged if they are allowed to re-grow undisturbed by further intensive human land-use activities.[25]

Mackey's work encourages us in the south-west to allow logged forests to grow back fully and to realise their sequestration potential to store vast and hitherto misunderstood amounts of carbon. Unfortunately this perspective has not been widely adopted by the Forests Products Commission, the Western Australian government body responsible for logging in the south-west.

In 2013 a Forests Management Plan was released for the years 2014 to 2023 which sets aside sixty-two per cent of forests for conservation while the remaining thirty-eight per cent will be available for timber harvesting. However, as almost half of the forests of the south-west have been cut down to date, the sixty-two per cent of forests put aside for conservation is in actual fact only around thirty per cent of the original forests of the south-west.[26] This management plan signalled an increase in logging in the south-west, while, as the climate of the south-west is drying year by year due to global climate warming, many commentators recommend that Western Australians should be cutting jarrah forest less rather than more.

*

But it hasn't only been government agencies that have had it in for the southern forests. *Phytophthora cinnamomi* was first discovered on cinnamon trees in Sumatra. It has gone on to become one of the worst plant diseases in the world. Phytophthora means 'plant destroyer' in Greek, and it turned out to be the worst plant disease to arrive in south-western Australia. The fungus, known as cinnamon fungus or phytophthora dieback, had started to kill jarrah trees in the south-west by the 1920s. The pale threads of the fungus cling to fine roots and kill them. It attacks the host plant, causing lesions (areas that appear rotten or dead). This weakens or kills the plants by reducing uptake of water and nutrients within the plant. The plant often dies of thirst. Jarrah trees are vulnerable, but it is usually shrubs that suffer most, especially banksias, heaths, peas and grass trees.[27] Orchids, sedges and some other plants survive by replacing their roots. So the colourful understorey of biodiverse shrubs gets replaced by monotonous sedges. The soils of the south-west are so infertile that the native plants have evolved vast rootstocks, and this makes them easy targets for the fungus. After some heavy rains the fungus gives out millions of spores. These spores can then spread out through the soil in flowing water. Or they can hitch a ride on the boots of bushwalkers, or the tyres of logging, road clearing and fire fighting vehicles that criss-cross the south-west jarrah forests and heathlands. If we had much more fertile soils in the south-west the microorganisms in the soil would destroy the fungus. Unfortunately the area contains exactly what the fungus thrives in: sandy, poorly drained soils, low in humus. Up to forty per cent of south-west flora is susceptible to infection by phytophthora dieback. Nowhere else on the earth are so many species of plants vulnerable to exotic disease. Tim Low describes dieback as 'a stealthy underground scourge that advances a metre a year'.[28] As a general rule the disease is only found in areas that receive more than 400 millimetres annual rainfall. In areas that receive between 400 and 600 millimetres annual rainfall, the disease is generally associated with water courses such as swamps, drainage areas and streams. In areas that receive over 600 to 800 millimetres annual rainfall, the disease can cause very high impact.[29] Since the 1970s, the Stirling Range National Park, a storehouse of biodiversity, has been heavily hit by the fungus. Disease-free areas of the park can only be visited in the dry summer months when the spores are inactive, and frequent signs warn the visitor of the dangers of spreading the disease. A quarter of the south-west is infected by the fungus. Forty per cent of the plants here are susceptible to it, including grass trees, zamia palms, hakeas, banksias and dryandras. Animals are affected as a flow-on effect – for example with the loss of banksias, birds and honey possums have less nectar to feed on. The state's Department of Environment and Conservation has been developing methods to fight the fungus, including spraying phosphonate onto plants and creating plastic-lined ditches to stop the underground spread of the disease through the soil, but the battle is largely one of containment and public education.

In 1870, the enthusiastic W.H. Knight wrote of jarrah that 'vast forests [of it] exist on the face and at the foot of the Darling Range sufficient to furnish any quantity that is likely to be required for centuries to come'.[30] Knight was wrong. What is more, such zealously pro-development attitudes were to create great damage over the next 100 years. To use Stephen J. Pyne's description of environmental change in New Zealand, the arrival of Europeans in south-west Australia has caused our biota to be 'smashed in a geological heartbeat'.[31]

Conservation here needs to be understood in its broadest context. When considering conservation, today's politicians might pause and remember that they are only picking up leftover shards of green when they choose to protect natural environments in their homeland. But even this metaphor does not suffice. Even the shards of green are not yet safe. As Jamie Kirkpatrick once wrote of grasslands in Australia, residents of the south-west are currently experiencing 'the steady attrition of the pathetic shards of a once extensive ecosystem'.[32] In some cases this is because the flora will not replace itself when it dies – for example many of those big old trees you see in paddocks as you drive through farming country are the living dead – and in some cases this is because of the invasion of non-native plants into the edges of these areas of natural vegetation. Even the shards that we are looking at on the satellite image are not yet safe. Understood in its historical context, the defence of nature in south-western Australia becomes not the luxury of overly demanding special-interest groups, but a cautious and long-awaited rearguard action to protect and to stabilise what remains of a once-glorious whole.

CHAPTER 10
WHERE HAVE ALL THE ANIMALS GONE?

In 1835, explorer Alfred Hillman walked through what is today the western edge of the Wheatbelt. He looked around himself, and then wrote down what he saw in his journal. The thickly wooded jarrah forest of the Darling Ranges thins out on its eastern edge into wandoo woodland, and some areas of this woodland, nearly all cleared today, would have been open enough to enable a broad view of the country all around. Walking up a hill near the Hotham River through open wandoo woodland and over native grasses, Hillman recorded that:

> as far as the eye could reach we saw the same beautiful country, with fine grass to the tops of the hills & abounding with herds of Kangaroo & an immense quantity of white cockatoo. At 5 o'clock we returned to our Bivouac, highly delighted with the appearance of the country.[1]

Hillman would see a different Australia if he were to rest in the same spot today. Most of the land would be cleared. The biggest and oldest wandoo trees would be gone, having been logged long ago for timber. There would be weeds, many of them of South African origin, such as watsonia and bridal creeper.

Part of what gives this scene from 1835 its attraction is

the presence of innumerable wild animals. In the above extract, the intrepid Hillman was seeing western grey kangaroos and western corellas (*Cacatua pastinator*), birds that move around in flocks of thirty to sixty individuals. The western corella hasn't done so badly, neither has the kangaroo. But their stories are not typical for most animals in this corner of the world.

In this chapter we visit the story of the animals of the south-west, a story little told or understood. A conservation reserve at Dryandra represents the largest fragment of what much of the western side of the Western Australian Wheatbelt used to be like. The wandoo woodland is open and easy to walk through. One walks among white columns under a blue sky, over tiny delicate white flowers that looked like stars in clusters on the ground. One night I camped there and bush stone-curlews sent a haunting and delicate cry out from the sclerophyllous black. This bird was called wilo by the Noongar people. The bush stone-curlew has been driven out of most of the western Wheatbelt through habitat loss and predation by foxes. The sound I was hearing came from an earlier, wilder Australia. Although I've never seen it in the wild (most people have not), I know from visits to wildlife shelters that the bush stone-curlew is a tall, large-eyed, phantom-like bird that feeds at night. Believe me, its call sounds nothing like any other birdcall you've ever heard, and is a signature note of darkness around here that should be widely known as such. In most of this area of Australia you hear no bush stone-curlews after dark. In most of this part of the world the night is quiet. Far too quiet.

Counting bird numbers in an ecosystem can act as an indicator of the health of that ecosystem. More than half of the bird species in the Wheatbelt have declined in range and/or abundance since broad-scale land clearing began.[2] This tells a sad story of habitat destruction. Carnaby's cockatoo (*Calyptorhynchus latirostris*), a big, intelligent, black-feathered bird, has become an endangered species. The first people here called it ngoolyak. Despite their great size and mobility, these birds have been simply unable to cope with the destruction and fragmentation of their home. They have been forced to move on when their home was knocked down, but now there is increasingly no home to move on to. Today there are less than half as many Carnaby's cockatoos as there were in the 1970s.

Most plants in the south-west are protected by thorns, thick and chewy leaf surfaces or aromatic chemicals. Native herbivores have had plenty of time to get accustomed to this, and have evolved in line with the adaptations of the plants. But when they are presented with soft, and lush European crops, they are effectively being presented with marsupial 'fast food'. Many show commensurate enthusiasm.[3] In the past if these animals had the gumption to eat vegetables, grain crops, or even young lambs, then they had to go. And they did, in their thousands. Under the 1896 Extermination of Native Vermin Policy, the Western Australian parliament voted for a small amount of money to be paid for the skin, tail or skull of each dead animal provided.[4] One of the most graphically violent episodes in this history came in 1932 when farmers in the north-eastern Wheatbelt asked the Commonwealth Defence Department for help in killing emus which they claimed were eating their crops. A machine gun unit was sent. The 7th Heavy Battery of the Royal Australian Artillery opened fire on around 1,000 birds at a waterhole. After firing 10,000 rounds at close range they had killed sixty to seventy of the enemy. The rest escaped.[5] This would surely rank as one of the low-points in the history of white Australia's relationship with its native inhabitants.

Of course the European red fox and the cat have also had an inestimable impact on the welfare of our small, furry marsupials. In the 1920s the fox was first seen in the south-west, and by the 1930s it was common.[6] We cannot give such a precise timeline for the introduction of the cat, but it was earlier. Cats are biological bulldozers: they can survive in arid areas simply by drinking the blood of their prey. My own family provides an early example of the introduction of this formidable predator being let loose. In 1858 my great-great-great-grandfather wrote to his daughter:

> I had almost forgot to tell my dear Fanny that the Cat that she used to lug about and call out 'Fats' and then fall down with the weight went into the Bush and was away more than two years he returned the evening your dear Mama was buried he staid about two Months very contented and then left we have seen nothing of him since that time till as I sat down to write this letter he walked in as fat as can be and has continued rubbing himself against my legs and purring the whole time I have been writing.[7]

Sadly behind the affectionate purr of Fats was the fact that he had almost certainly been glutting himself on increasingly rare Australian marsupials.

The cat and the fox are the most serious pest species in this region. However, there is a seemingly endless list of destructive introduced species in Western Australia. One of the more interesting is the rainbow lorikeet (*Trichoglossus haematodus*). At places like Cottesloe beach, vast and raucous hordes roost in the Norfolk pine trees. Like many parrots, these birds are garrulous, intelligent, pugnacious, and sometimes playful group animals. I have seen endless tourists, digital cameras swinging from the wrist, marvel at these 'Australian parrots'. They are Australian, but not Western Australian, and in this part of the world the lorikeets compete with native birds for the few remaining nesting hollows in the area.

In 1950 the government moved in a new direction, introducing the *Wildlife (Fauna) Conservation Act* which was to protect native fauna.[8] This act gave additional protection to rare fauna. Today the Department of Environment and Conservation has an extensive program, known as 'Western Shield', to bait and kill foxes using a poison called '1080' sourced from a local poison pea plant that native animals are not adversely affected by. Western Shield is an extensive and effective program. For example, in just two months in 2005, baiting and shooting of foxes from Geraldton to Albany resulted in 19,000 foxes being killed.[9] This has had some success at bringing native marsupials back from the brink of extinction in the south-west.

If you wanted to quickly and neatly summarise the environmental history of south-western, or even all, Australia, then you could choose to tell the story of the woylie (*Bettongia penicillata*). As Tim Winton says, 'the woylie belongs to the great treasury of marsupials that we revere and know nothing about'.[10] The woylie is a small, grey Australian marsupial about the same size as a rabbit, which hops around in the manner of a kangaroo. It has a curved tail it uses for carrying grass to build its grass nests. Up to the 1800s, woylies could be found over much of central, south-western and south-eastern Australia. Early settlers and explorers referred to them by the unflattering moniker 'kangaroo-rats'. By the 1960s only three remnant populations of woylie remained: in Dryandra, Tutanning and in the Upper Warren. The rest had been killed by feral animal predation and the effects of land clearing.[11] The government's conservation department does have a program to poison foxes in specific areas, which allowed woylies to begin to bounce back in the 1990s, but they have since crashed again to very low numbers (most recently a large fenced sanctuary in Perup, near Manjimup, has had some success at creating some hope for the future of the woylie). Today most Australians would be hard pressed to tell you what the woylie looks like. It has contracted in range from forty per cent of the Australian mainland to less than one per cent.[12] Their story gives you in highly condensed form an ecological history of white Australia: the destruction of functioning ecosystems and the living creatures that were part of them, and the consequent forgetting and loss of the bioregional identity that went with a great southern land. Where woylies have been brought back at a conservation reserve in the Darling Ranges managed by the Australian Wildlife Conservancy, some remarkable changes have taken place. According to scientists who have studied the area:

> The ground litter layer in surrounding long-unburnt areas, such as John Forrest National Park, is often deeper than within Karakamia. Woylies have effectively incorporated much of the leaf litter layer into the soil profile through their daily digging in search of subterranean fungi, which forms a large component of their preferred diet. Their staggering ability to turn over five tons of soil per year per woylie improves water penetration and soil nutrient levels – a vital component in improving the typically

nutrient-poor lateritic soils of the Darling Range. In turn, this results in lower leaf litter accumulation rates offering a lower fuel load, and thereby decreasing the bushfire risk within the sanctuary.[13]

Clearly the woylie is an important part of the ecosystem around here, and it is a cause for lament that it is no longer present in most areas.

Globally, ants often hide seeds underground, which end up growing into plants. One of the things that makes the south-west exceptional is that seed burial by other animals is both evident and accentuated. Both the boodie and the woylie like to dig down to eat underground fungi and soil arthropods, as well as to bury seed. Traditionally these actions would have played an important part in the ecology of the south-west. This ecological process is at great threat because of local extinctions of these animals in many areas.[14]

It turns out that the diligent woylie can even help the economy. In her 2002 Murdoch University thesis, Marie Murphy discussed the manner in which the woylie caches away seeds of the sandalwood tree.[15] This tree, native to south-west Australia, has a beautifully scented heartwood which is used to make sandalwood oil for the perfume market. Western Australia currently provides most of the world's sandalwood market (India and other traditional sources have been declining in their market share due to unsustainable extraction of the wood). The tree has a poor seed dispersal rate, but it is helped by the burrowing woylie. The woylie disperses and hoards sandalwood seeds away from the parent tree, to be used for food later on. The woylie doesn't always remember where it has hoarded all of its seeds, and sometimes the seeds germinate and grow into saplings. In areas where the woylie is present, the sandalwood tree flourishes, in comparison to where the woylie is absent. As this tree is of great monetary value, having the woylie around also is of benefit to the Western Australian economy.[16]

In 2008, Ian Abbott published a paper that presented a picture of the changing times, since white settlement has occurred for some conspicuous vertebrate species in the south-west. Abbott's paper was based on analysis of nearly 1,600 historical documents and, interestingly, interviews with more than 200 elderly Western Australians (over seventy years of age and with reliable long-term memories). As you'd expect from a careful scientific researcher, he found that it is not any one factor that has caused the decline in the distribution and abundance of Western Australia's animal heritage, but rather a synergy of a diversity of short- and long-term, more local and more widespread, influences. From the 1800s to the 1920s, Abbott lists these factors as including: drought; fire frequency; fire intensity and scale; Aboriginal predation, and the demise of tribal Aboriginal life; dingo predation, trapping and poisoning of the dingo; pastoralism; provision of water; vegetation clearing; hunting for food and sport; cat predation; introduced rodents; trapping, shooting and poisoning of native animals eating seed, fruit and crops and stored products; hunting and trapping for pelts and feathers; logging of forest; exotic animal disease; and rabbits.[17] In 2014, an Action Plan for Australian Mammals appeared and stated that, nationwide, the single greatest threat to Australian mammals was feral cats.[18] The report also stated that the next most important threats were coming from inappropriate fire regimes and predation by foxes.

*

The Middle and Upper Swan are the areas of most fertile soil to be found around Perth, and as such would have had relatively high biomass in its pre-European state and have been a productive hunting area for the First Australians. An Agricultural Society was formed in 1831, and paid bounties on hawks and dingos. Despite this, from the notes of John Gilbert who collected animals for science in 1839 to 1840, and 1842 to 1843, as well as the letters and diaries of colonists, there is no record of a sudden decline in the general fauna at this time.[19] In the 1840s the Europeans spread out from Perth, Augusta, Busselton, Albany, Toodyay and York, seeking grassy woodlands where cattle might graze.[20] Apart from in certain areas, such as the Avon valley, grassland was only found in small, isolated patches.

From 1847, attempts were made to stop the Noongar people from practising fire-stick farming. Around this time the effects of European diseases, such as influenza, were starting to show among dying Aboriginal men and women.[21] These diseases continued to cause a decline in the Aboriginal populations in the 1850s and 1860s. (As with semi-nomadic hunter-gatherer populations around the world, these people had little immunity to diseases that had evolved amongst densely settled populations back in Europe.) Aboriginal predation of kangaroo, wallaby and possum was thus reduced, and the abundance of these species increased, resulting in a profitable skin and hide trade in the 1870s.[22] Convict labour, starting in 1850 when convicts were first imported to Western Australia, had an environmental impact, as a new and more extensive network of roads was built. Roads facilitated further settlement away from the original white population centres, and thus aided further habitat clearance.

By the 1880s wire fencing (removing the need for shepherds and making paddocks possible), railways, broadscale land clearing and bird hunting were all having an impact on the landscape. The *Game Act (1874)* provided protection for many birds during their breeding season, and was introduced in response to a decline in bird numbers of species that had proved good for sport or food for the table.[23] A *Prevention of Cruelty to Animals Act* was passed in 1912, however it did not apply to marsupials and dingos and any animal not in a domestic state.[24] Rabbits became widespread in settled parts of the south-west around 1915, and foxes were soon to follow.[25]

Abbott notes that one of the most important events in the history of many animals of the south-west was the widespread establishment of foxes by the late 1920s. Major declines in native bird and mammal species were apparent by the 1930s and 1940s.[26] The destruction of the fox was prodigal. Ray Kitchener, a retired farmer and naturalist, said, 'I know a bloke who cut open the stomach of a fox down at Fitzgerald River National Park and found it full of honey possums. I think there were seven honey possums in this one fox.'[27] A knowledge of how endearing this diminutive nectar-drinking marsupial looks serves to accentuate the graphic nature of such rapacious destruction.

From the 1980s a large number of imminent extinct-ions – ones that had happened a long time before in most other parts of Australia – were averted by the government's management program of using 1080 baits to kill foxes. And yet it should also be noted that due to habitat destruction in the south-west over the course of the twentieth century, the successful reintroduction of many of these animals to large parts of this land area remains impossible.

Earlier I mentioned that Abbott's research was in part based on more than 200 interviews with elderly Western Australians, or what the author affectionately refers to as 'oldtimers'.[28] These people were generally in their seventies and were selected for interview if they had spent time on a farm in the south-west in the early decades of the twentieth century. This vein of information is one of the most interesting aspects of Abbott's study. According to Abbott one man remembered his father feeding the poultry wheat, while gnow (mallee fowl, or *Leipoa ocellata*; what the first white settlers called native pheasant) also pecked at the grains and mixed freely with the chickens.[29] Such a sight is almost unimaginable today. Historical records show that the Noongar men sometimes wore gnow feathers in a band on their arm.[30] Today very few people have seen the fascinating sight of a mallee fowl stalk to the top of his large piece of earth mounded architecture, stop, spread his dappled feathers to shake off the dust, then head down to the centre of the mound to check on the temperature of the sand with his beak.

Abbott notes that his study is of practical use as well as historical interest in that historical levels of distribution and abundance of species give an idea of where species might be reintroduced by conservation biologists, and what kind of numbers of the relevant bird or animal might be sustained in particular bioregions that are proactively managed. That's true, and it is also of interest to those who would like to know the history of their home. The bilby – or to use the original human name for the animal around here, the dalgyte – is a nocturnal, rabbit-sized animal with silky blue-grey fur, long naked ears, a pointed pink snout, and a long tail black near the base, white near the tip. Normally it is only found in the interior of the country, but interestingly enough it used to live in an area quite close to Perth, north-east of today's city.[31] Abbott's reconstruction of the dalgyte's original distribution shows that the little creature used to exist in many places across the south-west, including many parts of the jarrah forests. Burrows were so numerous in some areas that when, for example, cantering a horse through the bush near Moore River, north of Perth, one had to watch out for dalgyte burrows in case your horse stepped into one of the holes and broke its leg.[32]

Clearly gnow used to have a much wider distribution and greater abundance than they currently do. Historical records show that flocks of a dozen or more bustards used to run in their gangly way across the sands of the Swan Coastal Plain.[33] Picture a flock of twenty bustards running where a busy portion of Stirling Highway lies today, their ruffled feathers at the front of their necks all sifting in the oncoming sea breeze. Hungry settlers and foxes mean that such a sight is only a dim historical memory. The same goes for the previous distribution of the quokka on the Swan Coastal Plain. While watching these animals hop through the shadowy undergrowth on Rottnest, we forget that some of their ancestors hopped through the land that makes up our back gardens today.

Chuditch (*Dasyurus geoffroii* and known by early white settlers as the native cat) used to be numerous in the south-west. These beautiful, very agile and sometimes quite vicious carnivores were found in the roofs of suburban homes in Perth into the 1930s, and one was even found in a suburban kitchen in 1952.[34] Again foxes caused a decline in chuditch numbers from the 1930s.

Thankfully in the twenty years up to 2012, chuditch have actually increased in number, making them one of the conservation good news stories in the south-west.[35] I haven't dwelt much on this aspect of historical change here, but there has been some permanent extinction of native marsupials since the whitefellas set up camp. For example the pig-footed bandicoot, a small marsupial that bounded over the ground like a deer, is forever gone. It was last seen in 1898 near Youndegin. Abbott attributes its extinction to an epizootic, a disease prevalent among animals.[36]

The quenda (*Isoodon obesulus* or southern brown bandicoot) has done better than many marsupials, persisting in thickly vegetated regions of the south-west, including some southern suburbs of Perth. Unlike many local marsupials, female quendas can have ten to fifteen young per year (many other species would have only one or two), and this high reproductive rate has helped it to persist. Early white settlers complained of it digging up potato patches. With current fox-baiting programs, hopefully it will back digging in the vegetable patch once again.

The boodie (*Bettongia lesueur* or burrowing bettong) is a small rat-sized marsupial that lives in warrens. It was a significant part of the Noongar diet. In the nineteenth century it was so numerous that it was a significant pest on farm gardens, orchards and small paddocks of wheat. Stake fences were built to keep the boodies out. Farmers shot and poisoned them in their hundreds. In 1942, the last active boodie warren was photographed nearly Pingelly and hence forth they became extinct on mainland Western Australia.[37] I have walked past an old, vacant boodie warren on a hill in the Wheatbelt, far from any towns or human habitations. The warren, dug alongside a great pile of granite boulders, was silent and empty, and weeds covered many of its entrances. It was sad to realise that this was once a busy city, full of lively, gregarious, warm-blooded creatures. I was seeing a remnant of my homeland's former identity. Such warrens were dug under granite lintels, and, where you can find them, they are redolent of an earlier epoch when busy macropods pattered through the twilight. In 2003, twenty-one boodies were taken from Dorre Island in the north-west and put into the wild at Dryandra Woodland. Most have been taken by predators, but there are plans to translocate this species further.[38]

I have mentioned the woylie already. It was once called a kangaroo rat. Many of the old timers Abbott interviewed remembered keeping woylies as pets up until the 1930s.[39] The woylie used to be present in its thousands on the Swan Coastal Plain, and was a prized food item for the Noongar. First, an epidemic (epizootic), then poisoning by farmers around the end of the nineteenth century, and later fox predation caused the steep decline in numbers of woylies on their home range.[40]

The ecologist and writer Tim Flannery neatly sums up the impact of Europeans on the original four-legged Australians:

all of the land south of the tropics was devastated to the point that most Australians my age have never seen a wallaby or a bandicoot outside a zoo. Yet these creatures were once so common that bounties were paid on millions of their scalps, and they gave rise to such distinctively Australian sayings as 'on the wallaby track' and 'lousy as a bandicoot'.[41]

In Australia, 'all of the land south of the tropics' denotes a significant patch of dirt. Many animals that were once part of this land's identity have died and been forgotten. In 2006, Western Australia had 561 plant and animal species listed as threatened. In 2009 the Auditor General found that this number had increased to 601. As of 2015 there are 661 plant and animal species recorded as threatened by the Department of Parks and Wildlife, most of these are in the south-west.[42] In fact so many of our endemic species of plants and animals are rare and endangered that south-west Australia has the dubious distinction of having the highest concentration of rare and endangered species of plant and animal on the Australian continent.[43]

*

A great cause for hope is the concept of rewilding. This term refers to more than simply putting land aside to conserve nature. Proponents of rewilding hold the view that many of the world's natural ecosystems outside of Africa are a shadow of what they were before the first humans spread into them and wiped out key elements of their biodiversity. Such thinkers believe that at this late juncture in history one of our only hopes for restoring their original grandeur is through carefully reintroducing select large animals at or near the top of the food chain. Rewilding Europe currently has ten, 1,000-hectare areas that it plans to rewild by 2020. Ibex and red deer are already galloping through their sites along the border of Portugal and Spain. On Kauai (an island of Hawaii) giant tortoises have been introduced to a reserve where they mimic some of the ecological function of long extinct giant flightless ducks. These tortoises munch on rampant invasive plant species while leaving the beak-resistant native plant species intact.[44] Most famously for the rewilding movement, in 1995 wolves were reintroduced to Yellowstone National Park in the US. They reduced deer and elk populations, which allowed various trees species to return, in turn giving wood back to beavers for their dams and altering the flow of rivers. The flow on effects of reintroducing select species has more recently been demonstrated on Ile aux Aigrettes, a small island off the island nation of Mauritius. Here giant tortoises have been introduced to play the role of extinct native tortoises. Uncontrolled logging stopped on this island in the 1980s, but the trees were still not recovering adequately in 2000. After the tortoises were introduced seedlings proliferated, and the forest is returning.[45]

For much of Australia's history, large reptilian and marsupial carnivores played the role of apex predators. This megafauna became extinct around 50,000 years ago, about the time humans arrived on the continent. Today Australia is riddled with invasive species that have plugged the empty space left in the food web after the loss of the megafauna. This includes camels, goats, pigs, donkeys, horses, and so on. Since 1994, Australian of the Year Tim Flannery has promoted the idea of introducing the Komodo dragon, a large carnivorous reptile from the island of Komodo in Indonesia, to Australia. This animal would occupy the ecological niche that was formerly occupied by *Megalania prisca*, a goanna-like predator that disappeared from Australia around 40,000 years ago. This would be a bold and unambiguous example of rewilding: returning the country to a semblance of its former Pleistocene trophic cascades and consequent ecological balance through the reintroduction of an apex predator.

David Bowman from the University of Tasmania wrote in the journal *Nature* that Australia should stop 'spending millions on piecemeal control programmes that target one problem at a time', and take a more holistic approach to address our problems, an approach that includes rewilding.[46] He thinks that we must restabilise food webs that are currently out of balance because of the Pleistocene extinctions of the country's megafauna, as well as the loss of the Aboriginal traditions of patch burning and hunting, and the spread of invasive species. While he suggests that we introduce and manage predators to control the feral animals, he adds that we need to proceed cautiously with experimental studies that monitor the effects of these introductions. During a radio interview with David Bowman, he also proposed to me the concept of greatly increasing the part played by Aboriginal hunting, in controlling invasive animals in Australia.[47]

Another path to rewilding concerns a slender and intelligent dog. Dingos arrived in Australia 3,500 to 5,000 years ago, brought by human migrants from the north. The Noongar called these companions doot. Their scientific name is *Canis lupus dingo*, and they have been, and continue to be, significant predators in Australian ecosystems (although they rarely attack very large mammals such as horses). Foxes and feral cats are responsible for the extinction for around twenty species of native Australian animals. Dingos are very aggressive towards foxes and cats and will kill them. They will also eat them, but food consumption isn't the only reason for such killings. These species are not friends.

Katherine Moseby and colleagues demonstrated this by taking a thirty-seven-square-kilometre fenced paddock in arid South Australia. Within this area they placed a male and female dingo. Moseby then introduced seven foxes and six feral cats, with GPS collars on them, into the area. The dingos killed all of the foxes within seventeen days and all the feral cats died between twenty and 103 days after release, with the dingos causing the deaths of at least three of them.[48]

Studies to date have shown that their presence on the land has a beneficial effect on small animals of less than 5 kilograms. As they tend to hunt and kill foxes, they reduce the numbers of these 'mesopredators', thus indirectly benefiting the smaller and medium-sized Australian mammals whose tale of woe I have previously recounted.[49] They also reduce the numbers of grazing herbivores such as kangaroos, which reduces the grazing pressure on the native plants. Where dingos are found around Australia there are greater numbers of quolls: as the foxes are fewer in these dingo-rich areas, the quolls have less to fear from death by fox.[50] Elsewhere Mike Letnic and colleagues looked at sixteen sites on each side of the long dingo fence (a fence that traverses three states and extends 10,000 kilometres), and found consistent differences in the abundances of small mammals depending on which side of the fence was sampled.[51] The abundances of native rodents, and marsupials were greater in the presence than in the absence of dingos. Reintroducing the dingo would spell good news for Australia, and its suite of original inhabitants.

Unfortunately, sheep farmers are currently poisoning and trapping dingos to death. Even in national parks close to livestock areas, the government pays for dingos to be killed. And yet if you remove dingos, other dingos or wild dogs will move in, so it becomes a never-ending battle. One solution is guardian animals such as maremma sheep dogs. These are big cream-coloured dogs that have been used in the hills of Italy for hundreds of years to guard sheep from wolves. The Maremma sheepdogs are raised with the flock in a small yard and by the time the dog comes of age it sees its role in life as to live with those animals, whom it now regards as its intimate family, and look after them. The dog then makes its own decisions to look after the flock, decisions which happen to coincide with the interest of the sheep farmer. Guardian animals and dingos would enforce a separation of the sheep flocks, and reconcile the conflict between sheep farming and dingo conservation.

We should note that any free-roaming dogs one might see in the bush, in south-west Australia, will be feral animals, and as such they do not perform the same role as dingos. They have a less organised pack structure and can form large mobs that roam around and cause harm. They are not as smart as dingos or as good at hunting kangaroos. Feral dogs may not be able to exert some of the ecological control that dingos are able to exert on the landscape. These animals are also dangerous.

We should remember that the problem of feral dogs has been over-exaggerated. In over half the continent (mainly the northern half) we still have dingos. One solution for southern Australia that Australia's leading expert on the dingo, Professor of Conservation Biology Chris Johnson, suggested to me, would be to control the feral dogs and reintroduce dingo packs which would suppress the feral dog population and prevent the reestablishment of feral dogs (as it is very hard for them to gain a toehold when dingos are already present). We would have to breed dingos through captive breeding and restocking into the wild, while minimising the effects of being kept in captivity. At the same time we would have to stop implementing 1080 poison baiting in these areas, as such baiting would kill the dingos. This would be cheaper than a baiting program and would also reduce cat numbers, which to date are much harder to eliminate through baiting. We could then get dingo populations back into south-west Australia, preventing feral dog problems, suppressing foxes and cats, and thereby protecting our native animals.

So a key part of rewilding Australia means, if not actively putting dingos back on the land, at least leaving them alone. Johnson has another even more ingenious idea: putting Tasmanian devils (*Sarcophilus harrisii*) back onto the mainland. Within the past few thousand years devils lived throughout Australia. The oldest and most detailed picture of human life in south-western Australia is found in a cave known as Devil's Lair. It is called this because bones of 'Tasmanian' devils are found in some of the strata of the cave floor. Introducing devils to south-western Australia isn't such a crazy idea as it might first sound: it is rather a matter of reassembling an incomplete ecological jigsaw puzzle. In Tasmania, as the abundance of devils has been going down with the recent disease in devil populations, the number of feral cats has been going up. Chris Johnson is involved in ongoing research to find out what is going on with this shift in populations. If we put devils back into south-west Australia, they may exert control over cats and aid the plight of small marsupials. Johnson suggests that we trial the introduction of devils under controlled conditions (for example on a fenced peninsula) to examine the effects. They would probably reduce the abundance of feral cats. Scientifically this sort of thing makes sense, but it may be that many conservationists would baulk at the idea as it does not conform to their strict ideas of what is 'native' (a notion of the country frozen in ecological time, and frozen, unfortunately, at a time of chronic dysfunction).

Farmers object that the reintroduction of dingos to large parts of southern Australia would endanger their sheep. However, through the use of guardian animals such as large dogs reared with the flock, the impact of dingos on sheep can be minimised. What is more, according to Mike Letnic, 'effects that dingos have on populations of kangaroos and feral goats, it is probable that dingos help to relieve total grazing pressure and thus contribute positively to pasture and soil management strategies'.[52] Currently sheep farmers and their representatives spread uninformed scaremongering in the national media whenever the word dingo is mentioned. It is time for governments to stop acting as though sheep farmers are the only voices that matter. Reintroducing the dingo, or at least stopping the persecution of this animal, could be one way to bring this country back to life. On this issue it would seem that current legislation encourages a reckless killing, which is against the national interest.

If you care about returning this country to its former inhabited state, and bringing back the small furred scurrying and pattering things to the plains and forests of south-west Australia, then you would do well to support the cause of the dingo. I am sceptical of agriculturalists not always familiar with this newly emerging field of conservation research, and I long for the day when ten breeding pairs of beautiful dingos will be set free in the larger national parks of the south-west. If encouraged to return to the land and be maintained in healthy populations and packs, these lanky roamers would take on the beneficial role of indirect guardians of our national treasury of unique and threatened animal icons, especially those native species weighing less than a kilogram.

As for fearful campers worrying about dingos, they would have little to worry about a program of rewilding, if one ever was put into motion. We need not fear a vital wilderness. As John Muir wrote of one visit to a wild region of another land:

> When Lewis and Clark made their famous trip across the continent in 1804–05, when all the Rocky Mountain region was wild, as well as the Pacific Slope, they did not lose a single man by wild animals, nor, … were any of them wounded seriously. Captain Clark was bitten on the hand by a wolf as he lay asleep; that was one bite among more than a hundred men while traveling through eight to nine thousand miles of savage wilderness. They could hardly have been so fortunate had they stayed at home.[53]

As well as adding a refreshing tincture to our experience of nature, the ethereal howl of a dingo pack heard while camping at night would signal the return of the orange-furred guardians of an old Australia. It is not something to be feared, but rather something that would help, through trophic cascades, to re-establish an old order and diversity of creatures on the land, and thereby restore a sense of wonder and delight to our human experience of nature. Rewilding would help to heal a broken neighbourhood. Rewilding could make convivial a lonely household.

CHAPTER 11
ARRIVAL HOME

As I went walking I saw a sign there
And on the sign it said 'No Trespassing'.
But on the other side it didn't say nothing,
That side was made for you and me.
– *Woody Guthrie, 'This land is your land'*

It is 6 pm, Sunday evening. I am walking along the sands at the edge of the Swan River, the Derbarl Yerrigan. I walk in Freshwater Bay, below the expensive western suburb of Peppermint Grove. The sun has sunk to the west, below a limestone ridge to my right. Tranquil shade falls over the scene, even while cloudless blue sky may be seen directly overhead. Further up the bank to the right, grows a tangle of native cedars, tea-trees, acacias and tuarts. It is summer, and the water feels warm on my bare feet and ankles, and the shallows are clear over a sandy bottom. A strong wind blows from the ocean to the west, but this part of the river is sheltered from the south-westerly afternoon breeze. I am alone. As I look down at my feet in the clear water, I reflect on what it would be like to stand on this shoreline two hundred years ago. If I looked up at that time I would surely see the same flat water, but it would be empty of boats and moorings. There would be the same weed wrack along the shoreline below me, although rid of the motley sample of plastic human artefacts. Human movement might be spied amongst the trees. A different culture, alien to today's suburbs, would pass as light as a shadow over the land.

I look up anyway, and continue my stroll along the river's shoreline. Soon I come to an old casuarina that leans out over the water to my left. It is thick-trunked and its exposed roots spread out along the shore for a metre or two in matted tendrils of solid wood. They seem to be coiling over and under themselves at tree-pace. The lower roots are quietly lapped by river water, and have a wetter, darker, more polished patina, burrowing down into the sand. I put my hand forward to take hold of the leaning trunk of the casuarina, swinging myself around it without stepping too deep out into the water to the left. Halfway through the swing I arrest my motion.

Hand on trunk, pausing, I look up at the branches and needles of this old river patriarch. Despite the corrosive effects of salt, and the abrasive tides of European colonisation that have washed up the Swan over the years, this tree has endured. Its solid and entwined mass of roots speak of history weathered, of life undaunted. I look down again at the base of a tenaciously victorious casuarina and feel a sense of hope. The water chuckles amongst the roots.

Why lament the loss of Australian biodiversity? Why chart its history? Why write a book such as this one? Many conservationists will give you a perfectly sound list of scientific reasons to care about the natural world, from the provision of 'ecosystem services' such as clean air, water and food substances, to economic benefits to the nation and beyond. These are true and valid aspirations and goals. I share them. However we need to do more than just exist. I believe that having more ecological colour, diversity and mystery in our lives as human beings will make them more worth living for. I want to live in an interesting and exciting corner of the planet. I want to live in a corner of the globe that is unique and unrepeated. As ecologist and rewilding advocate Josh Donlan has said, 'history is the best guide we have for creating a roadmap for biodiversity and conservation in the future'.[1] By looking back we may look forwards. A rewilded south-west Australia will bring more colour, variety, and ecological enchantment to the lives of those of us who live here. I agree with Wendell Berry that 'healing is impossible in loneliness; it is the opposite of loneliness. Conviviality is healing. To be healed we must come with all the other creatures to the feast of Creation'.[2]

I want to see more of the wild in this part of the planet and, I also want to see rewilding progress to encompass our very identities as people.

*

There are moves afoot to reverse monocultures, and to rewild the land, and conservationists and concerned individuals are at the forefront of these. Many see the central Wheatbelt as an insuperably difficult place to rewild, with places such as Tammin being down to around four per cent of its original vegetation. Further south, where larger fragments remain, there is more hope. The Gondwana Link project was launched in 2002. It was a project to revegetate a large swathe of south-west Australia. The 'link' envisaged in the project is the reconnection of a continuous corridor of natural ecosystems, from the wet forests of the far south-west, to the woodland and mallee bordering the Nullarbor Plain far to the east of Western

Australia. Much of this area is still forested in the west, but two areas of surviving heath and woodland, Stirling Ranges National Park and Fitzgerald River National Park, stand out in the east amidst a sea of wheat and sheep.

It should be noted that rewilding the land in south-west Australia isn't quite as easy as in Europe or North America. In younger, more fertile landscapes you could leave the land alone – as happened after the Black Death of the 1300s for example – and nature would return, quickly and surely. These younger, more dynamic landscapes have floras that are weedy and easily dispersed. The fields would fill with a succession of vegetation associations, and the wild would return. In south-west Australia on the other hand, rewilding is harder. Much of the south-west is an old, climatically buffered infertile landscape. The flora's ability to disperse its seed is limited. Here more management is needed.[3] Here we need to get in there and appropriately replant the land to see quick results.

This is what conservationists have been doing. Since Gondwana Link began in 2002, the habitat gap between these two national parks has been reduced by almost forty per cent. Seven farms have been bought by various non-governmental organisations providing funding and several conservation covenants have been placed on private land. This translates into 9,000 hectares of land, of which around 2,500 hectares has been replanted and is now providing food and shelter for local wildlife.[4] In only five years, bare paddocks are now full of flowering and bird-loud shrubs and trees. I have walked through some of these newly rewilded lands. Where before the land was a blank and empty page, today diggings of small animals in the soil amongst the new vegetation are the first writings in a new chapter for our land.

Since 1996, the Western Shield project has seen 3.6 million hectares of conserved land where sausages have been dropped from planes on a quarterly basis. The sausages in question each have a three milligram dose of 1080 in them. The upshot of this is that if you were camped in the south-west in a national park in the 1980s and walked out at the right time of day or night you would not have seen a numbat, chuditch, tammar wallaby, or a bilby. Today if you took a spotlight and went out at night, you might well see some of these animals. Things have changed thanks to baiting programs in conservation areas. This is a real success story of human involvement with the natural world. Although not often commented on by city dwellers, it is indeed a major cause for celebration. Animals like chuditch, quenda and dibblers are all back in our lands, thanks to this Department of Environment and Conservation program. When I interviewed the principal zoologist at DEC in May 2010, Peter Mawson told me of reintroductions of recent tammar wallabies into Kalbarri National Park, and of woylies back into the Margaret River area in recent months.

Over the past few million years in Australia the forests have receded as conditions became more arid. Some of the wallaby groups in the forests took refuge in rocky outcrops. Isolated there, the wallabies evolved into the sixteen species Australia has today. These rock wallabies are beautiful and all are extremely acrobatic, jumping amazing distances and heights around their boulder-strewn homes. Now focus in on the south-west of the country. The black-footed rock-wallaby (*Petrogale lateralis*) is about half a metre tall with a dark coat and a white cheek stripe. Its first name around here was moororong. This old Australian wasn't seen in the Avon Valley (the patch of bush that surrounds the upper Swan as it makes a right turn into the Darling Ranges) after the 1940s. But in 1998, a not-for-profit group called the Australian Wildlife Conservancy bought a property between two national parks on the Avon-Swan River, and established the Paruna Sanctuary. The AWC, founded by English philanthropist Martin Copley, is today arguably the biggest player in the fight to save our native mammals, and should be applauded and thanked for its work across Australia. The AWC has reintroduced black-footed rock-wallabies into the sanctuary and these animals are doing well. In 2009 a new generation of black-footed rock-wallabies were born in the wild where they once lived, and are now hopping around the granite domes of the Avon Valley, where they haven't been for over fifty years. This is a wild ecosystem very close to Perth. Perhaps tonight a young black-footed rock-wallaby will be standing on a granite tor high above Bells Rapids, and looking down on the lights of the city in the distance. Here, very close to my home, nature, in benign collaboration with *sapient Homo*, is staging a comeback.

In a conversation in 2014, Stephen Hopper told me that when he was working in conservation biology in 1977 the south-west had 200 presumed extinct plant species. The good news is that today the south-west has around thirty extinct plant species. How could this happen? In 1977 the scientific knowledge of what was out there on the ground was so limited that many of those 200 plant species were indeed out there but had not been documented. So, around thirty extinct plant species isn't bad considering that the south-west boasts around 8,000 species. Most of the biological library of life is still here, with its genetic books firmly on the shelf. As Stephen Hopper said to me on the phone from Albany, 'Hope only ends when the last plant dies.'

Evolutionary biology has recently given us another reason to feel more hopeful about conservation in the south-west. I have reiterated many times that much of the south-west is an old, climatically buffered, infertile landscape. As the biota exists in small, genetically unique, fragmented populations, we have some reason to believe that it can be resilient to the fragmentation humans have forced upon it over the course of the twentieth century. In looking at a tiny reserve of original vegetation in the Wheatbelt, for example, somebody might say, 'Forget it, that remnant is too small to be viable.' This would be over hasty. Today we understand that if many of the organisms in these ancient, infertile landscapes have had millions of years to become accustomed to persisting in fragmented populations, then they may show unexpected resilience in the face of modern fragmentation caused by a growing Perth and widespread agriculture.[5] Taking this perspective means that every vestige of the original natural world, even if it is as small as a roadside verge, is worth retaining. Clearly larger is better for conservation reserves, as this decreases edge effects from invasive species, the wind-drift of fertilisers and disturbance from human access. And yet, even tiny remnants will contain some plants or animals that have persisted despite loss of the surrounding area. In south-west Australia more than in other younger, more fertile landscapes on earth, the small fragments of vegetation left in places like the Wheatbelt really can be resilient into the future.

About seven per cent of Western Australia's terrestrial area is currently reserved in the formal conservation estate. This is not enough. According to the 2007 State of the Environment Report the reservation target of fifteen per cent of each native vegetation type has only been met in twenty per cent of the terrestrial bioregions. Further, much of it is only reserved because it is in areas that farmers don't want. But it is better than nothing at all. It is wise to remember that we live in a world where some of the natural places we love have legal immunity from being cleared. In fact in 2007 the total area protected in Western Australia's conservation estate was 20.4 million hectares. This is something to give thanks for. Some of this land is the most beautiful land on the western third of the Australian continent, and if you are Western Australian, then it is yours as a citizen and resident. As Woodie Guthrie famously told the world in 1940 as a subversive yet deeply patriotic folk musician: *this land is your land*. It doesn't matter if you are rich or poor, this land is your land to be appreciated and treasured.

Although I won't discuss it in detail here, the Landcare movement is another good news story for the environment. Landcare groups are loose coalitions of farmers and community members around the state and the country who engage in activities that promote the sustainable use of the landscape. Since the 1980s those involved in Landcare have planted millions of trees, and fenced off many rivers and waterways. Around one in three farmers is a member of a Landcare group.

But what of us, the overwhelming majority of Western Australians, who live in the city? What actions can we take that will cause us to feel hope when we contemplate the natural environment that is Western Australia? I have spoken of the project of rewilding the land, now I will turn to the promise of rewilding of personal identity.

*

The domestication of grains in the Middle East around 10,000 years ago, and other parts of the globe with slightly different timing, led to behavioural changes in some human populations that mark some of the most important turning points in world history. Humans there and in other places invented agriculture, accumulated surplus food, developed large, materially complex societies.

Much later, in eighteenth-century Europe, the methods of science pushed back religious dogma and a democratic public sphere began to emerge. People with less melanin in their skin than was the historical norm colonised these northern realms after moving out of east Africa many millennia ago. In Europe they had a rich, fertile and weedy land. Unlike the first Australians they still had their large mammal species and domesticated some of them. Unlike the first Australians, they lived in a predictably seasonal, if severe, climate. Unlike the First Australians (whose range of artefacts were limited by their need for portability), these people differentiated themselves by their ownership of property and were comparatively materialistic. By the eighteenth century these pale-skinned people had began to travel on wooden vessels propelled by ocean winds from the Northern hemisphere to the Southern hemisphere. In 1791 the Englishman George Vancouver demonstrated his culture's emphasis on the importance of private property by naming an area around the present-day town of Albany 'Point Possession'.[6] Australia was the last of the world's continents to come under the influence of white 'civilisation', a comparatively recent elaboration in the behavioural patterns of some members of the primate species *Homo sapiens*. Some of what the newcomers brought to this land was potentially benign, with advancements in medicine, a reduction in the amount of cyclical inter-tribal physical violence, the introduction of a system of fewer than thirty signs known as the Roman alphabet and the written word (which allowed theoretic thought), and a banishment of the 'terrible spirits of the night' before the light of the physical sciences. It was also malevolent. In the 1720s, James Thomson sang of:

> Happy Britannia! where the Queen of Arts,
> Inspiring vigour, Liberty, abroad
> Walks unconfined, even to thy farthest cots,
> And scatters plenty with unsparing hand.[7]

It turns out Britannia did not only scatter plenty. The arrival of European 'civilisation' meant the importation of habits, attitudes, germs, animals and technologies that would massively impoverish the soils, rivers, forests, and airs of Western Australia, and which would almost obliterate many human societies already living there. Much intimacy with land, and ecological literacy, would be lost forever concerning the south-west corner of this country.

Australia has been geographically isolated for the past forty-five million years.[8] It has been geologically comatose during this time, and the soils of this continent have been leached of their nutrients. Most of the continent has low and variable rainfall. This has created a very harsh environment for organisms that demand much energy from the land, such as our own species. Australian plants, animals and indigenous human cultures have adapted to local conditions, and are generally very energy efficient as a result. Australia has a plethora of reptile species, animals that don't need to eat much as they are cold-blooded and have no need to warm their bodies internally. Australia has wallabies that can drink salt water. Australia has Aboriginal cultures that worked out long ago that soaking flowers in water and drinking the sweet liquid could provide a needed source of glucose. But when the British arrived en masse in Port Jackson (Sydney) in 1788 they started a process of colonisation in which foreigners tried to remake Australia in the image of England. They imported foxes, rabbits, sheep and cows. As farmers they replaced water-efficient native perennial plants with water-wasteful annuals. They chopped down vast swathes of trees, allowing groundwater to rise and bring poisonous salt to the surface. They did not understand the unique geological, hydrological and biological nature of the country they were emigrating to, and they did not understand that their land use changes and animal introductions would wreak biological havoc. The soft paws of macropods always trod lightly on the soil. You can see the land eroding under the sharp hooves of foreign organisms in Tom Roberts' 1891 painting *A Break-away!,* an iconic painting of Australian droving history that is held in the South Australian Museum of Art.

In *Preoccupations in Australian Poetry* Judith Wright writes that:

Australia has from the beginning of its short history meant something more to its new inhabitants than mere environment and mere land to be occupied, ploughed

Goanna. THOMAS M. WILSON

and brought into subjection. It has been the outer equivalent of an inner reality; first, and persistently, the reality of exile; second, though perhaps we now tend to forget this, the reality of newness and freedom.[9]

Early British immigrants might have been confronted by 'the reality of newness', but did they properly appreciate this newness?

Since the beginning, the colonists, apart from a few enlightened botanists, have shown a remarkable blindness to the native flora and fauna of this land. Amongst the abundance of bizarre life forms such as quokkas and goannas, the founders of Perth chose the black swan

223

as the city's emblem. While they had the opportunity to celebrate any of the more unique species of life in this place, they preferred to choose a bird that was only different in colour to the swans of the British Isles. In our cultural repertoire of animal symbols, the choosing of, for example, a monitor lizard might have required too great a receptivity to the newness of the environment our ancestors found themselves in.

In the early twentieth century, the New South Wales poet Dorothea Mackellar famously wrote, 'I love a sunburnt country'. As historian Geoffrey Blainey remarks, 'most Australians did not love a sunburnt country. Farmers certainly did not; most city people preferred green lawns to brown'.[10] In 1880s Australian art, the outback was not frequently represented until the advent of the work of Tom Roberts, Arthur Streeton and others. As Blainey notes, 'Who would wish to display on the walls of a dining room or club a parched landscape when more homely or fertile scenes could be framed and hung?'[11] In the first decades of the twentieth century, schools taught the geography of Britain as well as Australia, to the extent that, as Blainey writes, 'clever schoolgirls knew by heart the names of all the rivers and mountains of Britain'.[12]

John Simons writes that today Australia's urban middle classes 'motor around the freeways ... delivering their children to school in mighty Japanese four-wheel drive, off-road vehicles which could cope with the most rugged of bush terrain'. He concludes that Australia has inherited from England an urban 'nostalgia for the greenwood', and that this dream has difficulty being 'transformed into a colonial dream of the parched yellow landscapes of the Heidelberg School of painters and the red outback scenes of Russell Drysdale'.[13] In wishing for us all to truly become

Australians, Gammage laments, in a similar vein, that we are 'still exporting goods and importing people and values'.[14]

Most people still eat polluting beef rather than more environmentally benign kangaroo, which is often available at local supermarkets and butchers. It is also true that most people plant foreign plants in their gardens, and tend a huge mosaic of wildlife-unfriendly green lawns throughout the suburbs. They work hard to pay large mortgages on detached suburban homes, watch American television and Australian sport, shop, garden or go on holidays to New York City or Bali or Thailand in their annual four weeks of holidays. They are busy, urban, and often Eurocentric or culturally centred on some other land from which they or their family have emigrated, such as Britain or Ireland or India or Malaysia. For most people, Perth is a sunny, modern metropolis where they own, or aspire to own, real estate, to work and to raise children. Some of this might be lamentable, but it is all understandable.

In 2014 the Lord Mayor of Perth, Lisa Scaffidi, was reported as saying that:

> A 'Perth brand' is needed to tell the city's story to the rest of the world. Just as some people feel more stylish when they buy a designer item or get a great feeling as they post pictures of themselves in New York or the Amalfi coast, we want to be very focused on creating that feeling about being in or visiting Perth.[15]

Perhaps this is typical of a wider culture that presents the ultimate goal as the display and consumption of material status symbols. In this narrative, Perth takes the form of a 'brand' that is envied by consumers. Let us forget for a moment about how the ideology of conspicuous consumption in a post-industrial economy leads to a generation of worried, anxious and dissatisfied human beings (or 'affluenza', as Clive Hamilton has called it[16]), and let us consider what a typical inhabitant of 'brand Perth' might look like:

> His sense of his whereabouts is abstract: he is in a certain 'line' as signified by his profession, in a certain 'bracket' as signified by his income, and in a certain 'crowd' as signified by his house and amusements. ... Geography is defined for him by his house, his office, his commuting route, and the interiors of shopping centers, restaurants, and places of amusements – which is to say that his geography is artificial; he could be anywhere, and he usually is.[17]

Despite the aspirations of some, the story of Perth can be much more than that of a 'designer item' or an envy-inciting photo posted to a social media site. Thankfully, an increasing number of people are starting to rewild their very personal identities in relationship with this place (and I will speak more of this in the final chapter). Some of this 'personal rewilding' comes from visiting the natural places that are left on the Swan Coastal Plain. Some of it comes from engaging with the history of the place – both recent and ancient. And some of this process of self-rewilding involves harvesting the plants and animals of our home for human uses, much as Noongar families have done for millennia.

When Daisy Bates travelled through Western and South Australia in the early part of the twentieth century, she often came upon areas of the country where none of the original inhabitants remained. Bates reported that such areas were considered by the Aboriginal people to be 'orphaned' lands. How could a wild natural environment in Australia be considered to be without a parent or guardian? Because, simply, the first Australians used the land, and felt that the land was incomplete without their presence on and amongst it. As Adrian Franklin writes, the first Australians had a 'dwelling-doing perspective rather than one based on the visitor-viewer' of today's average National Parks tourist.[18] Franklin writes of how, upon beginning a tour in a National Park led by an Aboriginal Ranger, those in the group suddenly, and with pleasure, saw the land differently: the 'flora changed from a picturesque backcloth to a larder and workshop'.[19] We have much to learn from the first natives of south-west Australia.

Hopefully we all know what the smell of a crushed eucalyptus leaf is like. But today most people in Perth have less knowledge and, in many cases, respect for the natural environment than would have been encouraged and indeed, required, as a matter of survival, in the old Noongar culture that existed around the Swan River. For most modern Western Australians 'nature' is a collection of objects 'out there' beyond the subdivisions, residing in national parks, not a community of ever-present subjects all around us.

While I believe that we have much to learn from the original inhabitants, I am not suggesting that we try to adopt an Aboriginal cosmology. Across the Australian continent, the first inhabitants thought that at the time of the creation of the world unique ancestral spirits shaped the landscape. These ancestral spirits shaped into being plants, rivers, water holes, rock outcrops, and even the people themselves.[20] Such creation myths also provided templates of correct behaviour towards other plant and animal species, as well as other people. Noongar people might be dingo totem people if they were living near York, or fungus totem people if they had a special relationship with edible fungus in the karri forests. If you were a dingo totem man, the dingo would be considered as something like your elder brother. This wouldn't always stop the Noongar as a whole from eating the totem of course, or of eating the even more tender dingo pups, but at least the 'dingo men' had a sacred relationship with the totem as another member of the community of living beings. The white colonisers believed in an entirely different Christian philosophy that placed humans outside the natural world, and gave them rights to use nature as recorded in ancient scripture from the eastern Mediterranean.[21] European settlers liked their dogs, it is clear, but the philosophical framework behind much of their imported worldview meant that their dogs were part of a different order of being. The Noongar people, with creation myths rooted in the phenomenal world around them, did not have the same tradition of seeing themselves as distinctly separate from the natural order, or as being created in the image of a Judeo-Christian monotheistic God figure. The animistic world-view of the first Australians was cyclical and produced song-narratives in which spirits frequently are represented as inhering in the natural world. Most modern Westerners no longer lead lives that understand the physical universe through the lens of mythic beliefs (this is not to say that are lives are now uninfluenced by myths: think, for example of the widespread belief in the myth of economic growth and a fetishisation of the rising dollar).

Even so, it would be inappropriate for modern Australian society to make a wholesale adoption of Aboriginal mythic cosmology.

There are however many lessons that modern inhabitants of south-west Australia *might* learn from the first locals of this place. George Grey writes of the Noongar that they had a custom of never taking plants in seed:

> The natives have ... a law that no plant bearing seeds is to be dug up after it has flowered; they then call them (for example) the mother of *Bohn*, the mother of *Mud-ja*, &c.; and so strict are they in their observance of this rule, that I have never seen a native violate it, unless requested by an European, and even then they betray a great dislike to do so.[22]

This aspect of Noongar culture gives us an early example of a culture of sustainability. Conservation was achieved through a taboo being placed on the use of certain resources that would ensure ongoing productivity of the land. This gives us an example of environmental stewardship as an integrated cultural norm.

One of the key lessons from evolution in old, climatically buffered, infertile landscapes, is that we might encourage humans to live in the newer more fertile parts of the landscape, and leave the old bits alone. The Noongar were ahead of Europeans by thousands of years in that they consistently did just that. Old, climatically buffered, infertile landscapes are easily disturbed. According to Stephen Hopper:

> the top 5 cm of soil in Southwest Australian Floristic Region Banksia woodlands contains 90 per cent of all

seed and micro-organisms that sustain the above ground vascular plant communities. The next 5 cm deeper contains a further 5 per cent. Removal of this thin layer of topsoil compromises the ability of the community to persist and recover from other disturbances for very long periods of time.[23]

In fact, after such disturbances, invasive plants from younger, more changeable landscapes are quick to colonise the empty and depleted soil left on the land This is a lesson from ecology that Western researchers have only recently fully absorbed. For millennia the Noongar clustered around the younger and more fertile parts of the south-west such as estuaries, drainage lines and the Darling Scarp. In doing so they minimised human disturbance of the rich flora found on old, infertile parts of the landscape. In a key conservation strategy the Noongar provide a way of habitation for us to emulate.

Of course the original Australians were not ecological saints. Practices such as casually and regularly kicking over hundred-year old balgas in order to extract and eat the bardi, the small white grubs that lived in the trunk of the balga, are clearly sustainable when the human population on the Swan Coastal Plain was nomadic and numbered in thousands and not hundreds of thousands or millions. Ian Abbott hypothesises that the historically recorded absence of gnow – mallee fowl – from much of the Swan Coastal Plain and along the Avon river – the areas where Noongar populations numbers were historically highest – was due to Aboriginal predation of the fowl eggs and not a naturally low occurrence.[24] Sylvia Hallam points out that successive levels in Orchestra Shell Cave in south-west Australia show fewer and fewer taxa, 'a gradual depletion of mammal species from eleven to six'.[25] These first Australians were fire-stick farmers and kangaroo pastoralists, and had altered the landscape through their firing of the bush to create good pastures for kangaroos (and as an unintended consequence, for the cattle of white colonisers).

And yet these first West Australians were native to this place: culturally as well as physically. Irene Cunningham has written of the Aborigines who lived in an area of land north-east of modern Perth:

> Others living at 'Gnowlialup' where gnows nested, and some whose home was along the fish-filled tree-shaded freshwater river [the Moore river], near the rich soil of the twining warran fields which they cultivated, what happened to them? The respected flower-wearing warriors, owners of balka [grass tree] gum, gnow feathers, emu eggs, buy-yu [zamia palm] fruit and parsnips, turtle frogs and fat tortoises, gnow eggs, karak [red-tailed black cockatoo] feathers, spear and shield wood, dingo pups and wallaby mobs, why did they vanishfrom their seal-rich river mouth and birded watery hinterland?[26]

These people were gone from Cunningham's small area of land in the Midlands north-east of Perth, but their status as intimately acquainted with the natural environment in south-western Australia shines out in her portrait of this area, *The Land of Flowers*.

More than contemporary citizens of this country, the first Australians had kalip of the south-west. Kalip is an old Noongar word meaning 'a knowledge of localities; familiar acquaintance with a range of country... also used to express property in land'.[27] It is an important concept,

and one that we might today express as 'bioregional consciousness'.

So who has kalip?

You could claim that the red-necked stint *(Calidris
ruficollis)* has kalip. Each summer multitudes of these
birds come down from above the Arctic Circle in
northern Russia, crossing thousands of kilometres of
diverse forests, oceans and mountains. They settle along
the tidal flats of the Swan River with their fellow inter-
continental travellers. There they wade, probing the mud
for little worms with their bills.

Even Captain James Stirling had kalip, at least more
than many contemporary citizens of Perth. Stirling drew
a simple map of the Swan River in 1827 that shows key
aspects of the landscape around the river, including
Mount Eliza and the reef that used to block the entrance
until the end of the nineteenth century. Of course, clearly
the sailing captain didn't have as much kalip as the first
Australians with their ecologically attuned awareness of
seasons, animal behaviours and local landforms.

I try to have kalip. Where I live is not just a street name
and number: I live on a sandy, limestone hill close to the
Indian Ocean, near the mouth of the slow-flowing Swan
River, or the Swan estuary as I should call it when I write
this in the middle of a Perth summer. Captain Stirling's
old map is interesting to me as it captures many of the
important aspects of the landscape, such as Mount Eliza,
the prominence where today's Kings Park stands, and
most importantly, the river. Unlike most maps you will
see today, which depict the area on a north-south axis,
this map makes the river a central point and vertical axis
and a part of the landscape that stretches out before you,
the observer. The Swan is the centre – just as it was for

much of the year for the first people here.

Part of kalip may be said to be ecological literacy. The Noongar were ecologically literate. The concept of ecological literacy has been illustrated most poetically by the American eco-philosopher David Abram. In his book *The Spell of the Sensuous* he writes that:

> The human mind is not some otherworldly essence that comes to house itself inside our physiology. Rather it is instilled and provoked by the sensorial field itself, induced by the tensions and participations between the human body and the animate earth. The invisible shapes of smells, rhythms of cricket song, and the movement of shadows all, in a sense, provide the subtle body of our thoughts.
>
> Humans, like other animals, are shaped by the places they inhabit, both individually and collectively. Our bodily rhythms, our moods, cycles of creativity and stillness, even our thoughts are readily engaged and influenced by seasonal patterns in the land. Yet our organic attunement to the local earth is thwarted by our ever-increasing intercourse with our own signs. Transfixed by our technologies, we short-circuit the sensorial reciprocity between our breathing bodies and the bodily terrain. Human awareness folds in upon itself, and the senses – once the crucial site of our engagement with the wild and animate earth – become mere adjuncts of an isolate and abstract mind bent on overcoming an organic reality that now seems disturbingly aloof and arbitrary.[28]

David Abram's analysis of our modern Western loss of ecological literacy and our deafness to the dynamic interactions of the nonhuman, natural world are significant. They suggest that we might learn from cultures like the Noongar culture and become more attentive to the nonhuman lives native to our home ground. We might perceive such lives not as a collection of inanimate, abstract objects, but rather as a dynamic community of subjects. When one stands in front of Robert Dale's vast painting *Panoramic View of King George's Sound and the Princess Royal Harbour, 1834,* one is struck by the participation of the human bodies represented in paint with drama of the animate earth. One character climbs the trunk of a dead tree, another kneels on the brown earth. This vision of human life and landscape is salutary for modern inhabitants of Perth, transfixed by glowing or humming technologies.

Historian and farmer Eric Rolls recounts the story of a man, Bert Ruttley, who accompanied an Aboriginal dingo shooter on hunting trips when he was a boy:

> The dogger took up a post in sight of a waterhole and seemed to go to sleep. When Noisy Miners (Soldier Birds) cried out, young Bert would nudge him. The dogger did not even open his eyes. 'Goanna', he'd say. To other nudges he might utter 'Kangaroo' or 'Eagle'. But when a dingo approached he would have the rifle in his hands. The Noisy Miners had told him what was coming. No one believed such stories until recent scientific work confirmed that these birds give seventeen warnings that are understood by other inhabitants of a woodland.[29]

Here is a clear example of the way in which the first Australians could perceive and understand the nonhuman natural world as a community of dynamic subjects, not as a mere collection of determinate objects. We would only hear birdcalls, not comprehend their meaning.

We modern citizens, with sophisticated technology and rational minds, remain undeveloped and obtuse in significant respects. Understanding our limitations as modern inhabitants of settled Western cities, we might learn from these first Australian habits of thought and perception.

CHAPTER 12
PERSONAL REWILDING

Dreams come true. Without that possibility, nature would
not incite us to have them.
– *John Updike* [1]

We can surmise that the spatial and ecological intelligence
of the first Australians was, through greater and more
frequent use, far more developed than that of the white
colonisers. We are increasingly discovering the ways
in which humans really can be diminished when they
leave behind a hunter-gatherer lifestyle and sink into the
'soft bed of civilisation'. Highly sedentary and urbanised
peoples are more likely to suffer from a deficit of
ecological intelligence. We might consider retraining our
minds to understand the dynamic community of living
beings, birds, animals, trees and snakes, in our peculiar
and unique natural environment. Taking the long view of
history, Gary Snyder writes, 'nature is not a place to visit.
It is home'.[2] We all have the potential to become natural
botanists and zoologists, as the overwhelming majority
of our ancestors have been for the past few million years.
Learning from Noongar culture might mean not only
learning a trick or two about which plants you can eat in
the wild, but actually changing the wiring of your brain's
neural circuitry in significant and long-lasting ways. The

acquisition of local ecological intelligence means that we will be rewilding our very identities.

There are other directions in which you might take a program of personal rewilding, profitably following the lead of the first Australians. The average hunter-gatherer climbs trees, digs tubers, walks and runs around fifteen kilometres a day without shoes, experiences a stable and close bond with a community of other humans, gets plenty of sunshine and dirt and time in wild natural environments. They experience less type 2 diabetes, coronary heart disease, hypertension, osteoporosis, myopia, cavities, hearing loss, collapsed arches, allergies and auto-immune diseases. With civilisation,

> we mature faster, our teeth have gotten smaller, our jaws are shorter, our bones are thinner, our feet are often flatter, and many of us have more cavities … people sleep less, experience higher levels of stress, anxiety and depression, and are more likely to be short-sighted.[3]

Green exercise is defined as exercise in natural environments, and hunter-gatherers certainly do plenty of that. Large amounts of evidence have accumulated over the last few years to demonstrate that green exercise improves mental health and markers of physiological health.[4] In brief, we can say that moving more, outdoors in natural environments, perhaps without shoes and with the sun on our skin, will lead to many improvements in physical and mental wellbeing.

Food resources are an important channel of human interaction with the Australian environment. Chapter fourteen of Grey's fascinating nineteenth century journal is devoted to the food resources and technologies of the first people of the south-west and vividly brings to life scenes that would have been repeated for thousands of years in our home is remarkable. Here is an example where he describes a hunt for birds in a wetland:

A reedy lagoon lies at your feet, almost surrounded by rocky cliffs and dusky woods; there are some small open spaces of water, but generally it is so thickly overgrown with high reeds that it looks rather like a swampy wood than a lake; in the distance you see curling up a thin cloud of blue smoke, which indicates that a native encampment is at hand. The forms of many wild-fowl are seen swimming about among the reeds, for a moment caught sight of, and in the next lost in the dusky green of the vegetation. Every now and then a small party of them rise up, and after winging their way two or three times round the lagoon, at the same time giving a series of their 'quack, quack', which are loudly responded to from the recesses of the reeds, they again settle down in another part of it.

This circumstance, and a few other signs, induce a sportsman to suspect that there is some mischief afloat, and his doubts are soon set at rest: upon some bough of a tree, which stretches far out over the water, and thus affords its occupant a view of all that is passing in the lake below, he sees extended the form of an aged native, his white locks fluttering in the breeze; he is too old to take a part in the sport that is going on, but watches every movement with the most intense interest, and by well-known signs directs the movements of the hunters, who may now be seen creeping noiselessly through the water, and at times they appear so black and still, that even a practiced huntsman doubts for a moment whether it is a man or the stump of a tree which he looks on.[5]

Hunter-gatherers around the world have traditionally used plants and animals in ways most modern, urban citizens have little understanding of. Thousands of generations of Australians developed an intimate and complicated knowledge of the plants and animals upon which they depended. This intimacy only ceased in the last few generations when our recent ancestors fenced off nature and headed for the city. The results of this loss of intimacy with wild plants and animals are manifold. Richard Louv has coined the term 'Nature Deficit Disorder' to describe a rise in mood disorders among children increasingly cut off from wild ecosystems and surrounded by a world of electronic media and manmade artefacts, and much recent research has bolstered the notion that an intimacy with the natural world is beneficial to the mental health of all of us, adults included.[6] Elsewhere the microbiomes of the human gut have been radically altered, with unexpected flow-on effects. Unlike the Noongar of Grey's passage, we mostly do not eat wild foods, and drink spring and pond water. The decreased diversity and mass of the bacteria and other organisms in the human gut that has resulted has caused maladaptive immune system functioning, and consequent altered central nervous system processing, manifested in some cases as increased rates of anxiety and depression.[7] While we can no longer hunt and gather wild foods for our calorific intake, we might grow more of our own fruits and vegetables, and in doing so expose our digestive tracts to more soil microbes than the industrial food chain brings to the table.

Apart from their harvesting the natural world for food and shelter, and their dreamtime cosmology, there were other ways in which the Noongar related to their natural environment. Native animals were often kept as pets, for thousands of years presumably, by these first Australians. The Benedictine missionary Dom Rosendo Salvado learned much about these people during his time north-east of Perth in the 1840s. He had kangaroos and emus as pets, and they would dutifully follow him as he walked around the place. Salvado's relationship with his pet kangaroos and emus was one way in which he developed his intimacy with the place where he lived. Woylies were kept as pets by some European Australians until the 1930s. Many such animals could today be more widely considered as companion animals. The Noongar people kept dingos as pets. Hammond also records them cherishing 'woo' as pets, an animal he describes as a kind of wombat (likely a quenda).[8]

In one survey it was revealed that ninety-four per cent of Perth residents considered animals they kept as members of their family.[9] In today's lonely suburban world, where one's tribe is geographically fragmented, divorce rates are high, and to use the American poet Tony Hoagland's words, people's 'lives intertwine and divide with hysterical finality', companion animals increasingly play a significant role in the home, adding needed warmth and continuity to the emotional lives of many. These animals are part of the 'family' – indeed, a 2011 study in the *Journal of Personality and Social Psychology* found that, 'One's pet was every bit as effective as one's best friend' when it came to providing support and buffering the effects of social rejection.[10] Imagine then that it was a south-west Australian animal that was owned by hundreds of thousands of Perth residents. What would this look like? The evolutionary biologist Michael Archer gives us a classic first-person account of what keeping a chuditch as a pet is indeed like. Archer writes that during the course of writing his PhD in the 1960s:

> a friend offered me the chance to raise at home a laboratory-bred baby Chuditch or Western Quoll (*Dasyurus geoffroii*). The experience quite simply changed my life. At the time I lived in a Perth flat, with two Domestic Cats, the only animals I thought at the time to be suitable as flat pets. … over the next six years the relationships that developed between that Quoll, me and all others who came in contact with him was catalytic. He was obsessively clean, never failing to use a box of kitty litter for all excretions, dog-like in his love of play throughout his life (viz Ogden Nash: 'The trouble with a kitten is that; Eventually it becomes a cat'), bright and quick to learn, far more affectionate and attentive than a Cat, intently curious, happy to play on his own but clearly happier to play with me, active particularly in the late afternoons and evenings and asleep at more or less the same times as me (one early morning activity period overlapped with my sleep but play-tussling with a hand kept him happy), puppy-like when playing even as an adult, careful to mouth without biting, content to fall asleep in my lap, generally very quiet with only 'purring', clicks or 'Nark!' sounds rather than yowls or barks …[11]

There are many reasons to consider keeping native animals as pets. Archer's example might provide a role model for how pet ownership could progress into the future. Most modern Australian children cannot name many Australian mammals, apart from the generic 'kangaroo' (a hold-all term which covers dozens of unique species of animal). If they had the chance to have their lives intertwined with animals such as the woylie or chuditch, then not only would they know of these animals, they would also care about their plight. As Archer and Beale write:

> Bonding through pictures and visits to zoos is a start but it's simply not the same as that powerful emotional buzz that comes from touching, hearing, smelling and feeling the real thing. And because most Australian animals are nocturnal, fleeting glimpses of a streak of fur darting through the bush at a distance are also not likely to engage the average person. Bonding encounters with lasting value need to be up front and full on. And the best way to do this is to intertwine lives.[12]

Archer believes that it is likely that the thylacine would not be extinct today if that animal had been kept as a companion animal, even while it was being persecuted and eradicated in the wild.[13] He proposes that threatened mammals such as the chuditch would greatly benefit from having breeding populations kept going outside of their natural habitat, a habitat that has been almost entirely destroyed or degraded. In America, perhaps embarrassingly for Australia, Australian sugar gliders (*Petaurus breviceps*) have been kept as excellent companions for some time. They are the most popular 'pocket pets' in the United States and have the support of care manuals, experienced vets and breeding facilities.[14]

The alternative to keeping native animals as pets is, of course, generally to have cats and dogs. This is the business as usual option currently taken by the vast majority of pet-owning Australians. A survey found that seventy-five per cent of Perth residents kept animals on their property, and

Man with joey. IAN BERRYMAN COLLECTION

we can presume that most of these were cats and dogs.[15] These are placental mammals, like humans, and have been known to transmit a variety of diseases to humans. Marsupials diverged from our genetic line one hundred million years ago, and as such are far more distantly related to us, and much less likely to transmit diseases to humans. Further, cats cause significant environmental damage. According to The Australian Wildlife Conservancy, there are around fifteen million feral cats in Australia, and they kill an estimated seventy-five million native animals every night across the country.[16] In 2014, the

Action Plan for Australian Mammals found that feral cats were *the* single greatest threat to the country's amazing diversity of mammals. Thirty per cent of all of the world's mammal extinctions since 1600 AD have occurred in Australia, and the majority of mammal species continue to decline, thanks in large part to predation by feral cats. Cats need to be controlled across rural areas – and I've already championed the dingo as one of its enemies – and current government policy governing cat ownership in urban areas also needs to be reshaped, and urgently. In the words of Archer, 'Why is it that we can earn accolades, trophies and money for breeding and selling introduced Cats, but be fined for breeding native animals?'[17] Looked at historically and in the light of 'conservation through sustainable use', we can see that Salvado was in some senses ahead of his time in his choice of kangaroos and emus as favoured companion animals. For modern Australians to inhabit their country with good faith in the twenty-first century, the lessons of conservation through sustainable use of native species will have to be properly absorbed, and in relation to pet choices. Considering that the suburbs are increasingly lonely places for many people, and that companion animals are increasingly important in our lives, why not consider forming a bond with a local?

A boxing kangaroo flag was created for Alan Bond's attempt to win the yachting race the America's Cup, and his subsequent victory in 1983. There are other examples of the kangaroo having a symbolic role for Western Australian and Australian self-identity during the course of the twentieth century. Culture is made up of more than flags and slogans, and the diet of the majority of Australians also has a cultural dimension.

Although Australia is highly multicultural today, in the 2006 census nearly half of the population reported British ancestry. This has been reflected in the national cuisine for many years. In the 1950s *The Argus* proposed a prize for the best recipe for a national dish. The judges of the competition commented that:

> Our quest for Australia's national dish proved overwhelmingly that Australians regard the sheep as our national food as well as our most important source of national wealth! Almost every entry opened mentioned lamb![18]

I have already listed some of the environmental ills caused by sheep farming in this country. What of the virtues of kangaroos? The idea of putting a human food value on native kangaroo as a way of providing an economic incentive to secure more natural bush, and thereby enhance the survival capacity of millions of other native species has been around for some time. Despite this Australians continue to eat more lamb (defined as sheep less than twelve months old) than almost any other nation on earth (more than twice as much as the British).[19] When *The Sydney Morning Herald* surveyed people's thoughts on a national dish in 2010, roast lamb and meat pie, as well 'spag bol' made it onto the list.[20] Australians consume a high amount of meat in general by international standards. It has been calculated that in terms of fat content per 100 grams of raw meat, kangaroo contains only 1.3 per cent while beef has 6.3 per cent; and in terms of methane emissions contributing to global climate warming, cattle contribute 1.67 tonnes per head per year (carbon equivalent), while kangaroos add 0.003.[21]

If Australians are to eat meat (which of course we all need to be eating less of in general), I advocate what John Simons calls 'kangatarianism'.[22] This is a diet that excludes all meat products except kangaroo on the grounds of it being a healthier meat; that it is more humane to kill free range animals than to raise animals for slaughter; for the environmental benefits of the food being local; and from the animals having soft paws (reducing soil erosion) and low-green house gas emissions (negligible methane output compared with cattle and sheep). As I have already mentioned, selling kangaroo meat gives private landholders an incentive to conserve natural bush land, rather than purely focusing on introduced monocultures. Tim Flannery has publicly longed for the day when a multicultural Australia will happily encompass both the meat pie and the souvlaki, as long as both are made with kangaroo meat. And yet one survey revealed that only two per cent of Australians describe themselves as frequent kangaroo-consumers.[23] It is unknown if or when Australia will make this cultural adaptation to a unique continent.

There are many examples of native Australian plants that might also fill an ersatz conservation role, including seeds of various wattles (in fact the first Australians ate around fifty species), bush tomatoes (Solanum centrale), quandongs, and native tubers. Recent research has also shown that native legumes may have an important role in Australian food production. For example many of the nine species of the Kennedia genus that are native to south-west Australia might be grown for their large and highly nutritious seeds.[24] These plants have some tolerance to drought and poor soil fertility, and are better adapted to the local seasons and rainfall than

Quandong fruit. THOMAS M. WILSON

introduced grains. Quandongs have been a major part of Western Australian diets for thousands of years. In 1838 Georgiana Molloy wrote of the local habit of making marmalade out of them.[25]

Sandalwood is also of great value for its oils. In 1870 W.H. Knight wrote in typically imperialistic style that 'sandalwood has a very powerful and pleasant odour, and the chief use to which it is applied in China is for making the incense used in heathen worship'.[26] Today, as previously noted, Western Australian sandalwood is a major supplier of oils for the global perfume industry. Putting a human value on such native species encourages private landholders in rural areas to put some of this land's biodiversity back where it belongs. Australians should be making quandong marmalade again. The nineteenth century rumble of wagons loaded with sandalwood is a sound we might wish to hear again, assuming that this time around the rumble comes from vehicles full of sustainably grown and harvested logs.

In 1830 James Stirling wrote to the Secretary of State for the Colonies about the Noongar that, 'They are a strange unaccountable people, and appear to be as unlike the rest of the world, – as the Country in which they live'.[27] From today's more ecologically informed perspective, in writing these words Stirling was unintentionally praising these original Australians for having adapted to their environment and taking on a new and unique bioregional identity. In his review of human prehistory, Chris Gosden writes that:

> the llama, the sweet potato, and the chilli formed the nutritional basis and the zest for people's lives in South America in a manner analogous to, but nevertheless different from, the cow, millet, and beer in Africa. The continents saw different explorations of human capacities through local involvements with the world.[28]

The Noongar came from a different corner of the planet, one unlike any other, and their identity was deeply interfused in a similar way with the south-west's plants and animals. Their local involvements with the world were also unique. The descendants of Stirling and his kind have mostly failed to make a local diet part of anything like a new, bioregionally grounded sense of identity.

My great-great-great-grandfather Henry Edward Hall arrived on the sands of Western Australia in February 1830. He was granted 126 acres in Fremantle as a base from which to choose a much larger parcel of land. This block of land is today the southern half of South Fremantle, and strangely, South Fremantle is where I grew up. In the words of historian Michael Berson:

The *Protector* had put Hall and his entourage ashore of Catherine Point, surrounded by the clutter of his property. On the beach the 38 year-old Hall presented a striking figure, his short barrel-like frame topped with a tall Robinson Crusoe type hat. His wife, Sarah, 11 years younger, had one child in her arms and five others aged from 4 to 10 years around her. Hall strode among his servants, two men, two women and six apprentice boys sweating and heaving to move his goods across the sand. His blood mare was hitched to the horse drill, cultivator and ploughs as the servants struggled by with saddles, sacks of seed and flour, barrels of salt meat, pieces of furniture and chests of linen, earthenware and plate. Milling around in makeshift pens were Saxon sheep, goats and pigs and racing pell-mell through the sand hills were a dozen dogs. At Catherine Point his sloop swung low at anchor and drawn up to the water's edge was a small jolly-boat.[29]

When I first read this, I was stunned. Catherine Point is at South Beach in South Fremantle. Not only had I grown up in South Fremantle, but I had spent countless summer's afternoons after school making sand castles with my dog and my friends on South Beach as a young boy. It was at this very spot, where I had played, that my great-great-great-grandfather and mother, some of the first settlers to Western Australia, had first stepped ashore, surrounded by noisy hogs and barking hounds. It was off this shore, where I still swim regularly with my friends, that my ancestor's 'sloop swung low at anchor', and where his small jolly-boat was drawn up to the water's edge. Two worlds collided in that long passed moment of arrival on an alien shore. My ancestral past and my living present are, it was revealed as I first read these words, entwined in geographic as well as cultural and genetic ways. The thought still fills me with awe.

The main reason that I share this passage, beyond simple shock at a recognition of change and continuity through the generations, is that Henry's sacks of seeds, his Saxon sheep, his goats and pigs, all graphically speak of British environmental baggage that would become cumbersome over the next two centuries. These animals do not adjust their breeding to cease during a drought, their hard hoofs slice up and compact fragile top soils, they excrete fewer viable native seeds, and they crop grasses lower than native animals.[30] Although he didn't know it, the garrulous cargo my ancestor unloaded onto the beach at Fremantle were agents of imperial power. Henry's plough, his goats, his sheep, his pigs, his sacks of seed would bring economic gain and ecological degradation to much of this southern continent. Earlier, I mentioned how Fats, the family cat, escaped from the Hall farm in the 1850s and went into the bush to fill his stomach. Culturally, these were English men and women, and their suite of livestock, crops and companion animals were in many cases ill-suited to this new world. An acclimatisation society was established in Western Australia in 1895, which explicitly sought to place British animals into the environment, and as Adrian Franklin remarks, 'the Britainisation of nature was seen as having a civilising influence'.[31] Perhaps my ancestors saw these plants and animals in a similar light. Australians have more generally and for a long time, at least up until the 1960s, seen themselves as a people of British descent living on a southern continent.

How much adaptation to the environment has there

been so far? Early on, ironically, white Australia was more bioregionally conscious than it is today. Of course part of this was forced upon the people of the Swan River Settlement. Verandas rather than air conditioning helped to keep residents of houses cool. Without running water from the tap or hose settlers knew that for more than half of each year they were living in an extremely dry corner of the world. Drawing water from a well enforces a sense of the aridity of the local bioregion in a way that is hard to repeat. And occasionally the early whites did learn something from the first Australians. For example, in 1835, Joseph Harris records in his journal from an expedition through the Darling Ranges that 'It was our habit to cut the tops of grass trees, and long grass to rest upon: down beds could not have enabled us to sleep more soundly'.[32] Cutting the leaves from the grass tree to create a mattress was a Noongar habit, and clearly these explorers had picked it up from Aboriginal guides they had known in the past.

As Aldo Leopold wrote, 'we grieve only for what we know. The erasure of Silphium from western Dane County is no cause for grief if one know it only as a name in a botany book'.[33] In the past many early settlers knew the plants and animals of the south-west through their own sorties into the natural world. In 1883, Margaret Walpole went for a short walk near Albany. She wrote:

> It was a lovely walk and I shall never forget it though its beauty did not lie in any far reaching landscape but merely in the beauty of the creepers and blossoms peculiar to the Australian or I might say West Australian bush, for in no other part of Australia are there so many such beautiful flowers and shrubs.[34]

The flowers of south-western Australia are rightly loved. In spring in the early bush huts of the white settlers the women would sometimes tie pink everlasting flowers up in thick bunches and place them in a compact row along the top of the hut wall and the sloping edge of the rafters.[35] This would have brought the colours and scents of the Western Australian land into the domestic sphere of white immigrants.

These early adaptations slipped away over the course over the years. Much of the woodland around Perth has been bulldozed in the last few decades, to be replaced by freeways that take hasty and oblivious commuters to look-alike houses and chainstores gleaming in the sunlight. Figures like the television presenter and landscape gardener Josh Byrne are attempting to move contemporary approaches to building design in the suburbs into more ecologically adapted shapes. He advocates using grey water from showers and sinks to be diverted onto shrubs and fruit trees, diverting rainwater collected in a tank in winter into water for toilet and washing machine use, thereby reducing one's water usage during winter and letting one use adequate water on their vegetable garden in summer. He suggests that homeowners install ponds for native frogs and fish and nesting boxes for native birds. Like other organic urban farmers, Byrne advocates underground drip irrigation, and planting high-yield, fast-growing vegetables in the garden, as well as a compost bin and worm farm. In a series of well-publicised gardens around Fremantle he has championed planting indigenous plants, such as grass trees, on the front verge not only for their low fertiliser and water needs, but also to bolster a Western

Australian 'sense of place'.[36] Grass trees planted on urban front verges have been transplanted from land that was going to be cleared, mostly, for an expansion of low density, environmentally insensitive suburbs. Despite Byrne's inexhaustible, media-friendly enthusiasm, it is easy to view these hundred year old trees on urban verges with a sense of melancholy if you think too deeply about their past and the greater context of current housing development around Perth's fringes.

Byrne and others champion a new kind of housing development, and we may and should join them in doing so. Growing one's own vegetables is part of this environmentally benign vision, and yes, the beans push up out of the dirt in my own garden as I write, snow peas unfurl their leaves, and tomato plants climb bamboo stakes. Such an involvement in backyard agriculture is part of what makes a healthy community. And yet, as I hope is by now clear, more than organic, water-efficient gardening and passive solar designed houses are called for at the present juncture in history. Knowledge of the unique land we walk upon, and its largely forgotten past, is also sorely needed. In the words of Bob Beale and Michael Archer:

> nature has already conducted its own uniquely Australian research and development program over hundreds of millions of years. Through trial and error, virtually all the special traits and characteristics required for sustainable like in Australia have been developed. They are written in fine detail in the genes and life strategies of everything from pygmy possums to red kangaroos, from paper daisies to desert oaks.[37]

At this point in history, modern Australians need to bring some of the vast array of plants and animals native to the country they inhabit into their into their houses and into their culture, even onto their dinner tables, if we are to become better and more connected guardians of the place in which we live.

Our choices of pets and food items can lead to conservation through sustainable use of native plants and animals, and are readily affordable alternatives to the consumer products we already buy. Our choices can also affect our sense of cultural identity. Every few days I eat kangaroo. I use emu oil as a moisturiser. Sandalwood oil from our native sandalwood tree I find to have the most beautiful scent in the world, and I use it in a massage oil. Eucalyptus oil and tea tree oil are found in my cleaning products. My kitchen counter top is made from sustainably harvested jarrah. I have white and red-tipped black cockatoo tail feathers near my writing desk as talismans of the wild in Perth. I use native pepper in my cooking. If I find ochre on the Darling scarp on an afternoon's walk in the middle of summer I might take some home and, for fun, smear bold lines on the face of my friend. I have learned the names of many of the native plants and trees where I live in Fremantle. I grow native plants in my garden, for example kangaroo paws. I know I can eat native pigface, especially the fruits in summer. The paintings of Alan Muller are close to my heart, with their transcendent vision of human accommodation on the earth, centred around the Swan (Muller's series of canvases from 2012 and 2014 call back an ancient but not entirely passed world, and reinsert the viewer into this world as a nourishing home). When it becomes legal to own a chuditch as a pet in this state,

figure + plant 2. *THEO KONING*

I will be the first in line to add one to my family. I know I can pick and grind the seeds of *Acacia cyclops*, and am familiar with the beautiful smell of this seed roasting in my kitchen. When I find them on my ambles around the land, I pick quandongs and eat them off the bush. When I give flowers to someone I care about, I make sure that they are native: in winter it might be a large bunch of glowing red and purple *Banksia menziessi* framed by a spray of dark-green zigzagging leaves.

But most of all, I know the lay of my land. I know what the soils are like under my house. I know the ancient geological and biological history of this place. I know a little of the Noongar history of the terrain where I was born and the places where I tread each day. There are thousands of languages in the world, and each language represents a different way of approaching reality, and grows out of a different combination of the human spirit and unique bioregional ecology. For this reason perhaps we might take the time to read through a Noongar word list. We might experiment with using the names of local plants and birds and place names in lieu of their European ones. Consider towns and suburbs that have Noongar names and learn what these names mean: Mindarie – from 'mindar', the thin leaf of the balga tree; the town of Koorda, from the same word meaning 'friend' or 'mate'; Yongah Hill, the immigration detention centre outside Northam, recalling the yongka, the kangaroo. There are opportunities to take lessons in the local language of the place where you live so that you can learn how to say hello, goodbye and thank you in Noongar. Learn that 'boya' is both the word for 'rock' and 'money' and that there is no word for work, or holiday in Noongar. That the word for 'five', mara, is the same as the word for hand. These small acquisitions of knowledge are nonetheless important. A language is one way in which place speaks through human culture. These simple exercises will awaken you to a culture that is still very visible in our language, if you only take the time to look more closely.

Further, we might take the time to be with the natural world on the Swan Coastal Plain – to sit quietly and listen to the morning song of a tawny-crowned honeyeater (*Phylidonyris melanops*) ... to stand under a wandoo tree in Walyunga National Park and watch the black, tremulous eyes of a western grey yongka looking back ... to see a booldjit or western spinebill (*Acanthorhynchus superciliosus*), the apogee of the honeyeaters, feed as it clings to a giant, orange flower spike from a *Banksia prionotes* tree ... to be confronted by the mottled, bobbing head of a plucky yorndi, an ornate crevice dragon, on a granite monolith in the Wheatbelt ... to feel the padded paper rags of a leaning paperbark trunk underfoot, while balancing above the shadowy and long-necked tortoise-haunted waters of lake or wetland. This is not a land of thundering waterfalls and snow-clad peaks. Many of virtues of this place are sly, commonplace, and low down. Be patient. Perhaps while squatting down and looking around you will find that out of a tangle of navy green the curling and striped mouth of a dancing orchid (*Caladenia discoidea*) resolves into focus. This orchid's ancestors were here long before your ancestors were.

*

For a moment George Fletcher Moore looks up from the lamplight. The prehistoric print of an emu's foot takes shape amongst the cursive writings of a scribbling bachelor. The ecology of a place merges with a cultural heritage that hails from afar. Where we live might influence who we are. Today we may know this land and become a people unlike any other. Modern Australians of European or non-Aboriginal ancestry might aspire to

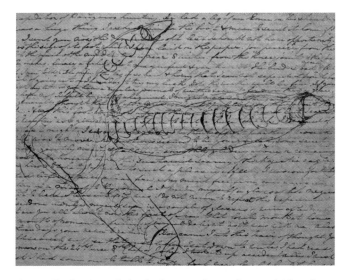

George Fletcher Moore's sketch of an emu foot outline overlaid on the writing in his personal diary. BATTYE LIBRARY

earn the distinction of being, in the long-dead Captain Stirling's words, 'as unlike the rest of the world, – as the Country in which [we] live'. This will happen by looking through the homogenous yet thin surface of concrete and glass, brick and tile, television and advertising, that has been smeared across the landscape of contemporary Perth, to see the durable and ancient realities of south-west Australia that lie underneath. This will happen through our interventions in the world: our choice of foods, garden plants, pets, flowers we give to those we care about. We can become more alert to the cadences and forms of our local, native ecology, be it plant smells or bird calls and, in doing so, change the nature of our consciousness and yes, even blow some fresh air and a new way of relating into our urban minds.

AFTERWORD
THE ULTIMATE GROUND

It has taken me half a lifetime of searching to realize that the likeliest path to the ultimate ground leads through my local ground.[1]

– *Scott Russell Sanders*

Humans drift around the world, on rafts or jumbo jets. We move and migrate, depart and arrive. Although we are a wandering species, we also bond to particular places. Again and again in history humans have developed a spirit of what it is to 'be here', whichever part of the planet 'here' meant. Gary Snyder calls this spirit, 'a direct sense of relation to the "land" – which really means, the totality of the local bioregion system, from cirrus cloud to leaf-mold'.[2] Societies that have developed this sense through centuries of willing and intelligent inhabitation of a savannah grassland, an alpine high country, or a coastal plain, may truly be said to be natives of their place. Natives really know where they are. They know the ways of small animals, which wood is hard enough for making a spear with, or at which time of year to expect the fruiting of a particular plant. The term 'native' is one beset by politics and loaded with controversy. However, I do not refer to being native by birth, by chance or by legality, but rather by knowing the creatures of the place and by being faithful to the beauty and richness of the world beyond the postcode. In this sense it is clear that we are at least a generation away from the time that the majority of locals can really claim to be native to south-west Australia.

The baseline of plants and animals that live here has shifted downwards with the coming of each successive human generation in modern times. Much violence has been done to this earth, and then forgotten about. Despite this, there have been, and continue to be, points of light, moments of accord between humans and the land. By knowing more of the history of our home and the nature of our bioregion, we develop towards becoming the kind of willing natives I have been describing, those who have a sense of belonging to their soils and their swamps in both spirit and in mind. We become one of the points of light in the surrounding darkness. Leaving behind the mind of the migrant and acquiring that of the whole-hearted and knowledgeable inhabitant, things begin to change.

The land undulates gently, and it is soft underfoot. We stop thinking that it would be better to be somewhere else. We realise that we are at the centre, encircled not only by human family but also by sundews and wetlands, by zamias and sou'-westers.

Finally, I return to the quote with which I began this afterword. What is the likeliest path to the ultimate ground?

*

The fresh smells of the eucalyptus forest after a night's rain. Soft coastal sands under bare feet. The promising glow of orange-yellow petals on the moodjar in December. With enough time and attention, such bioregional signatures might become strands in our consciousness, parts of who we are. Instead of sliding around a world made smooth by the effects of corporate homogenisation, transiting from airport terminal to suburban box without a glance en route, we might stop and wander away from the pavement. Over recent years, I have made time to navigate off the paved stones of civilisation and become conscious of the unique shapes of mallee buds and young eucalyptus leaves, the interlocking jigsaw of spider orchids, banksia cones, carpet pythons, dewy-nosed dibblers, and quiet yellow robins that make up the ecology of where I live.

For me this is a process of personal rewilding. Acts of personal rewilding can be both big and small, from climbing a tree to recognising a birdcall. Just as we begin to revegetate the land, and within a few years find fresh animal tracks amongst young trees, so too we can rewild ourselves, and within weeks find a renewed enthusiasm for inhabiting our homes. Personal rewilding is about going barefoot, spending more time in the natural world, and sleeping in the shadow of the earth. It is also about becoming more attentive to one's earthly locale, in a multitude of ways. We need to know the greater story of the clouds and trees and animals and plants of which we are a part in order to live in our place with graciousness and wisdom. Knowledge is power, both in indigenous thinking and Socratic thinking. *Stepping Off* tells this story in the manner of the south-west of Australia.

But rewilding can take place anywhere.

A partly rewilded Australia would stop rampant salinisation and species extinctions. It would bring back life to a sea of gaunt paddocks. Although there are enormous practical benefits to bringing back our unique plants and animals, there are also benefits that are less tangible. In rewilding Australia, we would bring more colour and meaning to our lives as human. In rewilding the country we would be helping to rewild ourselves. Over the past forty million years of natural history, and the past 47,000 years of human history, there has been much exquisite adaptation in the genes of organisms and the cultures of people to the soils, rainfall patterns, winds and temperatures that make up Australia. We can learn to use these adaptations, in our choice of food, pets, gardens, cultural symbols, and even our vocabularies, rather than to continue to remake our home with inappropriate cultural baggage. In our choices of food and shelter, of culture and even of history, we can refashion ourselves in detailed patterns in which our place suggests. From preserving quandongs, to having a quoll as a pet, to giving a friend a bunch of Geraldton wax, we begin to change. We move more through green spaces, suffer less hypertension, less heart disease, less chronic stress. We become happier. We become ecologically alert and literate. We have a clearer and more locally grounded sense of personal identity. We align ourselves with our place, and in so doing, we restore a sense of excitement and pleasure to our inhabitation of home.

*

It is evening. Stepping under the branches of the banksias, we return to the sandy shoreline. A group of humans are sitting by a slow-flowing river, clustered around a campfire. As the darkness advances upon the people, some of them look up. A large flock of black swans can be heard trumpeting overhead, out over mid-river. Some of the people see shapes move across a background of scattered stars. The darkness holds promise. It holds possibilities.

In glimpsing what this land was like before the advent of modernity, we see what parts of it may look like again. In knowing what we have lost, we discover what we may bring back. Once great flocks of black swans flew over the Derbarl Yerrigan, the Swan River. As well as recounting the past, this book calls back the swans. It is a story of loss, but it is also a chronicle of hope.

Much of the box-ironbark forest of south-east Australia is a distant memory. The once vast sub-tropical rainforests of north-east NSW and south-east Queensland are mostly gone, replaced by fields of grazing cattle. Most of the larger islands of the Pacific had their lowland tropical forests shipped off as timber long ago and replaced by sugarcane. Different losses and wounds underlie the histories of different places on the earth. But remember that in knowing the story of a particular place's history, we become able to imagine a rewilded future. In knowing a place's past, we can dream of a different future.

There is a warm, soft breeze passing over the heathland. I've stepped outside of a city of angles. I stand amongst the light navy greens of the plants, studded with the vivid reds and yellows of blooming flowers. My eye takes in the spiky leaf of a hakea, and then moves around to notice kangaroo paws, acacia flowers, macrozamias. I crouch down, taking the time to pause and look. I take a deep breath, and remember where I'm from. I'm from this land, this sandy, spiky, and warm part of the planet. This light navy-green ground, splashed with colour each spring, is my frame. In some ways I'm a colonial, speaking English in the heat of an island in a southern hemisphere. And yet I have a deep interest in understanding and loving the wilds of this 'new' ancient world. My cultural heritage comes from afar, but this land is my home. I crouch down amongst the hakeas and kangaroo paws, knowing and feeling that I am a south-western Australian. I am from emu country, banksia country, sandgroper country, blue-sky country.

Moyran Nungan II (Grandmother Mother); Swan River by night, aerial view with campfire smoke columns reaching up. ALAN MULLER

SUGGESTED FURTHER READING

Bush Tucker Plants of the South-West by Brad Daw, Trevor Walley and Greg Keighery (Department of Environment and Conservation, 2007).

Guide to the Wildlife of the Perth Region by Simon Nevill (Simon Nevill Publications, 2005).

The section on 'bush survival' at the back of W*ild Food Plants of Australia* by Tim Low (Angus & Robertson, 1988).

Chapter 14 of Volume 2 of George Grey's *Journals of Two Expeditions of Discovery in the North-west and Western Australia* (Thomas W. Borges & Co, 1969).

Dom Rosendo Salvado, *Historical Memoirs of Australia and Particularly of the Benedictine Mission of New Norcia and of the Habits and Customs of the Australian Natives* (edited and translated by E. J. Stormon, UWAP, 1978). Of particular interest is the bush-tracking incident recounted on pp. 150–152, which shows just how finely attuned to the natural environment the Noongar people were.

Daisy Bates, *The Passing of the Aborigines: A Lifetime Spent Among the Natives of Australia* (Pocket Books, 1973).

J.E. Hammond, *Winjan's People: The Story of the South-West Australian Aborigines* (reprint of 1933 edition, Hesperian Press, 1980 and 2005). A very short book that packs in a detailed description of much of this place's first human culture and its relations with the natural world.

Reg Morrison, *Australia: The Four Billion Year Journey of a Continent* (Facts on File Publications, 1990).

If you live in Fremantle as I do, then we don't have jarrah or banksia naturally growing here. We have native cypress and *Melaleuca lanceolota* creating stands that you can easily walk beneath. Take a trip to Garden Island to remember what our land used to look like. And of course we have tuart forest here and there behind the first row of hills. To understand tuart forest, the best thing you can do is to sit down and read a children's book. It is called *Tuart Dwellers* by Jan Ramage, illustrated by Ellen Hickman (DEC, Perth, 2007)

If you'd like to know the first human names for birds and animals in this region, including how to pronounce them, then look at the following two articles by Ian Abbott: 'Aboriginal Names of Bird Species in South-West Western Australia, with Suggestions for their Adoption into Common Usage' (*Conservation Science Western Australia* 7, 2009, pp. 213–278), and 'Aboriginal Names of Mammal Species in South-West Western Australia' (*CALMScience* 3, 2001, pp. 433–486).

ILLUSTRATION SOURCES

Illustrations are drawn from the following sources: p. 26: 'Bridal Rainbow': macro photograph of *Drosera macrantha* cating lacewings, Lilly Campe private collection; p. 31: Image of south-west Australia, NASA, <visibleearth. nasa.gov.>; p. 33: Granite boulder, Thomas M. Wilson; p. 56: Map of south-west language groups from Neville Green, *Broken Spears: Aboriginals and Europeans in the Southwest of Australia*, Focus Education Services, 1984; p. 63: Richard Atherton Ffarington, *Not titled [Aboriginal Camp]* c. 1840s, pencil, 22.4×14.6 cm, State Art Collection, Art Gallery of Western Australia, purchased 1984; p. 66: detail from *Panoramic View of King George's Sound, 1834,* by Robert Dale, engraved by Robert Havell, hand-coloured engraving, 19×247 cm, Kerry Stokes Collection, Perth; p. 74: detail of map of Swan River from J.M.R. Cameron, *Ambition's Fire: The Agricultural Colonization of Pre-Convict Western Australia*, UWAP, 1981; p. 80: tea tree grove canopy, Thomas M. Wilson; p. 103: William Shakespeare Hall, Thomas M. Wilson private collection; p. 127: aerial view of Perth prior to colonisation, Andrea Tate; p. 130: *Out of the Mist*, Fred Flood, from C.T. Stannage, *Embellishing the Landscape: The Images of Amy Heap and Fred Flood 1920–1940*, FACP, 1990; p. 137: Perth's geographic extent through time, from R. Weller, *Boomtown 2050: Scenarios for a Rapidly Growing*

City, UWAP, 2009; p. 143: *Djart Whadjuk Nyoongar Boodja*, Alan Muller, 2013–2014, acrylic and varnish on canvas, 20×20cm; p. 143: Mill Point in the 1926 floods, *Western Mail*, from *The West Australian*; p. 148: Real estate billboard, Thomas M. Wilson; p. 149: Vegetation clearing, aerial view, from R. Weller, *Boomtown*; p. 150: 'All you need is right here' from Nandi Chinna, *Swamp: Walking the Wetlands of the Swan Coastal Plain*, Fremantle Press, 2014; p. 162: Dead trees in salt-ridden valley, Thomas M. Wilson; p. 166: Wheatbelt from above, Richard Hobbs private collection, Perth; p. 171: Heath plants in the Stirling Ranges, Thomas M. Wilson; p. 171: Aerial image of native vegetation versus monoculture, Gwen Velge, Perth; p. 179: Jarrah forest from A*n Old Look at Trees: Vegetation of South-western Australia in Old Photographs*, R. Powell and J. Emberson, Campaign to Save Native Forests (WA), Perth, 1978, SLWA 816B/A/4268; p. 180: Karri, Thomas M. Wilson; p. 223: Goanna, Thomas M. Wilson; p. 243: Man with joey, Ian Berryman private collection, Perth; p. 247: Quandong fruit, Thomas M. Wilson; p. 255: *figure + plant 2*, lithograph, Theo Koning, pressed vegetation on paper, 12×30 cm, 2010; p. 257: George Fletcher Moore, Emu foot outline, Battye Library collection; p. 265 *Moyran Nungan II (Grandmother Mother)*, Alan Muller, 25×50 cm, acrylic on canvas.

ENDNOTES

INTRODUCTION – THE BOOK MY PARENTS
DID NOT GIVE ME

[1]   S.R. Sanders, *Writing from the Center*. Bloomington: IUP, 1995.
[2]   C. Hall, 'Red and Green Kangaroo Paw: A Floral Emblem of
Grace and Beauty'. *Western Wildlife*, 2013, 17(2):6.

CHAPTER 1 – GETTING THE LAY OF THE LAND

[1]   S.D. Hopper, J.A. Chappill, M.S. Harvey and A.S. George,
*Gondwanan Heritage: Past, Present and Future of the Western
Australian Biota*. Chipping Norton: Surrey Beatty & Sons, 1996,
p. 5.
[2]   *Historical Encyclopedia of Western Australia* [*HEWA*], J. Gregory
and J. Gothard (eds). Crawley: UWAP, 2009, p. 408
[3]   ibid.
[4]   A. Gaynor, M. Trinca and A. Haebich, *Country: Visions of Land
and People in Western Australia*. Perth: WA Museum, 2002,
p. 153.
[5]   Hopper, op. cit., p. 6.
[6]   P. Christensen and M.R.L. Lewis, *The Karri Forest: Its
Conservation, Significance and Management*. Como: Department
of Conservation and Land Management, 1992, p. 49.
[7]   M. Archer, I. Burnley, J. Dodson, R. Harding, L. Head and
P. Murphy, *From Plesiosaurs to People: 100 Million Years of
Environmental History*. Canberra: Environment Australia,
Department of the Environment, 1998, p. 7.
[8]   J.Beard, 'Evolution of the River Systems of the Southwest
Drainage Divsion, Western Australia', *Journal of the Royal Society
of Western Australia,* 82:147–164.
[9]   E.C. Rolls, *Australia: A Biography, the Beginnings from the Cosmos
to the Genesis of Gondwana, and its Rivers, Forests, Flora, Fauna,
and Fecundity*. St Lucia: UQP, 2000, p. 113.
[10] Hopper, op. cit., p. 17.
[11] Archer, op. cit., p. 17.
[12] W.J. Lines, *Taming the Great South Land: A History of the*

Conquest of Nature in Australia. North Sydney: Allen & Unwin, 1991, p. 7.

[13] Rolls, op. cit., p. 209.

[14] ibid, p. 163.

[15] ibid, pp. 167–168.

[16] S.D. Hopper and P. Gioia, 'The Southwest Australian Floristic Region: Evolution and Conservation of a Global Hot Spot of Biodiversity'. *Annual Review of Ecology, Evolution, and Systematics*, 2004, 35:623–650, p. 628.

[17] S.D. Hopper, 'OCBIL Theory: Towards an Integrated Understanding of the Evolution, Ecology and Conservation of Biodiversity on Old, Climatically Buffered, Infertile Landscapes'. *Plant Soil*, 2009, 322(1):49–86.

[18] ibid, p. 57.

[19] Rolls, op. cit., p. 159.

[20] ibid, p. 198.

[21] G. Seddon, *Sense of Place: A Response to an Environment, the Swan Coastal Plain, Western Australia*. Nedlands: UWAP, 1972, p. 102.

[22] Hopper, 2009, op. cit., p. 65.

[23] J.C. Taylor, *Australia's South-west and our Future*. Kenthurst, NSW: Kangaroo Press, 1990, p. 14.

[24] K. Breeden and S. Breeden, *Wildflower Country: Discovering Biodiversity in Australia's Southwest*. Fremantle: Fremantle Press, 2010, p. 28.

CHAPTER 2 – FORGETTING ABOUT 'WESTERN AUSTRALIA'

[1] W.H. Knight, *Western Australia: Its History, Progress, Condition, and Prospects; and its Advantages as a Field for Emigration*. Perth: 1870, p. 6.

[2] J.S. Beard, *Plant Life of Western Australia*. Kenthurst: Kangaroo Press, 1990, p. 45.

[3] T. Low, *Where Song Began: Australia's Birds and How They Changed the World*. Melbourne: Viking, 2014, p. 7.

[4] ibid, p. 10.

[5] ibid, p. 12.

[6] ibid, p. 64.

[7] ibid, p. 71.

[8] ibid.

[9] J.B. Kirkpatrick, *A Continent Transformed: Human Impact on the Natural Vegetation of Australia*. Melbourne: OUP, 1994, p. 20.

[10] G. Seddon. *Sense of Place: A Response to an Environment, the Swan Coastal Plain, Western Australia*. Nedlands: UWAP, 1972, p. 98.

[11] T.J. Entwisle, *Sprinter and Sprummer: Australia's Changing Seasons*. Collingwood: CSIRO Publishing, 2014, p. viii.

12   ibid, p. 4.

13   ibid, p. 25.

14   *Courier* [of London], 16.2.1831, reprinted in I. Berryman, *Swan River Letters*. Glengarry: Swan River Press, 2002, p. 202.

15   D. Bates, *The Passing of the Aborigines: A Lifetime Spent among the Natives of Australia*. London: Murray, 1938, p. 59.

16   S.D. Hopper, 'OCBIL Theory: Towards an Integrated Understanding of the Evolution, Ecology and Conservation of Biodiversity on Old, Climatically Buffered, Infertile Landscapes'. *Plant Soil,* 2009, 322(1):49–86, p. 62.

17   ibid, p. 60.

18   E.O. Wilson, *Letters to a Young Scientist*. New York: Liveright Publishing Corporation, 2013, p. 15

19   ibid.

20   K. Atkins, 'The South West: A Region for Global Conservation'. *Western Wildlife*, 2013, 17(4).

21   P. Christensen and M.R.L. Lewis, *The Karri Forest: Its Conservation, Significance and Management*. M.R.L. Lewis (ed.). Como: Department of Conservation and Land Management, 1992, p. 50.

22   K. and S. Breeden, *Wildflower Country: Discovering Biodiversity in Australia's Southwest*. Fremantle: Fremantle Press, 2010, p. 36.

23   T.H. Huxley, *On the Educational Value of the Natural History Sciences*. London, UK: J. Van Voorst, 1854, p. 64.

24   C. Drake. *Beyond the Swan: A Journey into South-Western Australia's Bush*. Nedlands: Wildflower Society of WA, 2000, p. 40.

25   Low, op. cit., p. 123.

26   ibid, p. 108.

27   S. Maxwell, A.A. Burbidge, and K.D. Morris, *Action Plan for Australian Marsupials and Monotremes. Recovery Outlines for Vulnerable Taxa*. Canberra: Wildlife Australia, 1996.

28   J. Shoobert, *Western Australian Exploration. Volume 1, December 1826 – December 1835: The Letters, Reports & Journals of Exploration and Discovery in Western Australia*. Victoria Park: Hesperian Press, 2005, p. 425.

29   *HEWA*. Crawley: UWAP, 2009, p. 331.

CHAPTER 3 – THE FIRST LOCALS OF THE SOUTH-WEST

1   E.O. Wilson, *The Social Conquest of Earth*. New York: Liveright Publishing Corporation, 2012, p. 287.

2   R. Dawkins, *The Ancestor's Tale: A Pilgrimage to the Dawn of Life*. London: Weidenfeld & Nicolson, 2004, p. 191.

3   M. Archer, I. Burnley, J. Dodson, R. Harding, L. Head and P. Murphy, *From Plesiosaurs to People: 100 Million Years of Environmental History*. Canberra: Environment Australia,

Department of the Environment, 1998, p. 17.

4 J. Dortch, *Palaeo-Environmental Change and the Persistence of Human Occupation in South-Western Australian Forests.* Oxford: Archaeopress, 2004, p. 42.

5 S.D. Arman and G.J. Prideaux, 'Behaviour of the Pleistocene Marsupial Lion Deduced from Claw Marks in a Southwestern Australian Cave'. *Scientific Reports,* 2016, 6(21):372.

6 D. Clode, *Prehistoric Giants: The Megafauna of Australia.* Carlton: Museum Victoria, 2009.

7 Hallam from *HEWA.* Crawley, WA: UWAP, 2009, p. 4.

8 Dortch, op. cit., p. 26.

9 J. Upton, 'Ancient Sea Rise Tale Told Accurately for 10,000 Years'. *Scientific American,* < http://www.scientificamerican.com/article/ancient-sea-rise-tale-told-accurately-for-10-000-years/>.

10 Dortch, op. cit., p. 32.

11 Archer, op. cit., p. 21.

12 J. Diamond, *Guns, Germs, and Steel: The Fates of Human Societies.* New York: W.W. Norton & Company, 2005, p. 310.

13 J.L. Kohen, *Aboriginal Environmental Impacts.* Sydney, NSW: UNSWP, 1995.

14 I. Keen, *Aboriginal Economy and Society: Australia at the Threshold of Colonisation.* South Melbourne: OUP, 2004, p. 256.

15 R.M. James, *Cottesloe: A Town of Distinction.* Cottesloe: Town of Cottesloe, 2007.

16 A. Tennyson, *Tennyson: Poems and Plays.* London: OUP, 1975.

17 D. Mackenzie and T. Nicol, 'New Conservation Collaboration Formed to Save Our Marine Life'. *Greener Times,* West Perth: Conservation Council, Autumn 2009.

18 S.J. Hallam, 'Peopled Landscapes in Southwestern Australia in the Early 1800s: Aboriginal Burning Off in the Light of Western Australian Historical Documents'. *Early Days,* 2002, 12(2):177–191.

19 J.E. Hammond, *Winjan's People: The Story of the South-West Australian Aborigines.* Victoria Park: Hesperian Press, 2005.

20 Keen, op. cit., p. 286.

21 *The Perth Gazette,* 2.4.1836, from I. Abbott, 'Historical Perspectives of the Ecology of Some Conspicuous Vertebrate Species in South-West Western Australia', *Conservation Science in Western Australia,* 2008, 6(3):1–214.

22 N.D. Burrows, '*Linking Fire Ecology and Fire Management in South-West Australian Forest Landscapes', Forest Ecology and Management* 255(7):2394-2406. Perth: Department of Environment and Conservation, 2008, p. 2396.

23 ibid.

24 ibid.

25 ibid.

26 ibid, p. 2397.
27 ibid, p. 2398.
28 ibid, p. 2399.
29 D.R.G. Sellick, *First Impressions: Albany 1791–1901: Travellers' Tales*. Perth: WA Museum, 1997, p. 45.
30 ibid, p. 93.
31 Dortch. op. cit., p. 11.
32 ibid.
33 J. Shoobert, *Western Australian Exploration. Volume 1, December 1826 – December 1835: The Letters, Reports & Journals of Exploration and Discovery in Western Australia*. Victoria Park: Hesperian Press, 2005, p. 422.
34 E.M. Thomas, *The Old Way: A Story of the First People*. New York: Farrar Straus Giroux, 2006, p. 10.
35 Shoobert, op. cit., p. 329.
36 LeSoeuf, *Portraits of the South West: Aborigines, Women and the Environment*, B.K. De Garis (ed.). Nedlands: UWAP, 1993, p. 9.
37 Hammond, op. cit., p. 45.
38 ibid, p. 26.
39 E.J. Eyre. *Journals of Expeditions of Discovery into Central Australia and Overland from Adelaide to King George's Sound* (Adelaide, 1845) in B. Gammage, *The Biggest Estate on Earth: How Aborigines Made Australia*. Crows Nest: Allen and Unwin, 2011, p. 152.
40 Hammond, op. cit., p. 40.
41 I. Cunningham. *The Trees That Were Nature's Gift*. Maylands: I. Cunningham, 1998, p. 26.
42 T. Low, *Where Song Began: Australia's Birds and How They Changed the World*. Melbourne: Viking, 2014, p. 119.
43 Thomas, op. cit., p. 102.
44 Hammond, op. cit., p. 40.
45 ibid, p. 31.
46 ibid, p. 28.
47 *Sydney Gazette*, 20.5.1830, reprinted in I. Berryman, *Swan River Letters*. Glengarry: Swan River Press, 2002, p. 184.
48 ibid.
49 de Garis, op. cit., p. 187.
50 Hammond, op. cit., p. 41.

CHAPTER 4 – 'OLD WORLD' ENCOUNTERS

1   L. Murray, *New Oxford Book of Australian Verse*. Melbourne: OUP, 1986, pp. 327–328.
2   S.D. Hopper, *South-Western Australia, Cinderella of the World's Temperate Floristic Regions 1*. Kew: *Botanical Magazine*, 2003, 20(2):103.
3   ibid, p. 103.

4   *HEWA.* Crawley: UWAP, 2009, p. 393.
5   J.M.R. Cameron, *Ambition's Fire: The Agricultural Colonization of Pre-Convict Western Australia.* Nedlands: UWAP, 1981, p. 24.
6   ibid.
7   G. Seddon and D. Ravine, *A City and Its Setting: Images of Perth.* Fremantle: Fremantle Arts Centre Press, 1986, p. 64.
8   L. Cullen and P.F. Grierson, 'Multi-decadal Scale Variability in Autumn–Winter Rainfall in South-Western Australia since 1655 BP as Reconstructed from Tree Rings of *Callitris Columellaris'.* *Climate Dynamics,* 2009, 33:433–444, pp. 440–441.
9   Cameron, op. cit., p. 52.
10 *Sydney Monitor,* 13.3.1830, reprinted in I. Berryman, *Swan River Letters.* Glengarry: Swan River Press, 2002, p. 113.
11 P. Statham-Drew, *James Stirling: Admiral and Founding Governor of Western Australia.* Crawley: UWAP, 2003, p. 151.
12 M.J. Bourke, *On the Swan: A History of the Swan District, Western Australia.* Nedlands: UWAP, 1987, p. 47.
13 Etherington from *HEWA.* Crawley: UWAP, 2009, p. 319.
14 *Courier* [London], 23.6.1830, in Berryman, op. cit., p. 139.
15 R. Powell and J. Emberson, *Woodman Point: A Relic of Perth's Coastal Vegetation.* Perth: Artlook, 1981, p. 44.
16 J. Simons, *Kangaroo.* Durrington: Reaktion Books, 2013, p. 74.
17 Cameron, op. cit., p. 60.
18 S. Chodorow, H.W. Gatzke and C. Schirokauer, *A History of the World.* San Diego: Harcourt Brace Jovanovich, 1986, p. 717.
19 M. Berson, *Cockburn: The Making of a Community.* Cockburn: Town of Cockburn, 1978, p. 8.
20 *Morning Herald,* 3.7.1830, in Berryman, op. cit., p. 21.
21 Cameron, op. cit., p. v.
22 ibid, p. 97.
23 G. Crabbe, 'The Village', *Selected Poems,* London: Lawson and Dunn, 1946, p. 3.
24 Hopper, op. cit., p. 11.
25 A. Marvell from R.J Demaria, *British Literature 1640–1789: An Anthology.* Oxford: Blackwell, 1998, p. 344
26 G.F. Moore, *Diary of Ten Years Eventful Life of an Early Settler in Western Australia, and Also a Descriptive Vocabulary of the Language of the Aborigines.* Nedlands: UWAP, 1978, p. 29.
27 ibid, p. 31.
28 P. Cowan (ed.), *A Faithful Picture: The Letters of Eliza and Thomas Brown at York in the Swan River Colony 1841–1852.* Fremantle: FACP, 1977, p. 38.
29 A. Burton (ed.), *Wollaston's Picton Journal (1841–1856).* Perth: Paterson Brokensha, 1975, p. 4.
30 ibid.
31 ibid, p. 5.

32 J. Davis, *Longing or Belonging? Responses to a 'New' Land in Southern Western Australia 1829–1907*. PhD thesis, School of Humanities, Department of History, UWA, 2008, p. 22. <research-repository.uwa.edu.au/files/3226789/Davis_Jane_2008.pdf>.

33 ibid, p, 38.

34 G. Grey, *Journals of Two Expeditions of Discovery in the North-west and Western Australia*. London, UK: Thomas W. Borges & Co., 1969, 1:298.

35 R. Giblett, *Forrestdale: People and Place*. Forrestdale: Access Press, 2006, p. 52.

36 J. Cross, *Journals of Several Expeditions Made in Western Australia During the Years 1829, 1830, 1831, and 1832*. Nedlands: UWAP, 1980, pp. 16–17.

37 J. Shoobert, *Western Australian Exploration. Volume 1, December 1826 – December 1835: The Letters, Reports & Journals of Exploration and Discovery in Western Australia*. Victoria Park: Hesperian Press, 2005, p. 209.

38 E.C. Rolls, *Australia: A Biography, the Beginnings from the Cosmos to the Genesis of Gondwana, and its Rivers, Forests, Flora, Fauna, and Fecundity*. St Lucia: UQP, 2000, p. 219.

39 Shoobert, op. cit., p. 376.

40 G. McLaren, *Beyond Leichhardt: Bushcraft and the Exploration of Australia*. Fremantle: FACP, 1996, p. 86.

41 Hopper, op. cit., p. 117.

42 ibid.

43 ibid, p. 119.

44 S.D. Hopper and P. Gioia, 'The Southwest Australian Floristic Region: Evolution and Conservation of a Global Hot Spot of Biodiversity'. *Annual Review of Ecology, Evolution, and Systematics*, 2004, 35:146.

45 ibid, p. 165.

46 ibid.

47 ibid, p. 167.

CHAPTER 5 – FAMILY

1 R. Richards, *The Murray District of Western Australia*. Perth: Shire of Murray, 1978, p. 60.

2 H.M. Wilson, *Sarah Theodosia and the Hall Family*. Perth: Helen Margaret Wilson, 1994, p. 11.

3 ibid, p. 12.

4 L. Talbot, 'Frank Hall: Wild Colonial Boy'. *Landscope: WA's Conservation Forests and Wildlife Magazine* 1994, 9(4):37–41, p. 38.

5 ibid, p. 41.

6 *Northern Times*, 9.12.1971.

7 D.R. Salvado, *Historical Memoirs of Australia and Particularly of the Benedictine Mission of New Norcia and the Habits and*

Customs of the Australian Natives, E.J. Stormon (ed.). Nedlands: UWAP, 1978, p. 150.

8   J.E. Hammond, *Winjan's People: The Story of the South-West Australian Aborigines*. Victoria Park: Hesperian Press, 2005, p. 39.

9   F.K. Crowley, *Australia's Western Third: A History of Western Australia from the First Settlements to Modern Times*. London: Macmillan & Co., 1960, p. 45.

10 *South African Commercial Advertiser* 17 & 21.4.1830, reprinted in I. Berryman, *Swan River Letters*. Glengarry: Swan River Press, 2002, p. 113, pp. 150–153.

11 N.J. Snell, *Landscapes and Land Uses: A Geography of Australia*. Sydney: McGraw Hill, 2003, p. 32.

12 K. Bradby, *A Park in Perspective: A Report on the Past, Present and Future of Fitzgerald River National Park*. Ravensthorpe: Fitzgerald River National Park Association, 1989, p. 30.

13 J.M.R. Cameron (ed.), *The Millendon Memoirs: George Fletcher Moore's Western Australian Diaries and Letters 1830–1841*. Victoria Park: Hesperian Press, 2006, p. 313.

14 Hall Family Letters, Thomas M. Wilson private collection, Wungong, WA.

15 J. Carter and B. Carter, *Settlement to City: A History of the Armadale District and its People*. Armadale: City of Armadale, 2011, p. 39.

16 B. de Garis, *European Impact on the West Australian Environment 1829–1979*. Nedlands: UWAP, 1979, p. 81.

CHAPTER 6 – SETTLING IN

1   J. Kaplan, K. Krumhardt and K. Zimmerman, 'The Prehistoric and Preindustrial Deforestation of Europe'. *Quarternary Science Reviews*, 2009, 28:82.

2   ibid, pp. 27–28.

3   ibid.

4   *Morning Herald* [London], 3.7.1830, reprinted in I. Berryman, *Swan River Letters*. Glengarry: Swan River Press, 2002, p. 104.

5   *Dublin Evening Post* 18.9.1832, ibid.

6   J.M.R. Cameron (ed.), *The Millendon Memoirs: George Fletcher Moore's Western Australian Diaries and Letters 1830–1841*. Victoria Park: Hesperian Press, 2006, pp. 235–236.

7   M.J. Bourke, *On the Swan: A History of the Swan District, Western Australia*. Nedlands: UWAP, 1987, p. 86.

8   Cameron, 2006, op. cit., p. 274.

9   ibid.

10 J. Host and C. Owen, *'It's still in my heart, this is my country': The Single Noongar Claim History*. Crawley: UWAP, 2009, p. 74.

11 J.M.R. Cameron. *Ambition's Fire: The Agricultural Colonization of Pre-Convict Western Australia*. Nedlands: UWAP, 1981, p. 199.

12 W.E.H. Stanner, *After the Dreaming*. Sydney: ABC, 1969,
    pp. 44–45, in B. Gammage, *The Biggest Estate on Earth: How
    Aborigines Made Australia*. Crows Nest: Allen and Unwin, 2011,
    p. 143.
13 S. Jones, *Almost Like a Whale: The Origin of Species Updated*.
    London: Anchor, 2000, p. 39.
14 G. Grey, *Journals of Two Expeditions of Discovery in the North-
    west and Western Australia*. London: Thomas W. Borges & Co.,
    1969, 2:263.
15 J. Sargeaunt, *Georgics, Book 1*. Edinburgh: William Blackwood
    and Sons, 1901, ll. 145–146.
16 J.E. Hammond, *Winjan's People: The Story of the South-West
    Australian Aborigines*. Victoria Park: Hesperian Press, 2005, p. 39.
17 H. Melville, *Omoo*. New York: Heritage Press, 1967, p. 165.
18 Marshall Sahlins, *Stone Age Economics*. Chicago: Aldine
    Transaction, 1974.
19 Grey, op. cit., p. 267.
20 J. Bohemia and B. McGregor, *Nyibayarri Kimberley Tracker*.
    Canberra: Aboriginal Studies Press, 1995, p. 61.
21 *The Perth Gazette*, 2.4.1836: 679 from Abbott, op. cit., p. 56.
22 J.M.R. Cameron (ed.), *The Millendon Memoirs: George Fletcher
    Moore's Western Australian Diaries and Letters 1830–1841*.
    Victoria Park: Hesperian Press, 2006, p. 127.
23 T. Griffiths, 'How Many Trees Make a Forest? Cultural Debates
    About Vegetation Change in Australia'. *Australian Journal of
    Botany*, 2002, 50:375–389, p. 380.
24 R. Weller, *Boomtown 2050: Scenarios for a Rapidly Growing City*.
    Crawley: UWAP, 2009, p. 19.
25 J. Watson from C.C. Florey, *Peninsular City: A Social History of
    the City of South Perth*. Perth: City of South Perth, 1995, p. 33.
26 A. Hasluck and M. Lukis, *Victorian and Edwardian Perth from
    Old Photographs*. Sydney: John Ferguson, 1977, p. viii.
27 G. Seddon, *Swan Song: Reflections on Perth and Western Australia
    1956–1995*. Nedlands: CSAL, 1995, p. 85.
28 Hasluck, op. cit., p. viii.
29 F.K. Crowley, *Australia's Western Third: A History of Western
    Australia from the First Settlements to Modern Times*. London:
    Macmillan & Co., 1960, p. 83.
30 Dora Hall to Sarah Bracher, Thomas M. Wilson private
    collection, Wungong, WA.
31 *The Perth Gazette* 2.4.1836, from I. Abbott, 'Historical
    Perspectives of the Ecology of Some Conspicuous Vertebrate
    Species in South-West Western Australia'. *Conservation Science in
    Western Australia*, 2008, 6(3):156.
32 Crowley, op. cit., p. 110.
33 S. Appleyard and T. Cook, 'Reassessing the Management of

Groundwater Use from Sandy Aquifers: Acidification and Base Cation Depletion Exacerbated by Drought and Groundwater Withdrawal on the Gnangara Mound, Western Australia'. *Hydrology Journal,* 2008, p. 9.

34   *HEWA.* Crawley: UWAP, 2009, p. 677.

35   Edmonds from *HEWA,* ibid. p. 321.

36   Dora Hall to Sarah Bracher, 15.12.1901 in Hall Family Letters, op. cit.

37   Gregory from *HEWA,* op. cit., p. 301.

CHAPTER 7 – A SNAPSHOT OF PERTH THROUGH MODERN TIMES

1   D.R. Salvado, *Historical Memoirs of Australia and Particularly of the Benedictine Mission of New Norcia and the Habits and Customs of the Australian Natives,* E.J. Stormon (ed.). Nedlands: UWAP, 1978, p. 31.

2   J.M.R. Cameron (ed.), *The Millendon Memoirs: George Fletcher Moore's Western Australian Diaries and Letters 1830–1841.* Victoria Park: Hesperian Press, 2006, p. 156.

3   D.R.G. Sellick, *First Impressions: Albany 1791–1901: Travellers' Tales.* Perth: WA Museum, 1997, p. 116.

4   M.J. Tyler and P. Doughty, *Field Guide to Frogs of Western Australia.* Welshpool: WA Museum, 2009, p. 36.

5   C. Thomson-Dans and G. Wardell-Johnson, *Frogs of Western Australia.* C. Thomson-Dans (ed.). Kensington: December 2002, p. 44.

6   C.C. Florey, *Peninsular City: A Social History of the City of South Perth.* Perth: City of South Perth, 1995, p. 5.

7   *Metropolitan Regional Authority. Perth City Link.* Perth, 2014.

8   I. Cunningham, *The Trees That Were Nature's Gift.* Maylands: I. Cunningham, 1998, p. 90.

9   Salvado, op. cit., p. 34.

10   A. Gaynor and I.A. McLean, 'Landscape Histories: Mapping Environmental and Ecological Change Through the Landscape Art of the Swan River Region of Western Australia'. *Environment and History,* 2008, 14:187–204, p. 187.

11   R. Lloyd, 'The Cit's Country Box', J. Barrell and J. Bull, *The Penguin Book of English Pastoral Verse.* Harmondsworth: Penguin, 1982, p. 351.

12   C. Miller, *After Summer Merrily: An Autobiographical Novel.* Fremantle: FACP, 1980, p. 78.

13   R. Weller, *Boomtown 2050: Scenarios for a Rapidly Growing City.* Crawley: UWAP, 2009, p. 23.

14   ibid.

15   ibid, p. 24.

16   Robert D. Putnam, *Bowling Alone: The Collapse and Revival of*

American Community. New York: Simon & Schuster, 2000.

[17] Miller., op. cit., p. 79.

[18] G. Blainey, *A Shorter History of Australia*. Port Melbourne: William Heinemann, 1994, p. 165.

[19] Moore from B. de Garis, *European Impact on the West Australian Environment 1829–1979*. Nedlands: UWAP, 1979, p. 132.

[20] A. Gaynor, M. Trinca and A. Haebich, *Country: Visions of Land and People in Western Australia*. Perth: WA Museum, 2002, p. 192.

[21] Miller, op. cit., p. 143.

[22] J. McEncoe, quoted in M. Uren, *The City of Melville: From Bushland to Expanding Metropolis*. Melville: Melville City Council, 1975, p. 33.

[23] A. Gaynor from *HEWA*. Crawley: UWAP, 2009, p. 369.

[24] W.J. Lines, *Taming the Great South Land: A History of the Conquest of Nature in Australia*. North Sydney: Allen & Unwin, 1991, p. 218.

[25] *Cultural Diversity in Western Australia: A Demographic Profile. Western Australia*. Perth, WA: Department of Local Government and Communities, and Office of Multicultural Interests, Government of WA, 2013. <omi.wa.gov.au/resources/publications/info_sheets/Cultural_Diversity_2013.pdf>

[26] R.G. Chittleborough, *Shouldn't Our Grandchildren Know?: An Environmental Life Story*. South Fremantle: FACP, 1992, p. 236.

[27] B. Ryan and P. Hope, *Indian Ocean Climate Initiative Stage 2: Report of Phase 2 Activity*. Perth: Bureau of Meteorology, Government of WA, 2005.

[28] *South African Commercial Advertiser*, 25.12.1830, reprinted in I. Berryman, *Swan River Letters*. Glengarry: Swan River Press, 2002, pp. 199–200.

[29] J. Betjeman, 'Motopolis', *The Best of Betjeman*, selected by John Guest. London: Penguin, 1978, p. 70.

[30] Department of Planning, WA: WA Planning Commission, 2002.

[31] ibid, 2006.

[32] W.L. Heat-Moon, *Blue Highways*. New York, USA: Fawcett Crest, 1982, p. 4.

[33] G.M. Hopkins, *Selected Poems of Gerard Manley Hopkins*. New York: Dove, 2011, p. 33.

[34] W. Berry, *The Unsettling of America: Culture and Agriculture*. New York: Avon Books, 1977, pp. 52–53.

[35] Western Australian Local Government Assocation Perth Biodiversity Project, unpublished data, 2007.

[36] Weller, op. cit., p. 124.

[37] J. Barton, M. Griffin and J. Pretty, 'Exercise-, Nature- and Socially Interactive-based Initiatives Improve Mood and Self-esteem in the Clinical Population. *Perspect Public Health*, 2012, 132(2):89–96.

38 N. Chinna, *Swamp: Walking the Wetlands of the Swan Coastal Plain*. Fremantle: Fremantle Press, 2014, p. 78.
39 W. Berry. 'In a Country Once Forested', *New Collected Poems*. Berkley: Counterpoint, 2012, p. 345.

CHAPTER 8 – FROM YORK/GUM BELT TO WHEATBELT

1   R. Herrick, 'The Hock-Cart, or Harvest Home' (1648), *The Penguin Book of English Pastoral Verse*. Harmondsworth: Penguin, 1982, p. 167.
2   J. Fowles, *The French Lieutenant's Woman*. London: Jonathan Cape, 1969, p. 157.
3   W.H. Hudson, *The Naturalist in La Plata*. New York: Appleton, 1895, p. 3.
4   J.B. Kirkpatrick. *A Continent Transformed: Human Impact on the Natural Vegetation of Australia*. Melbourne: OUP, 1994, p. 38.
5   B. Beale and P. Fray, *The Vanishing Continent: Australia's Degraded Environment*. Sydney: Hodder & Stoughton, 1990, p. 24.
6   J.S. Beard, *Plant Life of Western Australia*. Kenthurst: Kangaroo Press, 1990, p. 60.
7   G. Bolton, *Spoils and Spoilers: A History of Australians Shaping their Environment*. Sydney: Allen & Unwin, 1992, p. 19.
8   I. Cunningham, *The Trees That Were Nature's Gift*. Maylands: I. Cunningham, 1998, p. 276.
9   ibid, p. 2.
10 N.J. Snell, *Landscapes and Land Uses: A Geography of Australia*. Sydney, NSW: McGraw Hill, 2003, p. 62.
11 G. Blainey, *A Shorter History of Australia*. Port Melbourne: William Heinemann, 1994, p. 87.
12 *Lands Report*, p. 13, from Cunningham, 1998, op. cit., p. 39.
13 ibid, p. 40.
14 *The Perth Gazette*, 2.4.1836, from I. Abbott, 'Historical Perspectives of the Ecology of Some Conspicuous Vertebrate Species in South-West Western Australia'. *Conservation Science in Western Australia*, 2008, 6(3):156.
15 ibid.
16 A.J. Koutsoukis, *Western Australia: A Brief History*. Melbourne: Longman Cheshire, 1998, p. 69.
17 Abbott, op. cit., p. 291.
18 Koutsoukis, op. cit., p. 68.
19 Lindsay and Robson from *HEWA*. Crawley: UWAP, 2009, p. 54.
20 P.V. O'Brien from Cunningham, op. cit., p. 41.
21 *State of the Environment Report: Western Australia 2007: Overview*. Perth, WA: Department of Environment and Conservation, 2007, p. 56.
22 B.Y. Main, *Twice Trodden Ground*. Milton: Jacaranda, 1971, p. 34.
23 Abbott, 2008, op. cit., p. 157.

24   Tull from *HEWA*, op. cit., p. 302.
25   F.K. Crowley, *Australia's Western Third: A History of Western Australia from the First Settlements to Modern Times*. London: Macmillan & Co., 1960, p. 296.
26   C.J. Yates, D.J. Coates, C. Elliott and M. Byrne, 'Composition of the Pollinator Community, Pollination and the Mating System for a Shrub in Fragments of Species Rich Kwongan in South-west Western Australia'. *Biodiversity and Conservation,* 2007, p. 2.
27   K. Bradby, *A Park in Perspective: A Report on the Past, Present and Future of Fitzgerald River National Park*. Ravensthorpe: Fitzgerald River National Park Association, 1989, p. 16.
28   Cunningham, op. cit., p. 43.
29   Bradby from *HEWA*, op. cit., p. 520.
30   T. Winton, 'Silent Country'. *The Monthly* 2008:30–44, p. 30.
31   W. Berry, *The Art of the Commonplace: Agrarian Essays of Wendell Berry*. Washington DC, USA: Counterpoint, 2002, p. 202.
32   S. Holland, 'Life and Death in WA's Wheatbelt: A Farmer's Struggle', WA Today 2015. <watoday.com.au/wa-news/life-and-death-in-was-wheatbelt-a-farmers-struggle-20150225-13ounj.html>.
33   C. Drake, *Beyond the Swan: A Journey into South-Western Australia's Bush*. Nedlands: Wildflower Society of WA, 2000, p. 87.
34   R.J. Hobbs, 'The Wheatbelt of Western Australia'. *Pacific Conservation Biology* 2003, 9(1):9–11, p. 10.
35   E. Lefroy and T. Rydberg, 'Energy Evaluation of Three Cropping Systems in Southwestern Australia'. *Pattern Recognition Letters,* 2003, 161(3).
36   Beale, op. cit., p. 26.
37   C. Gole, *2006 Southwest Australia Ecoregion Initiative*. WWF-Australia. <wwf.org.au/publications/southwest-australia-ecoregion-jewel-booklet/>.
38   D.J. Coates, 'Priority Setting and the Conservation of Western Australia's Diverse and Highly Endemic Flora', *Biology Conservation,* 2001, 97:251–263, p. 252.
39   D.J. Coates. 'Defining Conservation Units in a Rich and Fragmented Flora: Implications for the Management of Genetic Resources and Evolutionary Processes in South-west Australian Plants'. *Australian Journal of Botany*, 2000, 48:329–339, p. 337.
40   D.J. Coates and K. Atkins, 'Threatened Flora of Western Australia: A Focus for Conservation Outside Reserves'. In P. Hale and D. Lamb (eds), *Conservation Outside Nature Reserves*. Brisbane: Centre for Conservation Biology, 1997, p. 10.
41   ibid.
42   ibid, p. 253.
43   ibid.

44 ibid, p. 255.
45 Lindsay and Robson from *HEWA*, op. cit., p. 55.
46 Tull, ibid, p. 300.
47 Bolton, op. cit., p. 154.
48 M. Archer, I. Burnley, J. Dodson, R. Harding, L. Head and
    P. Murphy, *From Plesiosaurs to People: 100 Million Years of
    Environmental History*. Canberra: Environment Australia,
    Department of the Environment, 1998, p. 22.
49 Hudson, op. cit., p. 2.

CHAPTER 9 – DOWN TO THE WOODS TODAY

1   W. Berry, 'The Dream', *New Collected Poems*. Berkley:
    Counterpoint, 2012, p. 72.
2   P. Christensen and M.R.L. Lewis, *The Karri Forest: Its
    Conservation, Significance and Management*. M.R.L. Lewis (ed.).
    Como: Department of Conservation and Land Management,
    1992, p. 42.
3   *National Forest Inventory. Australia's State of the Forests Report
    2003. Department of Agriculture, Fisheries and Forestry, Australia*,
    Bureau of Rural Sciences, Canberra: Department of Agriculture,
    Fisheries and Forestry, Bureau of Rural Sciences, 2003, p. 6.
4   I. Abbott and O. Loneragan, 'Ecology of Jarrah (Eucalyptus
    Marginata) in the Northern Jarrah Forest of Western Australia'.
    CALM Bulletin 1, 1986, p. 5.
5   J. Dortch, *Palaeo-Environmental Change and the Persistence of
    Human Occupation in South-Western Australian Forests*. Oxford:
    Archaeopress, 2004, p. 8.
6   ibid, p. 10.
7   ibid.
8   M. Calder, *Big Timber Country*. Melbourne: Rigby, 1980, p. 15.
9   Dortch, op. cit., p. 11.
10 ibid, p. 47.
11 ibid, p. 12.
12 ibid.
13 Calder, op. cit., p. 18.
14 A.J. Koutsoukis, *Western Australia: A Brief History*. Melbourne:
    Longman Cheshire, 1998, p. 62.
15 W.J. Lines, *Taming the Great South Land: A History of the
    Conquest of Nature in Australia*. North Sydney: Allen & Unwin,
    1991, p. 145.
16 Christensen, op. cit., p. 62.
17 F.K. Crowley, *Australia's Western Third: A History of Western
    Australia from the First Settlements to Modern Times*. London:
    Macmillan & Co., 1960, p. 173.
18 P.E.M. Blond, *A Tribute to the Group Settlers*. Nedlands: UWAP,
    1987, p. 49.

19 ibid, p. 50.
20 Lines, op. cit., p. 169.
21 C. Drake. *Beyond the Swan: A Journey into South-Western Australia's Bush*. Nedlands: Wildflower Society of WA, 2000, p. 16.
22 Hillier from A. Gaynor, M. Trinca and A. Haebich, *Country: Visions of Land and People in Western Australia*. Perth: WA Museum, 2002, p. 64.
23 G. Wardell-Johnson and M. Claver, *Toward Sustainable Management: Southern Africa's Afromontane, and Western Australia's Jarrah Forests*. Rotterdam: Millpress, Australian Forest History Society Inc., 2005, p. 6.
24 Hillier from Gaynor, op. cit., pp. 77–78.
25 B. Mackey and S.L. Berry, *Green Carbon: The Role of Natural Forests in Carbon Storage*. Acton: ANU E Press, 2008, p. 3.
26 P. Robertson, *Wilderness Society WA State Campaign*. Perth: RTR 92.1 FM Radio, 2010.
27 T. Low, *Feral Future*. Ringwood: Viking, 1999, p. 117.
28 ibid, p. 118.
29 *All About Dieback: Tackling Dieback*. GovPress <www.dieback.org. au>.
30 W.H. Knight, *Western Australia: Its History, Progress, Condition, and Prospects; and its Advantages as a Field for Emigration*. Perth: 1870, p. 30.
31 D. Garden, *Australia, New Zealand, and the Pacific: An Environmental History*. Santa Barbara: ACB CLIO, 2005, p. 172.
32 J.B. Kirkpatrick, *A Continent Transformed: Human Impact on the Natural Vegetation of Australia*. Melbourne: OUP, 1994, p. 43.

CHAPTER 10 – WHERE HAVE ALL THE ANIMALS GONE?

1 J. Shoobert, *Western Australian Exploration. Volume 1, December 1826 – December 1835: The Letters, Reports & Journals of Exploration and Discovery in Western Australia*. Victoria Park: Hesperian Press, 2005, p. 393.
2 I. Cunningham, *The Land of Flowers: An Australian Environment on the Brink*. Brighton Le Sands: Otford Press, 2005, p. viii.
3 J.B. Kirkpatrick, *A Continent Transformed: Human Impact on the Natural Vegetation of Australia*. Melbourne: OUP, 1994, p. 41.
4 Cunningham, op. cit., p. 99.
5 ibid., p. 113.
6 A.A. Burbidge, *Threatened Animals of Western Australia*. Kensington: Department of Conservation and Land Management, Government of WA, 2004, p. 17.
7 Henry Edward Hall to Sarah Bracher, 7.9.1858, Hall Family Letters, Thomas M. Wilson private collection. Wungong, WA.
8 Cunningham, op.cit., p. 102.

9   *The Perth Gazette*, 2.4.1836, from I. Abbott, 'Historical Perspectives of the Ecology of Some Conspicuous Vertebrate Species in South-West Western Australia', *Conservation Science in Western Australia,* 2008, 6(3):125.

10   T. Winton, 'Silent Country', *The Monthly,* 2008, p. 35.

11   S. Mitchell and A. Wayne, 'Down but Not Out: Solving the Mystery of the Woylie Population Crash', *Landscape: WA's Conservation Forests and Wildlife Magazine* 2008, 25(4):11–15, p. 15.

12   Department of Environment and Conservation. *Walpole Wilderness and Adjacent Parks and Reserves: Management Plan 2008*. WA: Conservation Commission of WA, 2008, p. 63.

13   J. Richards, T. Gardner and M. Copley, 'Bringing Back the Animals'. *Landscape: WA's Conservation Forests and Wildlife Magazine,* 2009, 24(3):11–22, p. 58.

14   S.D. Hopper, 'OCBIL Theory: Towards an Integrated Understanding of the Evolution, Ecology and Conservation of Biodiversity on Old, Climatically Buffered, Infertile Landscapes'. *Plant Soil,* 2009, 322(1):68.

15   *Hope for the Future: The Western Australian State Sustainability Strategy*. Perth: Department of the Premier and Cabinet, Government of WA, p. 95.

16   ibid.

17   Abbott, op. cit., pp. 140–142.

18   J.C. Woinarski, A.A. Burbidge and P.L. Harrison, *The Action Plan for Australian Mammals 2012*. Clayton: CSIRO Publishing, 2014, p. vi.

19   Abbott, 2008, op. cit., p. 153.

20   ibid, p. 154.

21   ibid.

22   ibid.

23   ibid, p. 155.

24   ibid, p. 156.

25   ibid, p. 157.

26   Abbott, 2008, op. cit., p. 153.

27   C. Drake, *Beyond the Swan: A Journey into South-Western Australia's Bush*. Nedlands: Wildflower Society of WA, 2000, p. 18.

28   Abbott, 2008, op. cit., p. 2.

29   Abbott, 2008, ibid, p. 7.

30   ibid.

31   I. Abbott, 'The Bilby *Macrotis Lagotis* (Marsupialia: Peramelidae) in South-western Australia: Original Range Limits, Subsequent Decline, and Presumed Regional Extinction'. *Records of the Western Australian Museum* 2001, 20:271–305, p. 278.

32   Abbott, ibid, p. 280.

33   Abbott, 2008, op. cit., p. 11.

34 ibid, p. 28.
35 Woinarski, op. cit., p. vi.
36 Abbott, 2008, op. cit., p. 36.
37 ibid, p. 45.
38 ibid.
39 ibid.
40 ibid, p. 48.
41 T. Flannery, 'The Third Wave'. *The Monthly,* April 2009, p. 2.
42 D. Mercer, 'Record Number of WA Species Under Threat'. *The West Australian* 2015, <au.news.yahoo.com/thewest/a/26366565/record-number-of-wa-species-under-threat>.
43 C. Gole. *2006 Southwest Australia Ecoregion Initiative.* WWF-Australia, <wwf.org.au/publications/southwest-australia-ecoregion-jewel-booklet/>.
44 S. Reardon, 'Return of the Wild'. *New Scientist* 2014, 221(2958): 40–43.
45 ibid.
46 D. Bowman, 'Conservation: Bring Elephants to Australia?'. *Nature,* 2012, 482(30).
47 Thomas M. Wilson interview with D. Bowman, 2013 for Understorey, RTR FM (radio).
48 K.E. Moseby, H. Neilly, J.L. Read and H.A. Crisp, 'Interactions between a Top Order Predator and Exotic Mesopredators in the Australian Rangelands'. *International Journal of Ecology* 2012, <hindawi.com/journals/ijecol/2012/250352/>.
49 M. Letnic, L. Baker and B. Nesbitt, 'Ecologically Functional Landscapes and the Role of Dingos as Trophic Regulators in Southern-eastern Australia and other Habitats'. *Ecological Management & Restoration,* 2013, 14(2). p. 3.
50 ibid.
51 ibid.
52 ibid.
53 J. Muir, *Steep Trails.* W.F. Badè (ed.). Boston: Houghton Mifflin Co., 1918, p. 211.

CHAPTER 11 – ARRIVAL HOME

1 S. Reardon, 'Return of the Wild'. *New Scientist* 2014, 221(2958):4.
2 W. Berry, *The Unsettling at America: Culture and Agriculture.* San Francisco: Sierra Club Books, 1977, p. 20.
3 S.D. Hopper, 'OCBIL Theory: Towards an Integrated Understanding of the Evolution, Ecology and Conservation of Biodiversity on Old, Climatically Buffered, Infertile Landscapes'. *Plant Soil,* 2009, 322(1):76.
4 Thomas M. Wilson interview with K. Bradby, Understorey, RTR 92.1 FM Radio, 2013.
5 Hopper, 2009, op. cit., p. 69.

6   S.D. Hopper, *South-Western Australia, Cinderella of the World's Temperate Floristic Regions 1.* Kew: Botanical Magazine, 2003, 20(2):112.

7   J. Barrell and J. Bull, *The Penguin Book of English Pastoral Verse.* Harmondsworth: Penguin, 1982, p. 310.

8   T.F. Flannery, *An Explorer's Notebook.* Melbourne: Text, 2007, p. 112.

9   J. Wright, *Preoccupations in Australian Poetry.* Melbourne: OUP, 1965, p. xi.

10   G. Blainey, *A Shorter History of Australia.* Port Melbourne: William Heinemann, 1994, p. 105.

11   ibid.

12   ibid, p. 150.

13   J. Simons, *Kangaroo.* Durrington: Reaktion Books, 2013, pp. 108–109.

14   ibid, p. 321.

15   P. Law, 'Future Perth: Blueprint for a Compact Capital'. *The Sunday Times* 5.10.2015 <perthnow.com.au/news/special-features/in-depth/future-perth-blueprint-for-a-compact-capital/news-story/6eb69ad56abd4831d464c91b8629a734?nk=4451409436337045edca34e9d524d77d-1462764840>

16   C. Hamilton and R. Dennis, *Affluenza: When Too Much is Never Enough.* Sydney: Allen & Unwin, 2005.

17   Berry, op. cit., p. 53.

18   A. Franklin, *Animal Nation: The True Story of Animals and Australia.* Sydney: UNSWP, 2006, p. 187.

19   ibid, p. 184.

20   C. Gosden, *Prehistory: A Very Short Introduction.* Oxford: OUP, 2003.

21   Genesis 1:28, King James Bible.

22   G. Grey, *Journals of Two Expeditions of Discovery in the North-west and Western Australia.* London: Thomas W. Borges & Co., 1969, 2:292.

23   Hopper, 2009, op. cit., p. 70.

24   *The Perth Gazette*, 2.4.1836, from I. Abbott, 'Historical Perspectives of the Ecology of Some Conspicuous Vertebrate Species in South-West Western Australia'. *Conservation Science in Western Australia,* 2008, 6(3):11.

25   S.J. Hallam, 'The First Western Australians', in C.T. Stannage (ed.), *A New History of Western Australia.* Nedlands: UWAP, 1981, p. 63.

26   I. Cunningham, *The Land of Flowers: An Australian Environment on the Brink.* Brighton Le Sands: Otford Press, 2005, p. 231.

27   Hallam, op.cit., p. 43.

28   D. Abram, *The Spell of the Sensuous: Perception and Language in a More-than-human World.* New York: Pantheon Books, 1996, p. 267.

29   E.C. Rolls, *Australia: A Biography, the Beginnings from the Cosmos to the Genesis of Gondwana, and its Rivers, Forests, Flora, Fauna, and Fecundity*. St Lucia: UQP, 2000, p. 228.

CHAPTER 12 – PERSONAL REWILDING

1   J. Updike, *Self-Consciousness: Memoirs*. New York: Random House, 2012, p. 45.

2   G. Snyder, *The Practice of the Wild*. San Franciso: North Point Press, 1990, p. 7.

3   D. Lieberman, *The Story of the Human Body: Evolution, Health and Disease*. London: Allen Lane, 2013, p. 163.

4   V.F. Gladwell, D.K. Brown, C. Wood, G.R. Dandercock and J.L. Barton, 'The Great Outdoors: How a Green Exercise Environment Can Benefit All'. *Extreme Physiology and Medicine* 2013, 2(3).

5   G. Grey, *Journals of Two Expeditions of Discovery in the North-west and Western Australia*. London: Thomas W. Borges & Co., 1969, 2: pp. 283–284.

6   E.M. Selhub and A.C. Logan, *Your Brain on Nature: The Science of Nature's Influence on Your Health, Happiness and Vitality*. Toronto: Collins, 2013.

7   E. Deans, 'The Gut–Brain Connection, Mental Illness and Disease. Psychobiotics, Immunology and the Theory of all Chronic Disease'. 2014, <psychologytoday.com/blog/evolutionary-psychiatry/201404/the-gut-brain-connection-mental-illness-and-disease>.

8   J.E. Hammond, *Winjan's People: The Story of the South-West Australian Aborigines*. Victoria Park: Hesperian Press, 2005, p. 45.

9   A. Franklin, *Animal Nation: The True Story of Animals and Australia*. Sydney, NSW: UNSWP, 2006, p. 208.

10   Selhub, op. cit., p. 133.

11   M. Archer, 'Confronting Crises in Conservation: A Talk on the Wild Side'. In D. D. and C. Dickman (eds). *A Zoological Revolution. Using Native Fauna to Assist in its Own Survival*. Sydney: Royal Zoological Society of NSW, 2002:12–52, p. 28.

12   M. Archer and B. Beale. *Going Native: Living in the Australian Environment*. Sydney: Hodder, 2004, p. 264.

13   Archer, 2002, op. cit., p. 30.

14   ibid, p. 33.

15   Franklin, op. cit., p. 201.

16   A. Ham, 'Cats Gone Wild'. *The Age*, 12.9.2014:18–19, p. 18.

17   Archer, 2002, op. cit., p. 33.

18   B. Santich, *Bold Palates: Australia's Gastronomic Heritage*. Kent Town: Wakefield Press, 2012, p. 21.

19   ibid, p. 151.

20   ibid, p. 25.

21   W. Zukerman. 'Eating Skippy: Is Kangaroo the Kindest Meat?'.
      New Scientist, 2010: 2781, p. 44.
22   J. Simons. *Kangaroo.* Durrington: Reaktion Books, 2013, p. 45.
23   Franklin, op. cit., p. 222.
24   L.W. Bell, R.G. Bennett, M.H. Ryan and H. Clarke, 'The Potential
      of Herbaceous Native Australian Legumes as Grain Crops: a
      Review'. *Renewable Agriculture and Food Systems,* 2010, p. 13.
25   Santich, op. cit., p. 50.
26   W.H. Knight, *Western Australia: Its History, Progress, Condition,
      and Prospects; and Its Advantages as a Field For Emigration.* Perth:
      1870, p. 73.
27   J. Richards, T. Gardner and M. Copley, 'Bringing Back the
      Animals'. *Landscope: WA's Conservation Forests and Wildlife
      Magazine* 2009, 24(3):25.
28   C. Gosden, *Prehistory: A Very Short Introduction.* Oxford: OUP,
      2003. p. 57.
29   Colonial Secretary's Records, 1831–1878, vol. 17, p. 173 in
      M. Berson, *Cockburn: The Making of a Community.* Cockburn:
      Town of Cockburn, 1978, p. 23.
30   Archer, 2004, op. cit., p. 129.
31   Franklin, op. cit., p. 101.
32   J. Shoobert, *Western Australian Exploration. Volume 1, December
      1826 – December 1835: The Letters, Reports & Journals of
      Exploration and Discovery in Western Australia.* Victoria Park:
      Hesperian Press, 2005, p. 400.
33   A. Leopold, *A Sand Country Almanac and Sketches Here and
      There.* London: Longman Cheshire, 1998, p. 48.
34   D.R.G. Sellick, *First Impressions: Albany 1791–1901: Travellers'
      Tales.* Perth: WA Museum, 1997, p. 151.
35   J. Davis, *Longing or Belonging? Responses to a 'New' Land in
      Southern Western Australia 1829–1907.* PhD thesis, School
      of Humanities, Department of History, UWA, 2008, p. 203.
      <research-repository.uwa.edu.au/files/3226789/Davis_Jane_2008.
      pdf>.
36   J. Byrne, *Small Space Organics: Creating Sustainable, Edible
      Gardens.* Richmond: Hardie Grant, 2013, p. 150.
37   Archer, 2004, op. cit., p. 12.

AFTERWORD

1   S.R. Sanders, *Earth Works: Selected Essays.* Bloomington: IUP,
      2011, p.126.
2   G. Snyder, *The Practice of the Wild.* San Franciso: North Point
      Press, 1990, p. 185.

ACKNOWLEDGEMENTS

I'd like to thank Alan Muller for letting me reproduce two of his memorable visions of the soul of Perth; to Theo Koning for his artwork, and Gwen Velge and Lily Kumpe for their photography. Thanks to Cheryl Macaulay, courtesy of Kwongan Foundation, for permission to reproduce her photograph of a black cockatoo on the back jacket of this book. Thanks to Neville Green for use of the language groups map, and to Andrea Tate for her image of Perth as a wetland. Thanks to Richard Hobbs, Richard Weller and Nandi Chinna for images reproduced. Thanks to Ian Abbott and all the other people who gave up their time to be interviewed by me on RTR FM's environmental radio show *Understorey* over the years. Thanks to the University of Western Australia for giving me space where I can focus on my writing. Thanks to Penguin Random House for letting me reproduce lines from *The Spell of the Sensuous* by David Abram. Thanks to Georgia Richter and Wendy Jenkins at Fremantle Press for their editorial help, to Zoe Barnard for copyediting, and to my cousin Ian Berryman for his proofreading. Thanks to my mother, Julia Denton-Barker, for early comments on the manuscript.

First published 2017 by
FREMANTLE PRESS
25 Quarry Street, Fremantle WA 6160
(PO Box 158, North Fremantle WA 6159)
www.fremantlepress.com.au

Editor Wendy Jenkins
Consultant editor Georgia Richter
Cover design Carolyn Brown, tendeersigh.com.au
Front cover Orien Harvey
Back cover Cheryl McAuley, Kwongan Foundation

Printed by Everbest Printing Company, China

National Library of Australia
Cataloguing-in-Publication entry:

Wilson, Thomas, 1978–, author.
Stepping off: rewilding and belonging in the South-West
ISBN: 9781925164329 (paperback)
Western Australia, Southwest—History.
Western Australia, Southwest—Environmental conditions.

Dewey Number: 994.12

Fremantle Press is supported by the State Government through the
Department of Culture and the Arts.

 Government of **Western Australia**
Department of **Culture and the Arts**

Publication of this title was assisted by the Commonwealth
Government through the Australia Council, its arts funding and
advisory body.

 Australian Government   Australia Council for the Arts